OTHER BOOKS

by Samuel Eliot Morison

THE STORY OF THE
"OLD COLONY"
OF NEW PLYMOUTH
[1620-1692]

Thomas Alva Edison

Foundation

for

Special excellence in

Portraying America's

Past

Winslow meeting with Quadequina

The Story of the

"OLD COLONY"

of New Plymouth

[1620-1692]

Samuel Eliot Morison

ILLUSTRATED BY CHARLES H. OVERLY

New York Alfred A Knopf 1960

Dedicated to my ancestress

PRISCILLA MULLINS

who said "yes" when John Alden spoke for himself

and to my beloved wife

PRISCILLA BARTON

who finally said "yes" when I spoke for myself

PREFACE

ALTHOUGH *everybody knows about the Pilgrim Fathers, the books that have been written about them in recent years leave them sitting on Plymouth Rock, as it were. One's natural curiosity as to where they went from there has not been satisfied. Historians seem to lose interest in the Pilgrims as soon as they were able to have three square meals daily, and own a cow. How many know that Plymouth Town, in fifty years' time, expanded into a colony of respectable size and strength? Or that it was a fighting colony after Myles Standish died, and "took the rap" in the toughest war ever fought in New England? Or that the Pilgrims were the first white men to establish trading posts on the Penobscot, Kennebec, and Connecticut Rivers? Or that a substantial part of Maine was for thirty years part of the Plymouth Colony?*

No history of the Old Colony, as it is still affectionately called in New England, has appeared for thirty-five years. And even those that were written for the three hundredth anniversary of 1920 taper off sadly after 1630, when the most brilliant and prosperous period of the Colony began. So in this book, written for young people of all ages, I have car-

ried the Story of the Old Colony right through to 1692, when the Colony was absorbed by Massachusetts. At the same time I have given a fresh but factual account of the early days, the Mayflower, *and all that; believing that readers are tired of souped-up stories of fictionalized Pilgrims in plug hats, and would like to know what sort of people they really were, and how they lived.*

After much cogitation I have decided to leave prices just as they are in the records, in pounds, shillings, and pence (£ s. d.), as the problem of translating them into the modern British or American depreciated currency offers too many difficulties. A pound, when the Mayflower *sailed, meant twenty shillings sterling, roughly five gold dollars; and a silver shilling (about twenty-five cents), contained twelve pence. But in 1652 the Massachusetts Bay Colony started to coin its famous New England pine-tree shillings which were lighter than the English shillings, and presumably the £ s. d. one encounters in Plymouth records thereafter are reckoned in this New England money. A pound therefore equalled, roughly, $3.33; and a shilling seventeen cents in gold or silver. The Spanish dollars imported from the West Indies, which later became the basis for our United States currency, were valued at six shillings.*

Many people have helped me in this work. First of all I wish to thank my secretary, Miss Antha Eunice Card, who has traveled through every town of the Old Colony, looking up landmarks and investigating records. It is owing to her pains that I have been able to direct my readers, in foot-notes, to some important historic spots. I am also much in-debted to Mr. W. Wallace Austin, Curator of the Old Colony Historical Society, Taunton; Miss Rose Briggs of Plymouth; Mr. and Mrs. Robert Davis of Yarmouth; Mr. Howard Man-dell of New Bedford; Mr. Joshua Nickerson of Orleans; Mr. Arthur Pyle, Secretary of Plimoth Plantation, Inc., which is putting up replicas of early buildings; the Sandwich His-torical Society; Mr. Warren Strong, Curator of Pilgrim Hall, Plymouth; Mr. George Tripp, Director of the Old Dartmouth Historical Society, New Bedford; and Dr. Douglas E. Leach, whose doctoral dissertation on King Philip's War (soon to be published as a book) has been of the greatest assistance.

I am grateful to Mr. Overly for his close cooperation with me in the matter of illustrations. He wishes to express his thanks to Dr. John O. Brew, Director of the Peabody Mu-seum of Archaeology and Ethnology at Harvard University, for his assistance in matters of Indian artifacts and costume; to Mr. William A. Baker, naval architect of Hingham, Massa-chusetts, for the drawing and description of the Mayflower; to Mr. Charles Hoffbauer, artist of the murals in the New England Mutual Hall, Boston, for permission to adapt his painting of Samoset's arrival at Plymouth, and for details from his other paintings. Mr. Nathaniel Hamlen of Boston has graciously given permission to use the painting of the three Mason children, which he owns, as the basis for one of our illustrations.

CONTENTS

THE STORY OF THE
"OLD COLONY"
OF NEW PLYMOUTH

[1620-1692]

HOW IT ALL STARTED

❀❀❀❀❀❀❀❀❀❀❀❀❀❀❀❀❀❀❀❀❀❀❀❀❀❀❀❀❀❀

THE TWO WILLIAMS

IN THE VILLAGE of Austerfield in Yorkshire, England, in the year 1604, there lived a somewhat puny fifteen-year-old lad named William Bradford. His father, who died when he was a baby, had been a well-to-do farmer; his mother was the daughter of a local shopkeeper. When she married again and moved away, Will boarded around with his grandfather and uncles. They brought him up to be a farmer, as they and their ancestors had been as far back as anyone remembered. There were no schools near by, but somehow Will managed to learn to read, and at the age of twelve he began to read the Geneva translation of the Holy Bible. He thought it the most wonder-

ful book in the world, and always did. He began to play
hookey from the little Anglican church where his family worshipped, because the minister gabbled through the prayer
book service and never read from the Bible or gave a sermon.
But Will lost no opportunity to hear a Puritan parson named
Clyfton who preached in the open air, or in people's houses.

From this Rev. Richard Clyfton, Will learned that the Bible
was not only the one true source of the Christian religion,
but the best guide to life. Mr. Clyfton declared that the official Church of England, a compromise between the Roman
Catholic Church and the Reformed or Protestant faith, was
completely off the beam. Will was ready to believe that, since
the only Anglican clergyman he knew was the dumb parson
of Austerfield. Pretty soon the lad began to attend private
meetings of a group of likeminded people, mostly local farmers and older than he. They assembled at the manor house of
near by Scrooby.

This manor house, which did duty as an inn for passengers
on the Great North Road between London and Edinburgh,
was kept by the leading man in the neighborhood, Mr. William Brewster. That gentleman, more than twice Will Bradford's age in 1604, was a graduate of the great University of
Cambridge, and a former secretary in Queen Elizabeth's diplomatic service. He knew both Latin and Greek and had
experience of the great world. Will looked up to him as an
educated gentleman, and when Mr. Brewster said that their
little group should separate from the Church of England and
set up a church of its own, Will naturally went along.

In those days, that was a dangerous thing to do; more so,
even, than it would be to join a Communist cell today. To
separate from the Church of England was regarded as treason, and three or four Separatists had already been executed.

For Will, his decision meant cutting himself off from his family and most of his neighbors. People said they had always thought little Willie was a no-good; and for him to join odd Mr. Brewster in defying King and Archbishop, setting himself up as purveyor of the Pure Truth, was just too much! Nobody foresaw that little Willie would become governor of the second English colony in the New World, and that Mr. Brewster would be his faithful colleague and assistant in that office as long as he lived.

Young Will Bradford listening to Mr. Clyfton
preaching at Brewster's home.

FAITH OF OUR FATHERS

∼§ BREWSTER and his friends were the nucleus of the group known to history as the Pilgrim Fathers. Religious controversies are not very interesting reading, but please listen a moment to the things the Pilgrims believed; or the story of their later struggles will make little sense. They could have stayed in England if they had even outwardly conformed to the Church of England; but it never occurred to them to do that. They could have had security in Holland if that had been what they wanted; but security was not what they were after. Their ambition was to found a community where they would have liberty to worship God in their own way and to follow the New Testament way of life.

One of the Pilgrim Fathers, William Wright, who died at Plymouth in 1633, made this confession of faith in his will, and it is the best expression we know of the "faith of our fathers":

I give and bequeath my body to the dust, and my soul unto the hands of God that gave it, being persuaded in myself that although my body shall be laid in the earth, there to return to dust from whence it came, yet at the last day when all flesh shall appear before the tribunal bar of God's justice, that then my soul and body shall be reunited, and that both soul and body shall receive recompense of reward. And whereas I am sensible of the wrath of God which I have incurred to myself by reason of my manifold failings and disobedience to my God, whereby He hath just cause to appear to me as an angry judge; yet I do believe that Jesus Christ, perfect God and perfect man, hath fully and sufficiently satisfied to God His Father for all my sins, and that by His blood alone I stand freely justified before God, and not by any desert, merit or worthiness of mine own, for in me dwelleth nothing that is good, and all my righteousness is filthy and abominable, and that this death is but a passage to life eternal. And I do desire my God to give me patience that I may bear His hand, and that all the days of mine appointed time I may wait until my change shall come. For I know my Redeemer liveth, and that I shall shortly see Him with these eyes, and I am willing to leave this frail and troublesome life and to be with Christ my Saviour, which is best of all.

There was nothing new or queer about this confession of faith; it was and is basic Christian doctrine, to which Catholics and Protestants alike subscribed, and in which they believe—or ought to believe—today. If anything is fundamental in the Christian religion, it is that triumphant prophecy of Job: "I know that my Redeemer liveth . . . And though . . . worms destroy this body, yet in my flesh shall I see God."

No, it was not faith that marked off the Pilgrims from their fellows; it was their idea of how the Christian Church should be *organized,* and how they should *worship* God. They insisted that the Church should be reorganized along New Testament lines, without regard to custom or tradition. This meant no more bishops or deans, no sacraments except baptism and holy communion, no set prayer book, no ritual, no altars, candles, organs, or incense. Each church must be independent, its ministers and other "elders" (officers) elected by the congregation. Services should consist only of Bible reading, a sermon, and extempore prayer; that is, a new prayer every Sunday. (However, "Our Father" was all right, because Our Lord told us to use it.) Thousands and thousands of people in England, Scotland, and Ireland came to

believe as Brewster and Bradford did. In derision they were
called Puritans because they were always talking about "pur-
ifying" the Church of England. They didn't like the name at
first, and Will Bradford doubtless had fights with boys who
shouted "Yah! Yah! Puritan!" at him. But in the course of time
they accepted it, just as the Society of Friends accepted being
called Quakers.

The greater number of Puritans were willing to bide their
time; to attend Anglican services provided they could hear
sermons on the side, and to hope for the best. But the Separatists, such as the Scrooby group, were unable to wait.
They agreed with the Rev. Robert Browne who urged "Ref-
ormation without Tarrying for Any" and who preached sermons on the text: "Come out from among them, and be ye
separate, saith the Lord, and touch not the unclean thing;
and I will receive you." That's what St. Paul said that the
Lord had said, so what else could a good Christian do?

Within a year after its "gathering" the Scrooby congregation obtained as preacher the Rev. John Robinson, a gentleman and a scholar, and a man of the world, "courteous, affable and sociable in his conversation." A graduate of Cambridge University and fellow of a college there, he embraced
the Separatist idea, renounced his Anglican orders, and
chose poverty and hardship in order to minister to the faithful few at Scrooby.

The situation of these Separatists was very uncomfortable
and even dangerous. What they were doing was illegal. Mr.
Brewster, to be sure, had powerful friends, but there was no
assurance that the whole congregation might not be thrown
into jail at any time, and the leaders tried for treason. Moreover, the rest of the community around Scrooby and Austerfield was hostile. Bradford later described the attitude of

these unfriendly neighbors as "ignorant and licentious." He had to endure "the wrath of his uncles" and the "scoff of his neighbors." He and his friends probably had to fight their way to their own meeting-place every Sunday, or dodge brickbats when they came out. Nobody would have anything to do with them. The girls they might have courted were ordered not to speak to them; merchants would not buy their farm products, and shopkeepers refused to sell them supplies.

PILGRIMS IN HOLLAND

◆§ THE SITUATION became so intolerable that, in 1607, the congregation voted to emigrate to the "Low Countries," the Netherlands. The Dutch, although not very tolerant among themselves, welcomed foreigners and let them worship as they pleased. Two other English Separatist congregations had already gone to the Netherlands and reported that they were not troubled by the authorities, and had found work.

To cross the North Sea to the Low Countries was no easy matter. Leaving England was illegal unless you had a passport from the authorities, and passports were not granted to "traitors," as Separatists were regarded. A sea passage cost money, and only Mr. Brewster had any. He sold most of his property and offered to pay the expenses of any members of the congregation who would go along. First and last, most of them did.

The first band of them that decided to leave, walked, with all the stuff they could carry, to the seaport of Boston in Lincolnshire, where they chartered a ship. The captain betrayed them to the authorities, who kept them in jail for a time and then sent them home. A second and smaller party made good its escape. In the spring of 1608 a Dutch captain consented to take the rest across, and met them off a lonely part of the English coast; but before he had embarked half of them, a sheriff's posse arrived and arrested those still on shore, including Brewster and Bradford. The last attempt, in which these two good friends took part, was successful. Their ship encountered a frightful storm in the North Sea and was almost driven onto the coast of Norway. Even the sailors cried out: "We sink! we sink!" But the Pilgrims prayed hard for deliverance and their prayers were answered. Thus, by the late summer of 1608 about 125 members of the Scrooby church, including the Rev. Mr. Robinson, had "gat over" to Holland, as Bradford wrote.

After a year's sojourn at Amsterdam the Pilgrims removed to Leyden, which Bradford described as "a fair and beautiful city and of a sweet situation, but made more famous by the university." The main business of Leyden was the spinning and weaving of woolen cloth. Most of the Pilgrims, being farmers, knew nothing of this occupation. "It was not long before they saw the grim and grisly face of poverty coming upon them like an armed man." But "at length they came to raise a competent and comfortable living, but with hard and continual labor."

The Dutch were very decent to the Pilgrims. They allowed a number of them to become naturalized subjects of the Netherlands. No effort was made to prevent them from earning their living in a humble occupation, although they could not join the trade gilds (corresponding to our labor unions) which monopolized the best-paying jobs. Some learned to comb or card wool for the spinners of yarn; others spun and wove. Bradford became a weaver of fustian, a coarse woolen cloth. Isaac Allerton, a London tailor who came over to join them, plied his old trade in Leyden. Mr. Brewster bought a press on which he printed Puritan books that the censors would not allow in England; Edward Winslow, a well-educated young man from another part of England, came over and helped him. That was still a dangerous thing to do. In Queen Elizabeth's reign, an English ambassador discovered that a Puritan book prohibited in England was being printed at Leyden. He sent an Anglican clergyman to burn the entire edition; and the authors of the book, Henry Barrow and John Greenwood, were tried as traitors in London

Pilgrims going to church—Leyden, Holland.

and executed.[1] The English Government now tried to have Brewster arrested and sent home for trial, but the Dutch protected him.

The Pilgrim congregation, numbering between 200 and 250 by 1615, bought a house for Mr. Robinson and held church services on the ground floor. Mr. Brewster was elected an "elder," which corresponded to a churchwarden of today; elders could preach and lead prayer meetings. They had deacons, too, and a deaconess: an old lady who visited the sick and helped the poor, and on Sunday, armed with "a little birchen rod," kept an eye on small children during service. William Bradford married a young girl named Dorothy May who arrived from England with her parents, and he, too, bought a house. Elder Brewster and the Rev. Mr. Robinson were welcomed at the University to take part in Latin debates on theology. No, the Pilgrims did not have too hard a time in Leyden. They were poor but respected, paid their bills, and never got in trouble. But they were not content to stay.

---

[1] Bradford "First Dialogue" pp. 7, 10. The Governor relates with great relish that the Anglican book-burner saved a copy for himself, intending to write a book to refute it; but instead he was converted by the arguments and became a Separatist.

WHY THEY CHOSE AMERICA

❧❧❧❧❧❧❧❧❧❧❧❧❧❧❧❧❧❧❧❧❧❧❧❧❧❧❧❧❧❧❧❧

REASONS FOR REMOVAL

AFTER OUR FRIENDS had been in Holland for about ten years, they began to talk about moving. Why? What was wrong with Leyden? For one thing, there was no future for them there, only hard indoor labor. They longed for fields and flocks and growing things; to go a-fishing as the Dutch sailors did. But they had no money to buy a fishing vessel or the scarce and expensive farm land of Holland. The older people were worried because the children were becoming little Dutchmen, forgetting their English language and customs and showing no respect for the Sabbath Day. Moreover, war was about to break out between the Netherlands and

Spain; the Pilgrims had heard about the cruelty of Spanish soldiers and wished no part of it. Last, and not least, wrote Bradford, they dreamed of having a community of their own in some "remote part of the world," where they could advance "the gospel of the kingdom of Christ," and attract likeminded people to join them. They had a vision of a colony overseas where they could make a decent living, worship as they thought right, and lead the New Testament life. That is hard enough to do anywhere, and almost impossible for poor workers in a crowded foreign city.

Then arose the great question: Where to go? Some suggested the vast, unsettled shores of South America, possibly Guiana which Sir Walter Raleigh had visited and highly praised. But the Dutch had published illustrated books of travels to America which described the Indians as cruel and bloodthirsty, tormenting captives and broiling and eating "collops of their flesh" before they were dead. Yet, if the Pilgrims stayed in Leyden, "the Spaniard might prove as cruel as the savages of America." The Spaniards were a menace in America, too; they had massacred a colony of French Protestant settlers on the East Coast of Florida, as the Pilgrims well knew.

So, Spanish America being off the list, why not try English Virginia? That seemed to be the answer to prayer. True, the English colony founded at Jamestown in 1607 suffered terrible hardships; but by 1618 the culture of tobacco had begun and Virginia was really getting on her feet and becoming known as an earthly paradise. Mr. Brewster had a personal connection with Sir Edwin Sandys, a prominent Englishman who was also the head of the Virginia Company. And the Virginia Company had begun to grant large tracts of land, called "Particular Plantations," to groups of Englishmen who would emigrate at their own expense. They were offered local self-government and other privileges.

Just the dish for the Pilgrims! But would the Virginia Company, an organization of loyal churchmen, allow religious liberty to despised Separatists? That was the rub.

Two leading members of the Pilgrim congregation, John Carver and Robert Cushman, went to England to interview Sir Edwin on the subject. Sandys said that his company would be delighted to grant their friends a Particular Plantation, but he could not promise religious toleration without the King's permission. He asked his friend Robert Naunton, a Secretary of State who sympathized with the Puritans, to see the King about it; and so he did. King James asked how the Pilgrims proposed to make a living. "By fishing," said Naunton. "So God have my soul," replied the King, " 'tis an honest trade, 'twas the Apostles' own calling!" But he would not promise them religious liberty without consulting the Archbishop of Canterbury. The Archbishop wanted definite assurance that the Pilgrims would acknowledge his and the King's supremacy over their church, and agree to other things that were against their principles. Sir Edwin Sandys urged them to accept these conditions, because they could then get a patent for a Particular Plantation near the mouth of the Hudson River and, once there, do pretty much as they pleased.

Most of the Pilgrims at Leyden thought this would be hypocritical and that they had better try to get a land patent in New England, as the "Northern Part of Virginia" had recently been renamed by Captain John Smith. But the Northern Virginia Company was just then being reorganized and could grant no land until it had a charter from the King.

Another thing that discouraged them about Virginia was bad news of the voyage of Francis Blackwell, an elder of the English Separatist church at Amsterdam, who attempted to carry out an almost identical plan. Blackwell chartered a ship, probably smaller than the *Mayflower*, and loaded her with 180 passengers "packed together like herrings." Starting for America in the fall, they were blown far south of their course, came down with scurvy, and ran out of fresh water. By the time they reached Virginia in March 1619, "after long seeking and beating about," only about fifty of the entire ship's company were alive.

After that news came through, it is no wonder that most of the Leyden congregation declined to go to Virginia at any price. But a resolute minority decided to accept the Company's offer in lieu of something better. For, as Robinson and Brewster wrote to Sir Edwin Sandys:

> It is not with us as with other men, whom small things can discourage, or small discontentments cause to wish themselves at home again. . . . We verily believe and trust that the Lord is with us . . . and that He will graciously prosper our endeavours.

RAISING THE MONEY

⮱ ON 2 February 1620, the Virginia Company issued a patent to them in the name of John Peirce, one of their London friends. It did not specify where the land was to be located—that was never done with "Particular Plantations" until the people actually reached Virginia. It was understood that the Pilgrims would settle somewhere near the mouth of the Hudson, handy for fishing and also for trading with the Indians.

But the patent was only half the matter. Who would pay for the voyage and advance supplies until the Pilgrims were self-supporting? All experience in Virginia showed that this required a big outlay of money, and the Pilgrims had barely enough to pay passage to England, let alone to the New World. In this quandary their agents were approached by Thomas Weston, a London ironmonger (we would call him a hardware dealer) and small capitalist. He was the sort of businessman who preferred to "chisel in" on some big enterprise rather than look for legitimate sources of trade. He had already barely avoided jail by doing just that. Now was his chance to organize a respectable "Company of Adventurers" (the word then used for merchant capitalists) and make good money by exploiting the Pilgrims.

The terms that Weston exacted were harsh, although similar to those for the first settlers of Virginia. The Adventurers would pay all expenses of ship hire, supplies, and transportation. The colonists must work for them at fishing, fur-trading, lumbering, or whatever means of profit they found, for seven years. All profits above bare subsistence would go to the Adventurers. At the end of seven years, each colonist sixteen years old and upward, who had labored for that space of time, would get one share worth £10 (about $50 in gold), and each Adventurer would receive one share for every £10 of his investment. All property in the colony would then be divided on that basis. Thus, a family of husband, wife, and three children who had worked seven years would get exactly the same dividend as a capitalist who had invested about $250.00.

In vain the Pilgrims asked to be allowed two days a week to work for themselves, and that the houses they built and the gardens they planted should be considered their private property instead of being thrown into the pot. Weston and his Company of Adventurers were adamant. The Pilgrims could take it or leave it.

Most of them decided to leave it. They lost heart at the prospect of working seven years in a wilderness and then getting nothing more than £10 worth of real estate. So the Rev. John Robinson had to remain with them, to the great grief of the emigrants.

But a minority of the Leyden congregation decided to take it, and to bring their wives and families with them. Brewster and Bradford, Carver and Cushman, Winslow and Allerton were the leaders in this decision and so became the leaders of the Pilgrim Fathers.

III

GREAT
PREPARATIONS

❦❦❦❦❦❦❦❦❦❦❦❦❦❦❦❦❦❦❦❦❦❦❦❦

FITTING OUT

ARRANGEMENTS should have been completed in time for
the Pilgrims to sail in April or May so that they could
plant a crop for the autumn harvest. But, what with one
thing and another, they did not even leave Holland until
22 July 1620; and their final departure for America was
postponed until September. They had to make all the prep-
arations themselves. Weston & Company (whom we will re-
fer to as the London Adventurers) advanced a part of the
money, but did nothing about fitting out, except to interfere.

Even today, in our highly developed industrial system, it is
a big business to fit out an overseas expedition under sail,

but little enough compared with what the Pilgrims' committee had to do. Their principal provisions were ship biscuit —"hardtack"—and pickled beef or pork, which sailors used to call "salt horse." For the one they went into the country, bought wheat, took it to a flour mill, and hired bakers to turn it into a kind of hard bread resembling dog biscuit. For meat they bought pigs and cattle on the hoof, drove them to a market town, paid butchers to slaughter them and salters to pickle the meat and pack it in barrels. For beer they must select a brewery which produced beer with enough alcoholic content so that the beverage would not sour. To make the barrels they hired a cooper who also sailed with them and inspected the casks daily, as an engineer checks the batteries of a submarine, to see that they were not leaking. That is how faint-hearted John Alden got his job and, eventually, his Priscilla. Then there were a hundred items that must be purchased—muskets, powder and shot, clothing and shoes, saws, axes, and other tools, and fishing gear. Everything cost more than was expected, more money had to be borrowed, and there were many unexpected delays.

The first thing, of course, was to get shipping. The English committee chartered the famous *Mayflower*, while the Leyden emigrants bought in Holland and fitted out the smaller *Speedwell*. She was to take them to England and carry some of them to America, where they would use her for fishing "and such other affairs as might be for the good and benefit of the colony."

When the time came for the Leyden Pilgrims—fifty or sixty in number—to depart, the entire congregation accompanied them to Delftshaven where the *Speedwell* lay ready. "So they left that goodly and pleasant city" of Leyden, writes Bradford, "which had been their resting place near twelve years; but they knew they were Pilgrims, and looked not much on those things, but lift up their eyes to the heavens, their dearest country, and quieted their spirits." Bradford continues:

> The next day (the wind being fair) they went aboard and their friends with them, where truly doleful was the sight of that sad and mournful parting, to see what sighs and sobs and prayers did sound amongst them, what tears did gush from every eye, and pithy speeches pierced each heart; that sundry of the Dutch strangers that stood on the quay as spectators could not refrain from tears. Yet comfortable and sweet it was to see such lively and true expressions of dear and unfeigned love. But the tide, which stays for no man, calling them away that were thus loath to depart, their reverend pastor falling down on his knees (and they all with him) with watery cheeks commended them with most fervent prayers to the Lord and His blessing. And then with mutual embraces and many tears they took their leaves one of another, which proved to be the last leave to many of them.
>
> Thus hoisting sail, with a prosperous wind they came in short time to Southampton, where they found the bigger ship come from London, lying ready, with all the rest of their company.

Of the "rest of their company," thirteen families and seven single men, some were Puritans like themselves; but others were not. Weston & Company, declaring that not enough Puritans had volunteered to form a colony—which was very true—had advertised for recruits. That is why there were intruded among the Pilgrims a group not interested in religion but who wanted some means to get to the New World and make their fortunes. Some of those who joined in London, such as the Chiltons, Eatons, Fullers, Hopkinses, and Mullinses, as well as Richard Warren, John Alden, and Myles Standish, became pillars of the Colony; but others, such as John Billington, who eventually was hanged for murder, turned out to be bad actors and troublesome citizens. These people the Pilgrims called "the strangers."

Myles Standish was hired to train the men in military exercises. Thirty-six years old, he had fought in the wars of the Low Countries and was well fitted to organize the Colony's defenses. Captain John Smith of Pocahontas fame, then unemployed, wanted the job; but the Pilgrims turned him down, saying that they had his book which was "better cheap." Doubtless they were right, for one cannot imagine the doughty Captain Smith taking orders from farmers who had never been overseas or seen an Indian.

Difficulties were not over when the entire company met at Southampton, where nowadays great passenger liners land and embark more passengers every day in the year than the entire Pilgrim band. Debts had been incurred, amounting to £100 over and above what Weston had advanced, and he would not give them another penny. So they sold some of their provisions, including several thousand pounds of butter, with which they were oversupplied, to get clear of the "land sharks," as sailors like to call ship chandlers; and they departed without enough weapons to arm every man, or proper fish hooks.

Fortunately, William Mullins, who had been a shoemaker at London, brought an extra supply of twenty-one dozen pair of shoes and thirteen pair of boots. This made a nice dowry for his daughter Priscilla when he died in 1621, and John Alden finally decided to "speak for himself."

FALSE DEPARTURE

◆§ THE COMPANY was divided beween the two ships, a governor appointed for each, and on 5 August they set sail. The *Speedwell* soon began to leak so badly that they had to put in at Dartmouth to have her repaired and calked. That consumed more time and increased the expense. Again they put to sea, about 25 August. But after they had sailed some three hundred miles into blue water, the master of the *Speedwell* complained that she was still so leaky that he dared not go on; they couldn't keep her dry, no matter how hard they pumped. So back again, this time into Plymouth. The trouble

Loading the Mayflower *at Southampton*

with the *Speedwell* was that she was overmasted and over-rigged, so that she strained in a seaway and her seams opened. The Pilgrims decided that it was too late in the year to do anything about it, so they sold her at a loss and some of her company crowded on board the *Mayflower,* while the others waited for another ship next year.

One of these, Robert Cushman, disgusted by the delays and by what he called the "bloodsucker" merchants, and by endless discussions among the Pilgrims themselves, wrote to a friend in London: "If we ever make a plantation, God works a miracle, especially considering how scant we shall be of victuals, and most of all disunited among ourselves and devoid of good tutors and regiment" (by which he meant leaders and discipline). . . . "I pray you prepare for evil tidings of us every day. But pray for us instantly, it may be the Lord will be yet entreated one way or other to make for us."

Cushman had good reason to be gloomy about the Pilgrims' prospects. No more desperate colonial venture was ever launched from English shores. The season was already too late for a fair voyage. The passengers had no knowledge of the New World. Simple farmers and artisans for the most part, they knew nothing about fishing or fur-trading, and were not trained to cope with pioneer conditions in a savage continent. But they had something better than money and skills—stout courage and firm faith. If no natural leaders appeared in England, forth they came when needed. Above all, they believed that God was for them. How true was Elder Brewster's boast: "It is not with us as with other men, whom small things can discourage!" All their troubles in getting to sea, they decided, had been planned by the Almighty to test them and weed out the weak and the timid.

No people who went out to form a colony were ever so ill-trained or so poorly provided with materials to make a success as these. Yet none came through so triumphantly. We may well echo the noble words of Bradford, written ten years later: "Our fathers were Englishmen which came over this great ocean, and were ready to perish in this wilderness; but they cried unto the Lord, and He heard their voice. . . . Let them therefore praise the Lord, because He is good; and His mercies endure forever."

THE *MAYFLOWER* AND HER CREW

❮❁

THE SHIP

"SEPTEMBER 6. These troubles being blown over, and now all being compact together in one ship, they put to sea again with a prosperous wind, which continued divers days together, which was some encouragement unto them." Thus begins William Bradford's brief account of the voyage of the *Mayflower*.

Before we tell the story, let us look at the famous ship herself.

There are several modern models of the *Mayflower*, and our English friends are now (1956) building a full-scale replica which they propose to sail across the Atlantic and moor in Plymouth Harbor. But reconstructing the *Mayflower* is like building the skeleton of a mammoth from one shinbone. The only facts we have are some records of her earlier voyages, a partial list of her crew in 1620, and her cargo-carrying capacity: 180 tons. This means that she could load 180 "tuns" or double hogsheads of wine in her hold. She had been in the wine trade with France for at least twelve years before the London Adventurers chartered her for the Pilgrims, and she was probably at least twenty years old when she sailed for America.

She was a fine, staunch vessel. Employment in the wine trade had made her a "sweet" ship. Leakage from the wine casks over a space of years neutralized the garbage and other filth that sailors in those days threw into the hold instead of bothering to drop it overboard. That explains why the Pilgrims lost only one of their number by illness on the long, rough, cold voyage. She was a fast ship, too, as her return voyage of thirty-one days Plymouth to Plymouth proves. That would be a good run by a sailing vessel of her size today.

On the basis of 180 tons' burden, historians familiar with the proportions and build of seventeenth-century ships have worked out a fairly reliable table of the *Mayflower's* dimensions, rig, and appearance. Her over-all length from bow to stern was around ninety feet; her beam (extreme breadth), twenty-five feet; the depth of her hold from the top deck to the inside of the keel, seventeen feet; and she drew, loaded, about two fathom (twelve feet) of water. The middle part of her main deck, which ran the full length of the ship, was exposed to the weather. This open part was called the "waist" of the ship, and canvas "waist cloths" could be rigged to keep out the spray. Below the main deck was the gun deck, with about five feet head room; and below the gun deck was the hold.[1]

At each end, the bow and the stern, there was a high superstructure. The forward one, called the forecastle, was where the crew lived and the cook had his galley—a crude brick stove which used wood for fuel. The larger stern-castle or poop had two short decks, one of which contained both the "great cabin" or wardroom, where the officers ate, and the master's stateroom; both had built-in bunks for the more important passengers. Here too was the bread room, where flour and hardtack were stored, since it was the dryest part of the ship. Under it was the steerage, where a sailor steered by a whipstaff, a vertical beam attached to the great tiller which ran through a sternpost to the rudder head. Steering-wheels and gear were not invented until the eighteenth century.

The helmsman couldn't see where the ship was going, or indeed anything but the foot of the mainmast and the lower clews or corners of the mainsail. He was "conned," as we still say in the Navy, by the officer of the deck (the master or one of the two master's mates) through an open hatch in the poop deck. Samples of such orders are: "starboard a little" —"steady now"—"full-and-by"—"luff her a little"—"keep her off." The officer of the deck had a compass before him in a square box called the binnacle, which was lighted at night; probably the helmsman had a second compass to help him keep the ship on a steady course.

---

[1] These dimensions have been kindly furnished by Mr. William A. Baker of Hingham, Mass., who designed the *Mayflower* now being built in England.

[OPPOSITE] *The* Mayflower.

The *Mayflower* had three masts. The mainmast, the middle one, together with the main topmast secured to it, extended about one hundred feet above the water. It carried a fifty-four-foot main yard to which the square mainsail, twenty feet tall, was bent. The mainsail's area and height could be increased by a nine-foot "bonnet" that was laced to its foot or lower edge, when the wind was light. The topmast carried a twenty-foot topsail yard upon which the topsail was bent, its lower clews being secured to the main yard; and above the topmast was a fifteen-foot flagstaff where the Union Jack could be displayed. Foremast and foretopmast, at least twelve feet shorter than the main, carried two sails similar in shape but smaller. The mizzenmast, about sixty feet tall with a forty-foot yard slung diagonally across it, carried a fore-and-aft lateen sail, like those still used by vessels in the Mediterranean Sea and the Far East. For headsails, since the jib had not been invented, she had a square spritsail bent to a short yard slung under the long, high-pointing bowsprit.

All the rigging was of hemp; there was not one piece of wire or Manila rope. Her sails were upheld by heavy lines called shrouds, crossed by ratlines like the steps of a ladder to enable sailors to climb aloft quickly. Her yards were hoisted by halyards, a word still used on sailing craft. They were adjusted to the direction of the wind by braces. Each square sail was set, furled, or trimmed by a complicated series of ropes—clewlines, buntlines, leachlines, tacks, sheets, and bowlines. In all there were probably seventy-five different lines in the running rigging of the *Mayflower*. They were secured to belaying pins at the foot of the masts or at the rail; and every sailor had to know how to lay his hand on the right one instantly in the dark—or else!

Every merchant ship of that day was armed, even in time

of peace, and the *Mayflower* carried several long guns called "minions" which fired a four-pound cannon-ball, and some lighter pieces called "sakers." Some of the larger ones were later mounted on the fort at Plymouth. She also carried muskets and cutlasses on racks for the men to use in case of a fight at sea. But that was one thing the Pilgrims did not have to go through, fortunately.

It is a puzzle how the *Mayflower* managed to accommodate all the passengers who, after part of the *Speedwell's* company joined, numbered 102. For she was a cargo carrier, not a passenger ship, and was not equipped to take many people. Some passengers, we know, slept in the shallop, a big ship's boat which was stowed on the gun deck. Double- or triple-tier bunks must have been built, or hammocks slung, on the gun deck. There can have been little privacy for anyone.

No live cattle or livestock of any kind were taken, but some of the passengers brought their pets. They used a mastiff and a spaniel to hunt deer the first winter ashore, and we may be sure that these were not the only dogs aboard the *Mayflower*. How they got on with the ship's cats—for every ship in those days had cats to cope with the rats—we don't know; but one can bet that any tough cat that had been on board ship for years could handle anything of the dog tribe.

MASTER, OFFICERS, AND CREW

⋖§ THE MASTER, as captains of merchant ships are called, was Christopher Jones of Rotherhithe on the Thames. He knew the *Mayflower* well, as he had commanded her for twelve years and had bought a quarter share of her with his savings. Master Jones has been depicted in a recent movie as

a brutal ruffian who spent most of his time on board making
love to Dorothy Bradford and the other girls, and who had
been bribed to take the Pilgrims to the wrong place. That is
sheer nonsense. The Pilgrims themselves spoke highly of him
and named the biggest stream that flows into Plymouth Bay,
Jones River, after him. Jones was an excellent seaman and a
humane gentleman who stood by them through their first
hard winter ashore.

The two master's mates, corresponding to our first and
second officers, had been in America before. John Clarke had
been kidnapped by a Spanish caravel at the Chesapeake in
1611, kept in a Spanish prison for four years, and later employed to carry a shipload of Irish cattle to Virginia. Robert
Coppin had previously been on a voyage to New England.
Besides these, there were four petty officers called quarter-
masters (as they still are in the Navy), a boatswain, a surgeon, a gunner, a cook, and twenty or more seamen. They
seem to have been the usual rough sailors of that era, religious in a way but disliking the frequent prayers and psalm-
singing of their Puritan passengers. One "very profane"
sailor, who was always cursing the seasick passengers and
threatening to throw them to the sharks, was stricken himself
and died at sea.

Just before weighing anchor at Plymouth, Master Jones
divided his crew into two watches—"starboard" and "lar-
board" (the old name for port, or left side of the ship), each
under one of the mates. Every four hours watches were
changed, except that between 4.00 and 8.00 P.M. they were
"dogged," i.e., divided in half so that different sailors would
alternate the tough "graveyard watch" from midnight to
4.00 A.M. Time was kept by a half-hour sand glass hanging
from a beam of the poop deck; for nobody on board owned a

watch, and the pendulum clocks of that era would not work on a tossing ship. Every half-hour, as the sand ran out, a sailor reversed the glass and struck a bell which hung in a little belfry at the break of the poop. At seven bells, or a little after, he woke up the relieving watch; and as eight bells struck, the officer of the deck bawled: "Relieve the helmsman and the look-outs!" Then the sailors who had been working on deck, or pumping, or looking around the horizon, went forward for something to eat and drink, and a well-earned sleep. But if the wind blew very hard or something carried away, it was "All hands on deck!" and the watch below had to turn out and lend a hand, no matter how tired, wet, and sleepy they were.

When the dog watches were changed, the seamen sang a psalm and said a prayer in which the passengers joined; for you needed all the help God would give you on a night at sea in 1620.

THE SIXTY-SIX DAY VOYAGE

❮❮❮❮❮❮❮❮❮❮❮❮❮❮❮❮❮❮❮❮❮❮❮❮❮❮❮❮❮❮❮❮❮❮

STORMY WEATHER

Luckily the *Mayflower* had fair weather for a week or two after her final departure on 6 September, so the passengers were able to shake down and get their "sea legs." Christopher Martin, one of the Pilgrims, was appointed their "Governor" on board ship to keep order among them. In those days people were used to being cold and uncomfortable on land, and the ship was not much worse except for drenchings and sea-sickness. There was no heat except in the galley, no chance to wash except in salt water. No plumbing, of course; if you were seasick or wished to ease yourself, you did it in a bucket and heaved the contents overboard, or you

hung in the nettings under the bowsprit and got soused by
the bow waves. There were no oilskins or rubber clothing for
passengers or crews; if you got wet you stayed wet until the
sun came out. People never undressed but wore the same
clothes all the way across; we would have found them very,
very smelly at the end of the journey! No mattresses or blankets were provided, except what the passengers themselves
brought. The food was nothing but ship biscuit, salt beef and
pork, and boiled peas or beans, although the leading passengers carried private stores of luxuries such as sugar and
raisins, and lemons to prevent scurvy. There was nothing to
drink but water and beer, except that Bradford and Brewster,
Martin and Carver brought a few bottles of wine and brandy.

The men and big boys among the Pilgrims helped the
sailors haul on ropes, partly to get exercise and partly to learn
how to sail; for they knew that in their new home the only
way to get about, until roads were built, would be in a boat.
The *Mayflower* had a well-balanced rig so that when the
yards and sails were trimmed properly she was as easy as a
small boat to steer; and often youths like John Howland
would be allowed to take a trick at the whipstaff, so long as a
professional seaman stood by. The boys were certainly allowed to climb the masts and sit in the crow's nest with the
look-out and listen to his yarns of the sea during the long
watches. When it blew hard and sail had to be shortened,
no "landlubbers" were wanted aloft. First the square sail
would be clewed; that is, pulled up in loose bunches on the
yard. It could not stay that way or it would slat and tear;
so a gang of sailors climbed aloft to roll it tight and fasten it
with short lines called gaskets. That was called furling.

Ships of those days could not sail closer to the wind
than six points of the compass. For instance, if the wind was

due west, the *Mayflower* could not sail nearer to west than north-northwest if on the port tack (wind blowing on her port side); or south-southwest if on the starboard tack (wind blowing on her starboard side). Master Jones had to judge which tack would get his ship nearer her destination, and when to "come about" on the other tack. For that complicated maneuver, all hands were called on deck. The mizzen was hauled in tight so as to kick her stern around, and the spritsail was furled. The helmsman put the tiller "hard down" and the great main yard was swung through an arc of about ninety degrees at the exact moment when the master shouted: "Let go and haul!" At that moment the crew were glad to have some "beef" from the passengers to apply to the main braces.

The women and children had the worst time on board. During the voyage a son was born to Elizabeth and Stephen Hopkins and appropriately named Oceanus; and just after arriving at Cape Cod, a boy was born to Susanna and William White and named Peregrine, the Pilgrim. Four persons, including Dorothy Bradford, died on board in Provincetown Harbor before the *Mayflower* left Cape Cod. Thus, only ninety-nine were delivered at Plymouth. Peregrine, many years later, received a land grant from the Colony as "the first of the English born in these parts"; he lived through the entire history of the Colony and died at Marshfield in 1704.

The *Mayflower* made a slow and rough voyage because she left at the wrong time of year. If the Pilgrims' plans had been carried out promptly, she would have started in May and enjoyed fair winds. But in September the season of westerly gales had begun, and she encountered plenty.

How did Master Jones find his way across this "vast and furious ocean," as Bradford called it? He had some inaccurate charts of the Atlantic, and knew the straight course for

Cape Cod; but for more than half the voyage the west wind prevented his steering the straight course. Every noon he checked his latitude by observing the sun with a crude instrument called a cross-staff, and applying figures from an almanac. But he had no means of measuring longitude or how far west he had sailed, except by tracing on the chart his compass course and estimated distance. He knew the *Mayflower* so well that he could judge the speed that she could make under various conditions.

In those days the usual route to Virginia followed that of Columbus, dropping down to the Canaries to get the easterly tradewinds to waft you across to the West Indies and Florida, whence you followed the coast. Some ships, however, had had good luck following the short route straight across, and Master Jones decided to try it. The *Mayflower* took sixty-five days to sail from Plymouth, England, to Cape Cod, and one day more to her first American harbor. That was exactly twice what Columbus took on his first voyage. The *Mayflower* might have made a shorter and easier passage by the southern route, but she would have run the risk of being captured by the Spaniards or wrecked off Cape Hatteras.

It is too bad that we have no log or sea journal of the *Mayflower;* it would be priceless now. Master Jones doubtless kept one, but since he died shortly after returning to England, his widow probably used it for wrapping-paper. All we know about the voyage, aside from a few incidents, is that after the first few days it was very, very rough. When half-seas over, a main beam (one of the thwart-ship timbers which strengthened the hull), cracked. This made the main deck leak rain or sea water and everyone on the deck below was drenched. Some of the sailors wanted to turn back; but the passengers broke out a "great iron screw brought out of Holland"—

probably for raising houses—and used it to shove the cracked beam in place. They then calked the deck, "committed themselves to the will of God, and resolved to proceed."

In some of the westerly gales the ship had to lie to, which meant taking in all sails and drifting with the wind. In one such gale John Howland fell overboard but managed to grab a trailing halyard and was pulled back with a boat hook.

LANDFALL AND CHANGE IN DESTINATION

✑ on 9 November 1620[1] at about 8.00 A.M., the *Mayflower* sighted the Highlands of Cape Cod, which made everyone "not a little joyful," says Bradford. No wonder, after two months and three days at sea! "And the appearance of it much comforted us, especially seeing so goodly a land, and wooded to the brink of the sea." All good Cape Codders will approve.

Master Jones, now knowing where he was, turned the *Mayflower's* bow south and sailed down the long, skinny arm of Cape Cod. He was on route, as he hoped, to the mouth of the Hudson River, the Pilgrims' intended destination. But by evening the *Mayflower* was off the elbow of the Cape, and involved in the dangerous shoals called Pollock Rip. The current was against her, the wind falling, and darkness coming on. Pollock Rip is a perilous passage for sailboats even today when it is well charted, buoyed, and dredged; but on 9 November 1620 it was terrifying to approach those "dangerous shoals and roaring breakers." Rather than become entangled in them, Master Jones held council with Carver,

---

[1] By the Julian calendar that the Pilgrims used. To find the equivalent date on our modern calendar, the Gregorian, add ten days.

Bradford, and other leading passengers, and decided to turn about and make for the harbor inside the tip of Cape Cod.

That was a sound decision. By next evening, 10 November, the *Mayflower* was off Peaked Hill Bar. The weather was clear and cold; the moon, in her last quarter, rose shortly after one o'clock, lighting up the white sand dunes of Race Point. Most of the passengers were below, the "graveyard watch" had charge, and on the high poop deck Master Jones and Mate Clarke walked briskly to and fro, watching the sails, peering into the binnacle, looking up at the stars, and conning the helmsman in the steerage. Every quarter-hour the leadsman in the chains hove the hand-lead and sang out

John Howland being rescued from the sea.

the depths. It was a night of watchfulness but not of danger; the passengers were thankful for their narrow escape from the shoals, and joyful over the prospect of landing on the morrow.

❧ VI ❧

LANDINGS AND
EXPLORATIONS

❧❧❧❧❧❧❧❧❧❧❧❧❧❧❧❧❧❧❧❧❧❧❧❧❧❧❧❧❧❧❧❧❧

THE LANDING AT PROVINCETOWN

DURING THE SMALL HOURS of 11 November the *Mayflower*
tacks to and fro, in order not to lose touch with the
Cape. Daylight, breaking around six o'clock, finds her on a
southeasterly course working in by Wood End with a fair
tide. At seven the sun rises red and clear above the Truro
hills; and by the time eight bells are struck and the watch is
changed, the *Mayflower* is south of Long Point and heading
into Cape Cod Harbor, as they then called it—Provincetown
Harbor as now renamed.

It is now nine or ten o'clock. The bulwarks are so crowded
with passengers eager to look upon their new Land of Ca-

naan that the mate orders them to stand clear of the tackle so
that he may work his ship. About a mile off the tip of Long
Point, Master Jones shapes a course southward for the land-
locked part of the harbor, feeling his way with lead-line so he
will not be in danger of running aground. At the same time
he is taking in sail. When the leadsman sings out, "By the
mark, five!" (meaning thirty feet, in land language), the master says to Mate Clarke: "Well enough." Clarke says: "Aye,
aye, sir," and bellows: "Hard down!" to the helmsman, who
answers: "Hard down, sir!" and presently: "Helm's a-lee!"
Now, with no sail to give her headway, the *Mayflower* glides
into the wind a couple of hundred yards from shore. At the
proper moment the best bower anchor is let go and the thick
hemp cable, which the seamen have been flaking on the
forecastle head since daybreak, is carefully paid out as the
anchor fluke bites into the bottom, and the ship begins to
make sternway. When the mate gives the word, the cable is
snubbed on the capstan. Now, as Bradford notes in correct
nautical language, "they rode in saftie." The *Mayflower* is
snugged down in one of the best anchorages of New England.

Now the ship's longboat is lowered and an armed party of
fifteen or sixteen men rows ashore, landing at the southern
end of the present Provincetown. Bradford tells us that they
promptly "fell upon their knees and blessed the God of
Heaven, who had brought them over the vast and furious
ocean, and delivered them from all the perils and miseries
thereof, again to set their feet on the firm and stable earth,
their proper element."

For all that, the Pilgrims were in a grim situation. It was too
late in the season to strike around Cape Cod again for the
Hudson. The settled part of Virginia, wherein they had per-

mission to plant, was hundreds of miles away. The nearest white men were the French at Port Royal, Nova Scotia. Behind them was the mighty ocean separating them from the civilized part of the world. Before them was the wilderness, whose only inhabitants were Indians "readier to fill their sides full of arrows than otherwise." Master Jones said they must make up their minds promptly where to pitch their colony, for his ship's stores were running low and he must keep enough to get home. It would be nine months, at least, before they could hope to reap a harvest. "What could now sustain them," writes Bradford, "but the Spirit of God and

Landfall at Provincetown.

His grace? May not and ought not the children of these
fathers rightly say: 'Our fathers were Englishmen which
came over this great ocean, and were ready to perish in the
wilderness; but they cried unto the Lord, and He heard
their voice and looked on their adversity.' "

THE MAYFLOWER COMPACT

❧ WINTER was coming on and the land off which the *Mayflower* anchored looked desolate and dreary. They had no
authority to settle in New England. On their last day at sea,
after turning back from Pollock Rip, some of the "strangers"
who had joined at London began to boast that, now being
outside Virginia, "none had power to command them," and
as soon as they got ashore it would be Hey, Ho! every man
for himself, and the devil take the hindmost.

The leaders soon fixed that business. Some genius among
them proposed that the thing to do was to draw up a compact
similar to their church covenant, but for political purposes,
and to persuade every responsible man to sign. The famous
"Mayflower Compact" was accordingly drafted, and before
they had anchored in Cape Cod harbor almost every able-
bodied man on board had put his signature to it. How the
"bad actors" were persuaded to "sign on the dotted line" we
don't know; but most of them did.

This Compact declared that the passengers, as "loyal subjects of our dread Sovereign Lord King James," having un-
dertaken to plant a colony, do hereby "covenant and com-
bine ourselves into a civil body politic for our better ordering
and protection," and promise "due submission and obedi-
ence" to officers elected, or laws passed, by themselves. That
done, the signers (who now became the voters) proceeded to

elect a Governor. Their choice was John Carver. They intended this government to be only temporary until they could obtain a patent from the Council for New England, or a charter from the King. But it remained the basis of their government for ten years; some will say for seventy years, since all their later government developed out of the Compact.

Governor Carver, forty-four years old at the time, was one of the wealthiest of the passengers. A merchant of London, converted to the Puritan point of view, he had emigrated to Holland and joined the Pilgrim church. He laid out almost his entire fortune to provide for such expenses as the Pilgrims could not induce Weston & Company to meet, and he brought along his wife Katherine and six servants. Almost this entire family died the first winter, but one of them, John Howland, the lad who fell overboard and was rescued, survived to found a family.

On board the *Mayflower*, stowed on the gun deck, was a shallop, an open sailing and rowing boat that could hold thirty or forty people. The Pilgrims intended to keep it for their own use and wished right away to explore the coast and find a good site for settlement. But the shallop had been so banged about in rough weather as to be full of leaks. So they hoisted it out and floated it ashore, where the *Mayflower*'s carpenter and some of the men went to work making repairs.

EXPLORING CAPE COD

ৎও IN THE MEANTIME, all hands made several trips ashore in the smaller longboat; the women to wash clothes in a little brackish pond that then lay behind the Provincetown beach, the men to cut fragrant juniper wood for the galley. The boys fished, dug clams, and picked mussels; they liked the clams but the mussels made them sick. And a party of men took off to explore the neighborhood.

Captain Standish and sixteen men, each armed with musket, sword, and breastplate, landed on 15 November. After they had walked about a mile along the beach they spied five or six Indians and a dog. The Indians scampered into the woods "and whistled the dog after them." Apparently the dog wanted to make friends with the Pilgrims' spaniel, but his masters had other ideas. The explorers, thrilled that the Indians were more afraid of them than they were of the Indians, gave chase. Armed as they were, and soft after the long voyage, they were no match for nimble redskins in a running race on Cape Cod sand. After following the tracks for two or three miles, they camped for the night on a sandy ridge overlooking Pilgrim Lake, where Cape Cod is only a few hundred yards wide.

Next morning they took up the Indian trail again, followed the narrow ridge between the ocean and East Meadow, and got lost in a thicket which tore their clothes. About ten o'clock, very thirsty, as they had brought "neither beer nor water with them," they had the good fortune to happen on a spring of water, "of which we were heartily glad," writes Bradford, "and sat us down and drunk our first New England water with as much delight as ever we drunk drink in all our lives."[1]

---

[1] This is quoted from the work known as *Mourt's Relation*, a small book printed in London in 1622, which was made up from extracts out of Bradford's and Winslow's Journals. The spring cannot have been the one now marked "Pilgrim Spring" on the south side of East Meadow, but one that feeds a little pond in Dyer's Swamp, surrounded by thickets.

Well refreshed, the explorers worked toward the Bay Shore and then walked south along the beach until they came upon the little pond which gives its name to Pond Village, Truro. Turning inland, they found the stubble of an Indian cornfield, then returned to the beach, passed the mouth of the Great Hollow, and reached a ridge rising from the shore that is still called by the name the Pilgrims gave it, Corn Hill. There they found some Indian graves and a great iron kettle which they thought the natives must have bought from some ship. Digging under a heap of sand, they found a store of Indian corn in baskets, some of which they appropriated, making a mental note to pay the Indians later.

After spending a second and rainy night in the open, near the Village Pond, the explorers started across the Cape again and managed once more to get themselves lost in the woods west of the present Cape Cod or Highland lighthouse. There the company had a great laugh at the expense of William Bradford. He was investigating an Indian deer trap made from a bent tree, when he accidentally sprang it and was caught up by one leg, his body dangling in the air. His friends soon released him, and by evening all were back at the harbor and on board the *Mayflower*. "This was our first discovery," says Bradford. They certainly had plenty to tell; but no doubt Will had to take a lot of teasing from Dorothy and the girls about getting caught in the deer trap.

Now the weather turned cold and rainy; and as the shores of Cape Cod harbor slope very gradually (which is why modern Provincetown wharves are so long), everyone who landed got wet wading ashore from the longboat, and many started to sneeze and cough. It was the general opinion that this was no place to pitch a settlement. Not enough fresh water, for one thing.

By 28 November, when the shallop was repaired, they decided to investigate the Pamet River, which the first explorers had sighted from Corn Hill. This time Master Jones commanded the expedition and some of his sailors went along—thirty-four men and boys in all. They crossed to the mouth of the Pamet River, which they named Cold Harbor, for "it blowed and did snow all that day and night, and froze withal." The hills were under six inches of snow. After some fruitless marching along the banks of the Pamet, followed by the shallop floating in on the flood tide, Master Jones decided to pitch camp under a pine grove. Fortunately his men with muskets shot three fat geese and six black ducks, which they cooked and ate for supper "with soldiers' stomachs."

On the third day the party marched cross-country to Corn Hill, and with their swords and cutlasses dug up the rest of the corn and a bag of beans. Some men then returned to the ship with ten or twelve bushels of corn, part of which they used for seed next spring.

While the shallop returned to the *Mayflower* with this treasure, on 30 November, the rest of the explorers followed an Indian trail until it became "a very broad beaten path, well nigh two foot broad." Realizing that Indians must be about, they lighted the matches for their matchlock muskets and prepared to fight if necessary. But the Indians still eluded them. Later in the day they dug up an Indian grave and marveled at the bows and arrows and wooden bowls and other things which were lying among the bones. Shortly after, they came upon their first Indian huts. These were not the tentlike wigwams that you often see in pictures. The Eastern Indians built long "lodges" in the shape of a Quonset hut. Bradford describes them as "made with young sapling trees, bended and both ends stuck in the ground; they were made round, like unto an arbor, and covered down to the ground with thick and well wrought mats." They also found a lot of Indian baskets and some tobacco. After they had spent a third night out, the shallop came to fetch them at Corn Hill, and brought them back to the *Mayflower*.

After the return of this second exploring expedition, there was a debate on board as to whether the Pilgrims should settle at Cold Harbor or look farther. Some were for Cold Harbor because corn grew there and the fishing promised to be good; whales played about the *Mayflower* every day, and Master Jones said he could have tried out a thousand barrels

Bradford caught in the deertrap.

of whale oil if he only had harpoons and try-works. One Pilgrim even tried to shoot a whale with his musket but the musket blew up in his face, providentially not hurting anybody; and when the whale got good and ready "she gave a snuff and away."

Others pointed out that Cold Harbor was only deep enough for a boat, not a ship; that good fresh water was scarce; and there were too many Indians about to make it a healthy locality for Englishmen, even though they had firearms and the Indians none. That was a sound argument. Samuel de Champlain, the French explorer, had been driven off by a group of these same Nauset Indians in 1605; and in 1617, a French vessel had been wrecked on Cape Cod and the Indians had killed all the survivors except three, whom they enslaved. That was how they got the iron kettle.

Robert Coppin, one of the mates of the *Mayflower,* who had already made a voyage to New England, told them about "a great navigable river and good harbor in the other headland of this bay," which his shipmates had called "Thievish Harbor" because an Indian there had stolen a harpoon from them. The Pilgrims decided to investigate this harbor. Coppin probably meant Gloucester Harbor on Cape Ann,[2] but he actually took them to Plymouth, already so named on Captain John Smith's map. On 6 December, after Johnny Billington had almost blown up the *Mayflower* by stealing some gunpowder and firing off "squibs," the shallop shoved off on a third exploring expedition.

---

[2] Coppin was so vague that we cannot be sure what he meant; but the distance he gives—"not much above 8 leagues [twenty-four nautical miles] distant," fits Cape Ann better than Plymouth; and by the "great river" he may have meant the Annisquam. But possibly he meant Boston Harbor and the Charles.

All the leading Pilgrims sailed—Governor Carver, Bradford, Winslow, Standish, Warren, Hopkins, John and Edward
Tilley, two mates, the gunner, three sailors, and several servants—eighteen in all. It was so cold that the spray froze on
their coats. After crossing Wellfleet Harbor they turned south
at sundown and went ashore on one of the beaches of the
present Eastham. Along the beach they saw some Indians
busy cutting up a school of stranded blackfish. So, after
throwing up a "barricado" of logs and boughs, and appoint-
ing sentries, the explorers spent the night ashore. All next day
they "ranged up and down," but found no place that they
liked, and plenty of evidence of Indians.

While spending a second night behind the "barricado,"
they "heard a hideous and great cry," sprang to arms, and
fired a couple of muskets. Nothing more happened. They
decided it was a pack of wolves, but undoubtedly it was
Indians who were frightened away temporarily by the shooting. For, around break of day, after they had carried their
weapons down to the beach to take them on board the shallop and were eating breakfast, suddenly arrows began to fly
among them and the cry of "Indians! Indians!" was raised.
Myles Standish, who had prudently held onto his flintlock
carbine, fired a shot. The others ran down to the beach to recover their weapons, carrying brands from the breakfast fire
to light the matches; and a real fight began. The Indians
uttered a yell which Bradford renders as *woath woach ha ha
hach waoch* (meaning, probably, "Kill the palefaces!") and
the Indian leader, "a lusty man, and no less valiant, stood
behind a tree within half a musket shot and let his arrows fly
at them; he was seen [to] shoot three arrows, which were all
avoided. He stood three shots of a musket, till one taking full

aim at him and made the bark or splinters of the tree fly about his ears, after which he gave an extraordinary shriek and away they went, all of them."

That place is still called First Encounter Beach.[3] The Pilgrims were mightily encouraged by driving off some forty Indians. They picked up eighteen arrows as souvenirs, some of them sticking in coats which were hanging on the barricade.

Again boarding the shallop, they sailed westward along the Bay shore of the Cape, passing Barnstable Harbor and the future entrance to the Cape Cod canal. "After some hours' sailing," says Bradford, "it began to snow and rain, and about the middle of the afternoon the wind increased and the sea became very rough, and they broke their rudder, and it was as much as two men could do to steer her with a couple of oars." But pilot Coppin "bade them be of good cheer for he saw the harbor." Night drawing on and the storm increasing, the shallop's mast broke and the sail fell overboard. "Yet by God's mercy they recovered themselves, and having the flood with them, struck into the harbor."

Plymouth Harbor is still a difficult place to enter in thick weather. Brown's Bank is the obstacle. It breaks all over at low tide in heavy weather; you must keep clear of it and run for the Gurnet, then make a ninety-degree left turn to shelter. Mate Coppin, who was piloting the shallop, lost his nerve "and said the Lord be merciful unto them, for his eyes never saw that place before." He probably thought he was entering Gloucester Harbor, and naturally did not recognize

---

[3] First Encounter Beach may easily be reached today. Samoset Road leads westward 1.3 miles off Route 6 between Eastham and Wellfleet, by a winding course to the beach. A stone marker has been placed on top of a sand dune there, with the names of the explorers inscribed.

any of the landmarks. The shallop was almost ashore "in a cove full of breakers before the wind," when a "lusty seaman" who had the tiller "bade those which rowed, if they were men, *about* with her or else they were all cast away; the which they did with speed. So he bid them be of good cheer and row lustily, for there was a fair sound before them, and he doubted not but they should find one place or other where they might ride in safety."

It is too bad we do not know the name of that "lusty seaman," for without him all would probably have been drowned. And with Carver, Bradford, Winslow, Standish, and Warren

The first fight with Indians—at "First Encounter Beach"—Eastham.

dead, the rest of the *Mayflower's* company would certainly have given up and sailed home. Elder Brewster could hardly have carried on without those five stalwart leaders.

THE LANDING AT PLYMOUTH

⚜ BEHIND the island later named Clark's the shallop found quiet waters on the night of Saturday, December 9. Everyone went ashore, "and with much ado got fire" with flint and steel; and were mighty glad of it as the wind whipped around to northwest and it froze hard that night.

In accordance with their religious principles, the Pilgrims "rested the Sabbath" on Clark's Island. On Monday, December 11, they rowed to the mainland in the shallop. The nearest land in Plymouth Bay where they might have landed was right where the Plymouth Cordage Company wharf now is; but they may have gone ashore anywhere between that point and the mouth of the Town Brook, where Plymouth Rock lies. From whatever place they did land, they marched for several miles along the shore, finding "divers corn fields and running brooks, a place very good for situation."

This is the day—December 11 in their calendar, the 21st in ours—that is celebrated as "Forefathers' Day," when the first of the Pilgrims landed at Plymouth.

After sounding the depth of water in the harbor, the exploring expedition sailed back to Provincetown Harbor and reported that Plymouth was the right place to settle. Their clinching argument was that of the cleared cornfields ready for tillage, and the absence of live Indians, with plenty of bones as evidence that the local natives were all dead. They

[OPPOSITE] *Landing on Plymouth Rock.*

had died in a pestilence a few years before, leaving their cornfields for the first comer to use.

For William Bradford, however, this return to the *Mayflower* was a tragic event, for during his absence his young wife Dorothy had fallen overboard and been drowned. One may suspect that she did it on purpose, disheartened by gazing on the barren sand dunes of Cape Cod. How many tender hearts of pioneer women must have grown faint when they first beheld the wilderness shores of New England, so different from those of the green and placid Old England that they knew!

On 16 December the *Mayflower* weighed anchor from Cape Cod, and that night she anchored in Plymouth Harbor. Since it was against Puritan principles to work on the Sabbath, everyone stayed on board during Sunday 17 December, and Elder Brewster conducted divine service. Exploring parties started going ashore on Monday the 18th.

Thus, if you wish to be exact about dates, the first landing took place at the site of Provincetown on 11 November; the exploring expedition landed at or near the present town of Plymouth on 11 December; the *Mayflower* anchored in Plymouth Harbor on the 16th, and the first people went ashore from her on the 18th. There was no immediate or wholesale "landing of the Pilgrims on Plymouth Rock" such as you see in popular illustrations.

PRIVATION AND PESTILENCE

❧❧❧❧❧❧❧❧❧❧❧❧❧❧❧❧❧❧❧❧❧❧❧❧❧❧❧❧❧❧❧❧❧❧

THEY SETTLE NEAR THE ROCK

FOR THREE DAYS the Pilgrims roamed the shore and discussed where to pitch their settlement. Some were for Clark's Island where the exploring expedition had spent a night. It was customary to establish your first American home on an island as easier to defend against Indians. But the Pilgrims decided that a small island would not do for them. So their choice lay between the mouth of Jones River, in the present town of Kingston, and Town Brook.

Jones River had the attraction of salt meadows where hay could be cut, but back of the meadows lay thick woods which must be cleared before there could be any planting, and in the meantime would be a fine cover for hostile Indians. Also, there was no good landing place at the mouth of Jones River. So their choice fell on the spot where Town Brook flows into the harbor. On either side were cleared Indian cornfields ready for planting; and just behind the shore, overlooking the brook, was a high hill from which you could look out to sea and view the country all around. The flow of the brook made a boat channel at low tide through the mud flats, and just outside its mouth was Plymouth Rock.

That famous boulder is the only one on this sandy shore. Although the range of tide here is about nine feet, the rock was covered only at spring high tides; so, connected with the edge of the boat channel and with the shore by square logs, it made a convenient landing at any stage of the tide. After their experience at Provincetown Harbor, the Pilgrims were mighty glad to be able to get ashore dry-foot and standing up. As proof of the value of Plymouth Rock as a landing, when the townspeople built the first wharf in the next century, they constructed it right over the Rock.

This decision to locate at the center of the present town of Plymouth was very wise. It was not only the most defensible locality on the Bay, and the best place to get supplies ashore; it had the advantage of cleared land ready for the plow.

On 21 and 22 December there was a cold, heavy rain and strong wind so that nobody could go ashore, and the *Mayflower* had to put out two extra anchors. On the 23rd most of the men landed with their tools and began to chop down trees for building. They worked all Christmas Day; some chopping, some sawing logs to make planks, and some splitting cedar to make clapboard. By the end of the day they had the sills laid for a storehouse twenty feet square. A few men stayed ashore to guard the tools and materials lest Indians steal them (for they had heard something that sounded like a war-whoop), while the rest went on board the *Mayflower* to spend the night. We are sorry to say that the children had no Christmas trees or stockings or presents, because Puritans did not believe in keeping Christmas;[1] but the men had beer for supper, which was something.

There was no time for Christmas holidays for anyone; shelter must be provided ashore, and every day the men worked at building. The weather was wet and cold, but no snow as yet; and the *Mayflower* with her twelve-foot draft could not anchor closer than a mile and a half from the Rock.[2] During one day the men leveled off the top of Burial Hill so that they could mount cannon; but for the most part they worked at building small houses on each side of Leyden Street, as they called the road that they laid out from the Rock up toward the Hill.

THE PILGRIMS AND THEIR FIRST HOMES

◄§ PLYMOUTH today has a replica of one of the first Pilgrim houses. It is built of squared and sawed timber, not logs, and very small. There is only one room, with a big fireplace, on the ground floor, and above it a loft reached by a ladder, where children could sleep. The Pilgrims did not build log cabins; they had never seen one and knew nothing of that

---

[1] Their reasons were (1) that the exact date of Jesus' birth was not known; and (2) that Christmas, as then kept in England, was a rowdy holiday when everyone ate and drank to excess.

[2] Her anchorage was probably at the five-fathom spot marked on our chart just inside Goose Point, or it may have been even farther out, north of the "Horse Race" where there is a tide rip.

way of building.[3] But they were great fellows with a saw.
They would dig a sawpit about six feet deep, lay a pine log
across it and saw it into boards with a two-man saw, one
standing in the pit and one on top, alternately pushing and
pulling. For splitting cedar logs to use as inside sheathing,
they used an iron hammer that they called a beetle, and
iron wedges; the resulting clapboard was also a good export
to England. Oak trees were squared off with axe and adze to
make posts and beams for the house frames, which were fastened with wooden pins called treenails or trunnels. When
the frame was fitted, the men joined in and had a house-
raising, after which the house was boarded in and roofed
with bulrush thatch. Chimneys at first were made of wood
daubed with clay, of which there was plenty around Plymouth.

Having taken a look at the houses and (we hope) wiped
out the log-cabin myth, let us turn to the Pilgrims themselves.
Only one of them, Edward Winslow, ever had his portrait
painted in England, and that was thirty years later; it shows
him as a handsome, ruddy-faced man with brown eyes, chest-
nut-colored hair parted on the side, and a mustache and
goatee of the same color. We have no picture or even description of any other *Mayflower* passenger. Since whiskers
were still fashionable in England in 1620, we may imagine
the Pilgrim men as bearded. Young men and boys doubtless
vied with one another on board ship to see who could grow
the most formidable beard, just as our sailors did in World
War II.

Unfortunately, popular illustrators—excepting ours—have

---

[3] Log cabins were introduced to America by the Swedes who settled
on Delaware Bay in the 1640's. No English or French settlers built
log houses until the late seventeenth century.

given a completely wrong impression of what the Pilgrims wore. They insist on clothing the men in black suits and tall black hats with silver buckle, and the women in shapeless mouse-gray dresses. Actually these people dressed like other English people of their class. Each man of substance had a black suit and hat (but not a buckle) for Sunday; on ordinary days and when working, every man wore a gray, brown, or blue linen long-sleeved shirt, a buff leather jacket called a jerkin, woolen or leather breeches, Irish knit stockings which covered the thighs, and either low shoes or high jack-boots. Instead of an overcoat he had a sleeveless cloak, and his usual headgear was the Monmouth cap. That was a wool stocking cap much like the traditional cap of Santa Claus. Most of these clothes were colored. Women wore long colored wool dresses, and children wore clothes of the same cut as those of the grownups. We shall describe their clothing in more detail later.

Brightly colored though their clothes were when new, the Pilgrims were not walking fashion plates. Their garments took an awful beating on the voyage, and from hard work ashore. Note the old ballad quoted later, in Chapter X, about how their clothes had to be patched over and over again.

Let us, then, think of the Pilgrims as dressed in rough but colored work clothes and wearing Monmouth caps. It is as absurd to picture them sawing wood, hoeing corn, or hunting game in black breeches and plug hats as it would be to show a farmer of today plowing in a tuxedo coat and Homburg hat.

THE GREAT SICKNESS

❧ THE WINTER of 1620-21 was an open one for New England, with little frost or snow, but miserably wet and clammy. Of course there was plenty of wood to keep roaring fires in the houses or out where the men were working, and they did appreciate that, because firewood was scarce and dear in Europe. They would have got along all right but for the "Great Sickness." Bradford says that the chief trouble was scurvy, a vitamin-deficiency disease which often attacked people on long voyages, for it was now a good four months since they had eaten any fruit or fresh vegetables. Some doubtless came down with pneumonia; others may have caught typhus, the "ship fever" of the day, from the lice on board ship. Their condition became worse, owing to the cold and wet and change of diet. Englishmen in those days were used to eating plenty of beef and wheat bread, and drinking beer. But salt beef and hard bread had to be saved for the *Mayflower's* return voyage, and the people had to get along as best they could on corn bread, shellfish, and game. Plymouth Bay is famous even today for clams and lobsters, so there was plenty of sea food—but try eating clams and lobsters three times a day for a week, and you will never want to look either in the face again! Fish were so scarce that when a sailor picked up a herring on the shore, Master Jones ate it for supper. No fish nets had been brought over, and the only hooks they had were too big to catch the tomcod, flounders, and other small fish that came into the Bay. A fishing party which ventured outside in the shallop on 8 January brought back three seals and "an excellent good cod" which were eagerly devoured. But how the sick people did crave a good slice of roast beef and a hunk of white bread!

Although the Pilgrims were rather clumsy and unenterprising about fishing, some of them at least were good shots; and this is surprising, as Englishmen of their class were not accustomed to shooting birds. Captain John Smith, for instance, admits that in early Virginia the woods were full of game, "but they so wild and we so weak we could not get at them." Whether it was due to Myles Standish or what, I do not know, but the Pilgrims were certainly able to kill plenty of wild duck, geese, and turkey. And one of their earliest laws was "that fowling, fishing, and hunting" be free—no fish and game laws for them, as in the Old Country! When Edward Winslow and a friend were on their way to call on Massasoit in 1621, they obliged the friendly Indians of Nemasket by shooting no fewer than eighty crows that were eating their corn, in one day. If you have ever tried to shoot a crow, you will agree that this was mighty fine gunning. And one thing the Pilgrims had plenty of was gunpowder and shot.

January and February of 1621 were the worst months at Plymouth. Some days, two or three died; and at times there were only six or seven healthy people to care for the rest. Bradford himself was laid low, and Governor Carver; while they were lying sick in the storehouse, its thatched roof caught fire from sparks out of the chimney, and they and the gunpowder were got out just in time to prevent a catastrophe. The *Mayflower* doubled as a hospital ship, and her surgeon, Giles Heale, did what he could for the invalids, but that was not much. Samuel Fuller, who brought over a chest of surgeon's instruments and a supply of "physic" was "a great help and comfort to them," but he had no cure for scurvy or pneumonia. Passengers who did not fall sick, including Elder Brewster and Myles Standish, cared with great tenderness for those who were stricken. They kept fires burning, cooked their food, washed their "loathsome clothes" and did "all the homely and necessary offices for them which dainty and queasy stomachs cannot endure to hear named," recorded Bradford. About half the *Mayflower* passengers died before spring, and by summer only twelve of the original twenty-six heads of families and only four of the twelve bachelors were alive. Three entire families were wiped out— the Martins, Tinkers, and Rigsdales. Of the eighteen married women who reached Plymouth, only three survived. Fortunately the young girls were more hardy; only one out of nine died.

It was tough for men to lose their beloved wives and see their little children pine away and die; and even worse for children to lose a parent. And there was no minister to read a burial service over them, though Elder Brewster doubtless said a few prayers and consoled the relatives as best he could. And the survivors dared not mark the graves lest prowling Indians suspect how many had been lost.

The crew of the *Mayflower* suffered almost as much as the passengers. So many of them fell sick that Master Jones decided to stay until spring to be sure of enough men to work his ship; as it was, the boatswain, the gunner, three other petty officers, the cook, and several seamen died.

SPRING RETURNS

OF COURSE it was not all bad, at least for the men and boys. There was the thrill of being in a new land, building houses, shooting game, and watching for Indians. Young Frank Billington climbed a tall tree, saw a "great sea" as he described it and came running home saying he had discovered the Pacific Ocean! The big pond that it turned out to be is called Billington's Sea to this day.[4] John Goodman and Peter Browne took the mastiff and the spaniel along when cutting bulrushes for thatch, and both dogs gave tongue after a big deer; the boys followed them far into the woods and got lost. That afternoon it snowed, and they spent the night at the foot of a tree, terrified by the howling of wolves which they imagined to be lions, and ready to climb the tree if attacked. Next afternoon they mounted a hill from which they sighted the Bay and laid a course for home. John's feet were so swollen that his shoes had to be cut off; but within a week he limped off to the woods again with the spaniel. Two big wolves chased the dog, which "ran betwixt his legs for succor," but John fended the beasts off with a stick "and they sat on their tails grinning at him a good while," then went away. John was quite a hero after that.

Nobody saw hide or hair of an Indian until 16 February when a man gunning for wildfowl saw a dozen braves marching "Indian file" in the direction of Plymouth. He ran home and gave the alarm. Nothing happened, except that Myles Standish and Francis Cooke, who left their heavy woodcutting tools in the forest, had them stolen by the Indians.

These events caused the surviving men to hold a meeting, elect Myles Standish their captain, and give him authority to drill and command. And a few days later Master Jones and

---

[4] Wiser men than Frank made the same mistake, which stemmed from an old chart drawn by the Florentine navigator Verrazano. Robert Cushman, writing in 1621, said that New England was an island, separated from the American mainland by "a great arm of the sea," but he didn't know whether it connected with the Pacific Ocean or the St. Lawrence.

his sailors brought ashore four or five cannon from the *Mayflower* and helped the men to mount them on the big hill—
the one called Burial Hill today. That was very generous of
Jones, because every ship in those days needed guns to beat
off pirates. He also brought a fat wild goose which he had
shot, and the Pilgrims produced a mallard duck, a crane, and
a dried ox tongue, which were the makings of a merry feast.

Fortunately there was an early spring in 1621. On 3
March (the 13th in our calendar) the weather turned warm
and "the birds sang in the woods most pleasantly." The Pilgrims began to plant garden seeds on the 7th. Red-breasted
American thrushes hopped about the garden lots, looking for

John Goodman holding wolves at bay.

worms, and the Pilgrims called them "robin red-breasts" after a small bird they knew well in England. The trailing arbutus put forth its fragrant pink flowers and the Pilgrims called it the mayflower after their ship. The shad-bush cast out its brilliant pink-white blossoms in the woods, small white flowers thrust up through the fallen oak leaves and pine needles, and the marsh marigold bloomed golden on the edge of Town Brook. Hope returned with spring, and the hearts of the Pilgrims lifted.

INDIAN ALLIES

SAMOSET AND SQUANTO

Now came another happy break for the Pilgrims in their relations with the natives. They had scared off the Nausets at "First Encounter," and they had found a place to settle where the Indians were all dead. But word of their arrival had spread to all the tribes along the New England coast; and as these had received very rough usage from English and French traders and fishermen, they were fearful of what this new crowd of Englishmen might do. There were Indian villages within fifteen or twenty miles of Plymouth— Nemasket in the present Middleborough and Manomet at the site of the Cape Cod Canal. The Indians had been so weakened by the great pestilence that they dared not attack, but "came skulking about" as Bradford wrote. There is no doubt, however, that the natives who lived between Cape Ann and Cape Cod and along Narragansett Bay, of whom at least two thousand were "pinses" (warriors), could have got together and wiped Plymouth Colony off the map, if they had tried. And the one man who could have led them was Massasoit, sachem of the Wampanoags or Pokanokets.

The event that turned this potential danger into an asset occurred on 16 March 1621. A stalwart Indian, "stark naked, only a leather about his waist," boldly walked into the settlement, to the terror of the children; for he was the first they had ever seen. But he called out: "Welcome, Englishmen!" to the first men he encountered, and held out his right hand. He was Samoset, sagamore[1] of a tribe that lived around Pemaquid Point in the future State of Maine. That part of New England had been frequented for twenty years by English fishermen, and Samoset had made friends with them and learned their language. After he had dined on ship biscuit, cheese, and butter, with a slice of wild duck and a bit of corn pudding, washed down with a glass of brandy, he became talkative and gave the Pilgrims valuable information on the tribes round about. He spent the night in Stephen Hopkins's house, and next day departed with a knife, a bracelet, and a ring as presents, promising to bring some of the Wampanoag tribe, with which he was sojourning, to call.

Samoset evidently sized up the Pilgrims as good people who had no intention of molesting the Indians, but possessed cannon and muskets that packed a terrific wallop against any enemy. On the 18th he returned with five Wampanoags clad in buckskin shorts and leggings. They "did eat liberally of our English victuals," wrote Bradford; and, as payment, put on a song-and-dance and returned Myles Standish's stolen tools. The children now began to think that Indians

---

[1] A sagamore was a chief next in rank below a sachem, whom the English often called a king, because he had nobody over him.

were good fun, and some of the boys begged a few beads or iron nails, to trade with them on the next visit.

On his next call, four days later, Samoset brought a most interesting redskin who stayed with the Pilgrims the rest of his life. This was Squanto (alias Tisquantum), sole survivor of the Patuxet tribe that formerly lived on the site of Plymouth. He owed his survival to the fact that he had been kidnapped, along with nineteen others, by a rascally English shipmaster, before the pestilence struck in. The Englishman had intended to sell his captives as slaves in Spain; but Squanto escaped and stowed away on a vessel bound for England, where he was taken in and kindly treated by a London merchant. At his request the merchant sent him to Newfoundland, where a shipmaster en route to New England picked him up as interpreter and landed him on the Maine coast. Thence he made his way to his old home, only to find that all his friends and relatives were dead.

Being a man without a country, as it were, Squanto decided to throw in his lot with the Pilgrims and make himself useful. And that he did, to such good purpose that Bradford called him "a special instrument of God for their good." He was familiar with the coast from the Penobscot to Point Judith. He taught them where and how to catch fish, how to tread eels out of mud, where to find succulent herbs in the forest, and, best of all, how to plant corn, of which they knew nothing. The cornfields were hoed, Indian fashion, into squares about six feet to a side, the earth heaped up in the middle, and three or four grains of corn planted in each hill, together with a fish or two as fertilizer. And Squanto taught them that the time to do this was when the oak buds had

[OPPOSITE] *Samoset's arrival.*

burst and the unfolding leaf was "as big as a mouse's ear."

Alewives, the fish he taught them to use for manuring their corn, were a kind of herring that swam up the streams every spring to spawn in the ponds, and in such numbers that they could be caught in a bucket or even by clubbing. They were good eating, too; fat enough to fry without grease and easy to cure by smoking, a welcome addition to the Pilgrims' fare. The only trouble with using them for fertilizer was their smell. This attracted the dogs, who dug up a lot of corn hills in search of rotten fish, before the Pilgrims knew what was going on. After that, the mastiff and the spaniel were hobbled—one front paw tied up so that they could not scratch or dig—until the corn was high.

MASSASOIT'S VISIT

MARCH was a great month for meeting Brother Redskin. On the 22nd, Squanto returned with Massasoit, sachem of the Wampanoags, with his brother Quadequina, and some sixty members of the tribe. They stopped on a hill across the Town Brook, within sight of the fort. That seemed a good many Indians for thirty or so Englishmen to handle; but they made the best of the situation and this meeting turned out very much to their advantage.

Massasoit's visit was conducted with as much ceremony as if he had been royalty. First, Edward Winslow, dressed in a full suit of armor and girt with his sword, crossed Town Brook with a few attendants and presented the "royal" brothers with knives, a copper chain with a jewel in it, an earring, a pot of brandy, and some buttered ship biscuit. While these gifts were being sampled, Winslow made a speech, stating that King James wished Massasoit to be his friend and ally, and that Governor Carver was prepared to make a treaty with him. The speech was translated by an Indian who knew a little English. Winslow then stayed with Quadequina as hostage, while Massasoit and twenty pinses (warriors), leaving their bows and arrows, crossed the brook. On the other side they were met by Myles Standish and six men who fired a musket salute and conducted the sachem to an unfinished house, where a green rug was spread on the floor, and he was enthroned on a pile of cushions. Governor Carver now entered with a drummer and trumpeter and "some few musketeers." He and Massasoit kissed hands and sat down; Carver called for drinks and Massasoit took a big swallow of brandy which "made him sweat all the time after." A feast of fresh venison was served. Massasoit, who wore a chain of white bone beads about his neck, was painted dark red in the face and oiled all over, so that "he looked greasily," and doubtless smelled very high. He carried a pouch of tobacco, which he shared with the Governor.

After the Governor and the sachem had smoked a pipe of peace, they concluded a treaty, in brief as follows:

1. The Wampanoag tribe would not injure the Pilgrims; or if any did, Massasoit would deliver up the offender for punishment. And if any of the Colony did harm to the Indians, they would be punished;

2. Each party would help the other if attacked, and Massasoit undertook to inform all the other tribes that he was the Englishmen's ally;

3. When Indians visited Plymouth, or English visited the Indians, they must not carry weapons to the meeting;

4. King James would accept Massasoit as a friend and ally.

Although King James was not consulted, this treaty was faithfully kept for fifty-four years. And that is longer than most Indian treaties—indeed longer than most treaties between civilized nations—have been kept.

Bradford, who had a keen sense of reality, remarked that Massasoit was friendly because his tribe had lost over half its strength in the great pestilence, which had not touched the powerful Narragansetts. They frequently crowded him, and he counted on the English with their firearms to keep them at bay. Massasoit doubtless regarded the Pilgrims as providential aid from the Great Spirit to take the place of the extinct Patuxets who had been his subjects. Be that as it may, Massasoit was a great and good man, by any standards. Winslow recorded that he always told the truth, he was neither bloody nor cruel, he ruled his tribe by reason and character rather than by force, and always made them leave the English alone. For the next few years the very existence of the Colony depended on Massasoit's good will and loyalty.

We may be sure that during these proceedings all the small boys of the Colony were clustered about the house, whispering and wishing they could tell the kids in Leyden and London how real wild Indians looked. Too bad they couldn't have seen the Indian children, too; but these were kept on the hill with their mothers.

Next, Governor Carver conducted Massasoit to the Town Brook, where they embraced each other. Presently Quadequina, the sachem's brother, came with Winslow, and the whole party, except the treaty-making, had to be repeated for him. The Indians, except Samoset and Squanto, spent the night on their hill half a mile away.

Now that this important Indian business was concluded, the Pilgrims went ahead with their building and planting.

[OPPOSITE] *The Peace Treaty with Massasoit.*

And the Great Sickness was not yet over—sixteen died in March.

Mayflower RETURNS

⌇ ON 5 April the short-handed *Mayflower* set sail for England. It speaks well for the fine spirit of the Pilgrims, and their loyalty to the Colony, that not one of them went home in the ship. Such a thing had never happened before in the history of American colonization. Usually, after the first winter on our shores, everyone wanted to go home, and many did. But there must have been many aching and homesick hearts among the people who watched the *Mayflower* spread her sails, pass the Gurnet, and disappear over the eastern horizon. It had been a comfort to see her at anchor, and to know that if the Indians moved in you could go on board and sail away. Now the Pilgrims' last link with civilization was broken.

In April, in the midst of their corn-planting, Governor Carver came in from the fields, "complaining greatly of his head," lost his senses, and died. The good gentleman must have had a stroke from overworking. Signers of the Compact now met, and elected Bradford Governor and Isaac Allerton his Assistant. So began the first term of William Bradford, at the age of thirty-one. He was re-elected to the same office thirty times—a record not since surpassed by any governor of an American colony or state—and he died in office.[2]

Now the wild strawberries were ripe, the pink lady's-slipper or moccasin flower bloomed in the woods; buds of the

---

[2] All except two of the elections were annual, the others biennial. Bradford was Governor of Plymouth Colony from 1621 to 1656 inclusive, except for five years when he begged off in favor of Edward Winslow or Thomas Prence.

wild rose were bursting; the first garden peas and herbs were gathered, shad and alewives were running up the rivers, and striped bass were plentiful.

A HUNGRY EMBASSY

BRADFORD and his counselors decided it was high time to pay a return visit to Massasoit. Edward Winslow and Stephen Hopkins were sent on the long overland journey to his seat at Sowams (in the present Barrington, Rhode Island), with Squanto as guide. They started on 10 June. At Nemasket the local Indians entertained the "embassy" with corn bread and a mixture of shad roe and acorns; that was when the two Englishmen obliged by shooting eighty crows. Their next stop was at Titicut, in the present town of Raynham, where the Indians had built a weir to catch bass; they gave the Englishmen plenty to eat and provided more guides. Finally the party reached Massasoit's "capital" at Sowams. The Pilgrims, it seems, had a laced scarlet horseman's coat among their clothing supplies. Figuring, doubtless, that many years would elapse before they would have a cavalry troop or a fox hunt, they sent the coat by Winslow to Massasoit, who was delighted with it and strutted about in great glee. But he had no food to offer. Indians always gorged when they had plenty, and then went hungry for days; and it was the bad luck of the English to arrive when nothing to eat was on hand. For two nights the "ambassadors" were kept awake by the Indians yelling, as well as by lice, fleas, and mosquitoes; and during the day, which was spent with much speechmaking and powwowing, they were given only a small piece of fresh fish. On Friday, 1 July, empty in stomach and lightheaded for want of sleep, they started home. Fortunately, on the way they acquired a handful of parched corn, a string of dried clams, and half a squirrel.

ASPINET AND CORBITANT

◄§ YOUNG Johnny Billington next distinguished himself by getting lost in the woods. After wandering about for five days with nothing to eat but last season's wintergreen and partridge berries, he reached an Indian village at Manomet near the present Cape Cod Canal. The Indians there sent him on to the Nauset tribe, with whom the Pilgrims had had their first encounter on Cape Cod. At Governor Bradford's request, Massasoit found out where the boy was, and the shallop was sent to the present Eastham to fetch him home. Aspinet, sachem of the Nausets, delivered Johnny all decked out with wampum; and the Governor, who commanded the shallop, took this opportunity to pay Aspinet for the corn the Pilgrims had dug up the previous December, and to make peace with the Nausets.

On the way back to Plymouth the shallop put in at Barnstable Harbor for fresh water, which was furnished by the local sagamore, named Iyanough. The squaws "joined hand in hand, singing and dancing before the shallop, the men also showing all the kindness they could, Iyanough himself taking a bracelet from about his neck and hanging it on one of us." All this trouble for one wandering small boy! Johnny Billington must have been insufferable after that adventure.

About that time a Wampanoag named Hobomok came to live with the Pilgrims, along with Squanto. These two, being sent with a message to Massasoit, encountered one of the latter's subject sagamores named Corbitant, who picked a quarrel and threatened to kill them both. Hobomok broke away and ran some fifteen miles to Plymouth, declaring that Squanto must have been slain; when last seen, Corbitant had him by the hair and was brandishing a knife. Bradford made the brave decision that Corbitant must not be allowed to get away with this; if the Pilgrims' messengers were molested or killed, the Indians would lose all respect for them. So Myles Standish, Hobomok, and fourteen armed men were sent with orders to cut off Corbitant's head if he had indeed killed Squanto. After a brief scuffle they ascertained that Squanto was still very much alive. He and two of Corbitant's Indians who had been wounded in the brawl accompanied Standish to Plymouth, where the Indians' wounds were healed by Dr. Fuller. This episode made a deep impression on all the Indians of southern New England. Corbitant asked Massasoit to intercede for him, and the Indians of Martha's Vineyard even sent an embassy to make a treaty with the Pilgrims.

❦ IX ❧

THE FIRST
THANKSGIVING

❮❮❮❮❮❮❮❮❮❮❮❮❮❮❮❮❮❮❮❮❮❮❮❮❮❮❮❮❮❮❮❮❮❮❮❮

VISIT TO MASSACHUSETTS

So the first summer at Plymouth passed with planting, hoeing, and fishing, and establishing relations with the Indians. Goldenrod, new to the Pilgrims, bloomed; asters, which they called Michaelmas daisies, were coming out. The wheat and peas planted in the spring did not do well, but the beans produced a good crop, and the Indian corn a bumper one. The cornstalks were cut and gathered into sheaves, which Squanto said was the way to ripen the ears; and the pumpkins he had taught them to plant among the corn hills were now in great golden heaps alongside the houses. So the men decided to make a combined trading and diplomatic trip to "the Massachusetts" in their shallop. It was high time they obtained a stock of fur to start repaying their London creditors; and the Indians up there needed attention.

The Massachusetts, meaning "at the hill" of that name in Milton near Boston (now called the Great Blue Hill), were a tribe that lived along the Neponset and Charles Rivers. "The Massachusetts is the paradise of those parts," wrote Captain John Smith in 1616, because the Indian population was thick, and as you sailed along the coast and through Boston Harbor you saw many cleared fields and "savage gardens." The tribe had been much weakened by the great pestilence, but their sachem still commanded several hundred pinses.

So Governor Bradford, Myles Standish, and eight other men, together with Squanto and Hobomok, set forth in the shallop on an ebb tide at midnight. Next day they went ashore at Copps Hill, Boston, where the old burying ground and Christ Church are now located. A squaw going down to the shore to get lobsters told them where to find the sachem. He proved friendly and said that his people were in mortal fear of the Abnaki Indians in Maine, who never bothered to plant corn for themselves but plundered the Massachusetts. Following his directions, the Pilgrims crossed Boston Harbor, went ashore at Squantum (later so named after Squanto) and found the place where the Massachusetts had concealed their stock of corn, guarded by squaws.

These squaws were wearing some remarkably fine beaver coats, which would bring big money in England. Squanto was so eager for beaver that he urged his English friends to cover the women with their matchlocks while he stripped them. Bradford and Standish refused, saying that was no way to start friendly trading relations; and as soon as the Pilgrims produced some glass beads and other trifles that ap-

pealed to the squaws, they "sold the coats from their backs
and tied boughs about them, but with great shamefacedness,
for indeed they are more modest than some of our English
women are," wrote Winslow. So this trip to "the Massachusetts" was looked on as very successful, and paved the way
for more profitable trading in the future. But, as we shall see,
the Massachusetts Indians were not consistently friendly like
Massasoit's people.

THANKSGIVING DAY, 1621

AT PLYMOUTH "they now began to fit up their houses
and dwellings against winter, being all well recovered in
health and strength and had all things in good plenty." Some
of the men went fishing for cod, which they cured for winter
use. Others ranged the shores and woods, now splendid
with brilliant autumn colors such as the English had never
seen, to shoot wild duck, geese, and turkey. And as Massasoit and ninety Indians arrived for a fall visit, the Pilgrims
took occasion to make it a thanksgiving feast.

The Indian guests contributed five deer, which were
"barbecued" in the open; the Pilgrims provided other game,
corn bread, and a little salt meat, ship biscuit, and butter
left over from the *Mayflower's* supplies. The men "exercised their arms," shooting at a mark to impress the Indians,
who were just as deadly at short range with bows and arrows.
Planks set on trestles or sawhorses made a big table in the
open; stools or stumps made good seats for the Pilgrim population. The Indians sat on the ground, gnawing on deer
bones, tearing fowl apart, and lapping up the very ancient

[OPPOSITE] *The First Thanksgiving.*

and rancid butter with grunts of appreciation. It is a pretty picture to think of—the blue waters of the Bay in the foreground and splashes of scarlet samphire on the salt marshes; and on the land side, gold maples, ruddy oak leaves, the new-thatched houses made snug for the winter, and Elder Brewster asking a blessing on this, the First Thanksgiving in New England.[1]

This time the Indian women and children mingled with the Pilgrims; it must have been amusing to see the small fry of each race eying the others warily and then playing together. The entire crowd stayed three days, feasting daily. When they departed, Governor Bradford doubtless said: "Thank God, they have left us *something* to eat next winter!"

---

[1] The exact date is not known; probably it was around 15 October. The Pilgrims did not have regular Thanksgiving Days as many suppose; the Governor merely declared one when he saw fit, and the traditional date of the last Thursday in November did not become fixed until the nineteenth century. It is now the fourth Thursday.

STRUGGLING
ALONG

❧❧❧❧❧❧❧❧❧❧❧❧❧❧❧❧❧❧❧❧❧❧❧❧❧❧❧❧❧❧❧

THE *Fortune* AND HER FATE

THE GOVERNOR did not know that he would soon have more hungry mouths to feed.

One day near the end of November, 1621, Plymouth seethed with excitement. A strange sail was seen standing in by the Gurnet—first to appear since the *Mayflower* departed in April. Was she friend or foe, English, French, or Dutch, honest trader or pirate? Captain Standish called his musketeers to arms and saw that the guns on the Hill were manned and shotted.

Presently a sharp-eyed lad made out the Union Jack flying at the mainmast. It was the *Fortune* which the London Adventurers had chartered to bring over recruits for the Colony. She carried thirty-five passengers. Some, such as Robert Cushman and his son, were former *Speedwell* passengers for whom no room had been found in the *Mayflower*. Some were relatives of the original Pilgrims. Edward Winslow's brother John came, and Elder Brewster's son Jonathan; also a young man named Thomas Prence who later became Governor of the Colony, and a Dutchman of French parentage named Philip de la Noye, ancestor of President Franklin Delano Roosevelt. And there were several unattached young men, "some of them wild enough," said Bradford.

It was good to have recruits, but the *Fortune*'s voyage was so lengthy (she started in July) that almost all the food on board had been eaten, and the passengers brought no extra clothes, bedding, or cooking pots. Fortunately the master had a chest full of ready-made clothing for the sailors, which he was willing to sell; for the Pilgrims by this time were in rags.

Cushman returned in the same ship to see what he could do about getting more supplies. Before leaving, he made a speech urging the Pilgrims to keep up their courage: "Here you are by God's providence under difficulties; be thankful to God it is no worse! . . . Comfort and cheer up one another, laboring to make each other's burden lighter." Probably some of his hearers said: "Very well for you, going back to England; but how about us, starting a second winter with all these new mouths to feed?"

The newcomers were quartered with families who had houses, but they made the food situation very serious. After the *Fortune* departed on 13 December, Governor Bradford and Isaac Allerton took stock of provisions on hand and found that they could be stretched to six months at best. So they put everyone on half-rations, eked out with clams, game, and the few fish that could be caught in winter. "They bore it patiently with hope of supply."

A valuable document delivered by the *Fortune* was a patent signed by the lords and gentlemen who made up the new Council for New England.[1] It gave the Colony legal standing by confirming the Mayflower Compact and promising that after seven years the Colony would be given definite boundaries, and every settler a hundred acres of land. On the other hand, the ship brought a letter from Thomas Weston, head of the London Adventurers, scolding the Pilgrims for sending home no cargo by the *Mayflower* and threatening to cut them off if they failed to ship valuable furs promptly! Bradford replied calmly and with dignity, telling of Governor Carver's death and of the great sickness. "At great charges in this adventure I confess you have been, and many losses may sustain; but the loss of his and many other honest and industrious men's lives cannot be valued at any price." And he sent the *Fortune* back with a full cargo of cedar clapboard (in demand in England for wainscoting rooms), topped off by two hogsheads of beaver and other skins, the whole worth £500.

Alas, the more valuable part of this cargo never reached England. A French warship captured the *Fortune* off the French coast and brought her into a port where the furs were confiscated, the ship rifled, the passengers and crew stripped of their valuables, and then allowed to proceed to England. Such was one of the hazards of sea voyages in those days, even in time of peace.

---

[1] The Dukes of Lenox and Hamilton, Earls of Warwick and Sheffield, and Sir Ferdinando Gorges. The original document is preserved in Pilgrim Hall, Plymouth.

Shortly after the *Fortune* sailed for England, Canonicus, sachem of the powerful tribe of Narragansett Indians, sent a messenger to Plymouth with a challenge to fight, in the form of a bundle of arrows wrapped in rattlesnake skin. Squanto told the Governor what that meant, so Bradford returned the snakeskin filled with powder and shot. Canonicus wouldn't even accept this token but sent it back; and that ended the correspondence.

The Pilgrims were too wise to expect God to protect them from hostile Indians without preparation on their part. Myles Standish, with some forty able-bodied men at his disposal, organized four companies, one of which constantly "watched and warded" against fire or enemy attack. Fire was an ever present danger to wooden houses with thatched roofs and clay-daubed chimneys. They also put a stout pale fence around the village, with a strong-point at each corner.

THE SECOND HUNGRY YEAR

❧ THE SECOND WINTER at Plymouth was not so bad as the first, since there was no Great Sickness; but half-rations caused discontent as well as hunger. In the meantime Squanto, partly out of jealousy of Hobomok and partly to increase his own importance, started rumors that Massasoit was about to break the treaty and attack Plymouth. The sachem, furious at this malicious gossip, sent messengers to the Governor demanding that he give up Squanto; they had orders to cut off Squanto's head and hands and bring them to Sowams. This demand put Bradford on a spot. The corn and English provisions were all gone and the people were weak; he hated to give Squanto up, but must he not do so, since the very existence of the Colony depended on Mas-

sasoit's good will? While he was debating with himself and
seeking divine guidance, a boy came running up and said that
a sail had been sighted outside the Bay. Bradford, fearing
it might be a French enemy such as the one that had seized
the *Fortune,* had the drum beat and the trumpet sound to
arms, and told Massasoit's messengers that they must wait.
The sail proved to be friendly; it was a shallop belonging to
a ship of Weston's that was fishing off the Maine coast. In the
meantime Massasoit's messengers, "mad with rage and im-
patient at delay, departed in great heat." So Squanto's life
was saved, to the Colony's great profit; and Massasoit, if he

Snake skin challenge.

planned to take revenge, soon changed his mind, as we shall
see.

The shallop brought seven passengers whom Weston had
sent to start a colony of his own, and whom he asked the Pilgrims to "entertain" and provide with seed corn. But they
brought no food of their own. "All this was but cold comfort
to fill their hungry bellies," wrote Bradford. This practice of
the London Adventurers was most unfair. They would send
out groups of men—the "Particulars," Bradford called them
—to trade and fish for their own benefit instead of pitching in
with the Pilgrims to help pay off the debt; but they always
expected the Colony to provide shelter and food.

And as if that were not enough, two more Weston ships, the
Charity and the *Swan,* arrived at the end of June 1622.
They brought the bad news about the *Fortune,* "sixty lusty
men" as passengers, and a letter from one of the London
Adventurers warning Bradford that Weston was aiming to
get all the profits from New England into his own hands. But
again, no food; and June was the worst month of the year for
food, because last year's corn was exhausted and the new
crop not yet ripe, and no wild fowl were then about. At this
crisis, when "famine now began to pinch them sore," a boat
sailed into the harbor with a letter from a jovial Virginia
shipmaster named Huddleston. His big ship, the *Bona Nova,*
was fishing from Monhegan, one of the big rocky islands off
the Maine coast. He sent this letter to his "friends, country-
men and neighbors," as he addressed the Pilgrims, to tell
them about the horrible Indian massacre in Virginia that
spring, and to warn them to be on their guard. Bradford sent
Edward Winslow in the shallop to accompany Captain Huddleston's boat to Monhegan. There he found some thirty
English and Virginian ships fishing, and from them he ob-

tained, as a free gift, a good supply of English provisions. These saved the Colony from starvation; for their corn was all gone and they were living on clams and a few fish.

DEFENSE AND TRADE

◀§ THE MASSACRE in Virginia was a terrible warning of what might happen if Massasoit turned ugly or Canonicus went on the warpath. So the Pilgrims devoted a good deal of their slender strength that summer to building a fort on Burial Hill.[2] "It was a great work for them in their weakness and time of want," wrote Bradford; and Winslow tells us that it caused much discontent. The Plymouth pacifists grumbled that the Governor was building a "castle" just for show; the Red Indians were all friendly, surely? Almost a year was required to finish the fort, but it was a good one, built of stout squared timber, mounting six cannon from the *Mayflower* on the roof, and commanding all approaches by land and by sea. Sentries guarded it day and night, and Elder Brewster held divine service there every Sunday until his death in 1643; the first meeting-house or church was built in the town itself in 1648.[3]

"Now the welcome time of harvest approached," wrote Bradford, "in which all had their hungry bellies filled. But it arose to but little." This was mostly because Weston's "sixty lusty men" were always stealing corn before it became ripe.

---

[2] A replica of this fort, following the several descriptions of it that have come down to us, has recently been built near Plymouth Rock. It has an interesting collection of weapons and armor such as the Pilgrims used.

[3] The familiar painting of the Pilgrims marching up the hill to service, with men on guard, is accurate; it follows the description given by a Dutch visitor in 1627.

At this juncture more help arrived from Virginia. The *Discovery* called at Plymouth to do a little trading on her way from Jamestown to England. She carried plenty of English beads and knives, which the Colony bought, though at one hundred per cent profit to the owner; and this "trading truck" enabled the Pilgrims to buy corn and fur from the Indians. John Pory, Secretary of the Virginia Colony, was a passenger on the *Discovery*. Bradford and Brewster lent him some books to read on the voyage home, and he wrote an account of the little Colony, full of praise for the Pilgrims' character, hospitality, and military preparedness.

With trading truck in hand, Bradford sailed in the shallop around Cape Cod, Squanto acting as pilot, to procure food from the Nauset Indians. Squanto died on this voyage, "desiring the Governor to pray for him that he might go to the Englishmen's God in Heaven," and asking that his few belongings be distributed among his good friends at Plymouth. He was very much missed, especially by the children.

The trading yielded twenty-six hogsheads of corn and beans. On the way home a northerly gale cast the shallop so far up the beach near Yarmouthport that Bradford had to hide the provisions in the ground and walk fifty miles home. And officials collected no "mileage" in those days! Myles Standish led a party back there in February 1623 and salvaged both the boat and the provisions.

WESSAGUSSET FIGHT

IN THE FALL of 1622, Weston's "lusty men," who had caused no end of trouble at Plymouth, removed to a place called Wessagusset (the site of Weymouth near Boston), and started a colony of their own, much to the relief of the Pil-

grims. But these men had no morale or ambition. They were
the riffraff of the London slums, unable to adapt themselves
to wilderness life. Hating honest work, they began to steal
corn from the near-by Massachusetts Indians, and to molest
their women. The Pilgrims heard about this with dismay, for
they knew it meant trouble and that they would have to do
something about it.

So they did, through a curious chain of events. In March
1623, Governor Bradford heard that Massasoit was sick unto
death and wished to see his friend Edward Winslow. So the
Governor sent Winslow with another man, and Hobomok as
guide. They found the ailing sachem at Sowams, the neck of
land between the Barrington and Palmer Rivers that flow into
Narragansett Bay. He was in his lodge, surrounded by
squaws and medicine men who were "making such a hellish
noise, as it distempered us that were well and therefore unlike to ease him that was sick," wrote Winslow. The two
Englishmen diagnosed the chief's malady as nothing worse
than severe constipation, following a bout of gluttony. They
administered a purge, with favorable results. Winslow then
shot some wild duck and made duck broth, and persuaded
a squaw to cook a dish of cornmeal mush in which wild
strawberry leaves and sassafras were boiled. Massasoit gob-
bled this mess so greedily that he threw it up; but gentle
doses of duck broth brought him back to health. The sachem
was so grateful for his cure that he disclosed the dreadful
news that the Massachusetts Indians had made a league with
the Nausets and others to wipe out the Weston colony at
Wessagusset and then attack Plymouth.

By the time this medical mission returned, one of Weston's
men had fled through the woods to Plymouth to tell about
the desperate situation at Wessagusset. Next a Massachu-

setts Indian was seized while skulking about Plymouth and chained up in the fort so he could not return to his tribe with news of how weak the Pilgrims still were. Although the Plymouth pacifists urged that nothing be done (Weston's men were a bad lot and had brought this trouble on themselves, so to hell with them!) Bradford was no isolationist; he knew "for whom the bell tolls." If Plymouth allowed these wretched fellows to be wiped out, it would be her turn next. So he decided to strike first, and hard. Myles Standish was sent off in the shallop with eight armed men—all that could be spared from the home guard. He found the Weston colony in a very bad way. The men had become beachcombers, living on shellfish. Some had become servants to the Indians to get an occasional meal; one even had been executed to please the Indians, who amused themselves by kicking over their poor pots of clams when they were about to eat, and whipping off their blankets as they slept.

For several days Standish and his men stayed with the beachcombers to size up the situation. Two big six-foot pinses who had been teasing the Englishmen, Witawawmut and Pecksuot, would whet their knives before the captain's face and threaten to kill the "little shrimp"—for Myles stood only about five feet two in his boots. Standish kept his patience until he managed to get both fellows and two other Indians into the house where his company lodged. Closing and barring the door, he snatched Pecksuot's own knife from his neck and stabbed him to the heart. The soldiers killed Witawawmut and another Indian and hanged the fourth. After another scuffle in the open, all the Indians fled. Some of the beachcombers returned to Plymouth with Standish, and the rest sailed to Monhegan in their own boat. Standish brought back, as trophy, Witawawmut's head which, according to the custom of those days, was displayed on the fort.

The story of these exploits of Myles Standish was carried all over southern New England, with great effect. Some Indians who had planned to join the Massachusetts "forsook their homes, living in swamps and other desert places." Aspinet, sachem of the Nausets, who was in the conspiracy, got bogged down and died miserably. Others sent canoes full of gifts to Governor Bradford; and there was no more trouble from Indians for many years.

"COMMON COURSE" MODIFIED

❧ SHORTLY AFTER this victory, which took place in March 1623, Governor Bradford and his chief advisers made an important decision in domestic policy. The London Adventurers, it will be remembered, had required the Pilgrims to work as a gang, with no private property, until 1627, when each would get a dividend worth £10. Everybody disliked this system. Young bachelors didn't see why they should work for other men's wives and children; married women hated to cook and wash for the bachelors; the strong and able got no more rations than the weak and lazy. So it was decided to assign to each family a definite planting-field in addition to the little kitchen gardens which they already had, and let each family grow its own corn. This, says Bradford, "made all hands very industrious . . . the women now went willingly into the field and took their little ones with them to set corn." And production was greatly increased.

This wise decision has been cited as a blow at communism and a start to the "American Way of Life." It was not, however, communism that was abolished, but a very degrading and onerous slavery to the English capitalists that was somewhat softened. The families still could not sell, nor their children inherit, the newly allotted fields. Trading furs with the Indians continued to be a Colony monopoly, in order to discharge the debts to the London Adventurers. But, just as soon as it could make a new deal with the Adventurers,[4] the Colony made land grants outright, for the owners to have and to hold, or to sell, provided always that the purchaser was acceptable to the community.

Until the next corn harvest the Pilgrims got along by netting striped bass, which in those days came into the bay in great numbers. In the winter, as Bradford says, "they were helped with ground nuts"—a wild vine with starchy tubers on its roots—by wild fowl, and "now and then a deer." And always there were clams. The humorist Bill Nye well described the Pilgrims' life as follows:

"The people were kept busy digging clams to sustain life in order to raise Indian corn enough to give them sufficient strength to pull clams enough the following winter to get them through till the next corn crop should give them strength to dig for clams again." John Pory, who visited the Plymouth Colony from Virginia in 1622, wrote that the lobsters there were "so large, so full of meat, and so plentiful . . . as no man will believe that hath not seen. For a knife of three halfpence value I bought ten lobsters that would well have dined forty laboring men." But you can't live on nothing but clams and lobsters.

The division of cornfields did not put the Pilgrims on "Easy

---

[4] See Chapter XIII below. Still, modern communist regimes might have profited by Plymouth's example. In Yugoslavia, Tito forced the peasants into soviet-style collectives in 1950, the result being outright famine, from which the country was saved by American aid. When Tito relented, about five out of six peasant families withdrew from the collectives and accepted farms of ten to twenty-five acres each.

Street." The region suffered a long and bad drought in May, June, and July. The corn withered away; it looked as if there would be no harvest. Elder Brewster then called for "a solemn day of humiliation." Immediately after, clouds gathered and "sweet and gentle showers" of rain "revived and quickened" the parched corn. "Behold another providence of God!" said Bradford. A special Thanksgiving Day was held for it on 30 July 1623.

The very next day more passengers arrived in the ship *Anne,* and a week later the *Little James* came in, which raised the number of new recruits to sixty. Some of them were the Pilgrims' wives, children, and friends from Leyden. They were so "daunted and dismayed" by the ragged and emaciated appearance of the settlers that "some wished themselves in England again; others fell a-weeping, fancying their own misery in what they now saw in others." The best dish the Pilgrims could offer the newcomers was "a lobster or a piece of fish without bread or anything else but a cup of fair spring water." We wouldn't think that too bad; but the English, as we have said, thought themselves very badly off without beef, wheat bread, and beer. And as yet there were no cattle in the Colony, nor any domestic animals except a few chickens.

If you still suppose that the Pilgrims were a grim, tight-lipped band of people, you are wrong. They were able to laugh at themselves and their troubles in the worst of times. As proof of it, take this ballad which was composed by some jolly member of the Colony around 1623, and passed down by word of mouth:

The place where we live is a wilderness wood,
Where grass is much wanting that's fruitful and good:

Our mountains and hills and valleys below
Being commonly covered with ice and with snow;
And when the northwester with violence blows,
Then every man pulls his cap over his nose; [5]
But if any's so hardy and will it withstand,
He forfeits a finger, a foot, or a hand.

When the spring opens we then take the hoe,
And make the ground ready to plant and to sow;
Our corn being planted and seed being sown,
The worms destroy much before it is grown;
And when it is growing, some spoil there is made
By birds and by squirrels that pluck up the blade;
E'en when it is grown to full corn in the ear
It is often destroyéd by raccoons and deer.

And now our garments begin to grow thin,
And wool is much wanted to card and to spin;
If we can get a garment to cover without,
Our other in-garments are clout upon clout; [6]
Our clothes we brought with us are often much torn,
They need to be clouted before they are worn;
But clouting our garments they hinder us nothing,
Clouts double, are warmer than single whole clothing!

If flesh meat be wanting to fill up our dish,
We have carrots and pumpkins and turnips and fish;
And, when we've a mind for a delicate dish,
We repair to the clam-bank and there we catch fish.

---

[5] A Monmouth cap, of course. You couldn't pull one of those black plug hats over your nose!

[6] Meaning; "the garments we wear indoors are just patch upon patch." This ballad was taken down from the lips of an old lady aged ninety-four in 1767 and printed in the *Massachusetts Spy,* 1774.

Instead of pottage and puddings and custards and pies,
Our pumpkins and parsnips are common supplies;
We have pumpkin at morning and pumpkin at noon;
If it was not for pumpkin we should be undoon.

If barley be wanting to make into malt,
We must be contented, and think it no fault;
For we can make liquor to sweeten our lips
Of pumpkins and parsnips and walnut tree chips.

Now while some are going, let others be coming,
For while liquor's boiling it must have a scumming;
But we will not blame them, for birds of a feather,
By seeking their fellows are flocking together.
But you whom the Lord intends hither to bring,
Forsake not the honey for fear of the sting;
But bring both a quiet and contented mind
And all needful blessings you surely will find.

The *Anne* was sent home with a good cargo of beaver and clapboard for the London Adventurers, while the *Little James* remained in New England to fish. The harvest of 1623 was bountiful, and never again did the Plymouth Colony feel famine. The winter of 1623-24 was the first in which there was no great suffering. Edward Winslow, who went to England in the *Anne*, returned in March 1624 in the *Charity*, bringing three cows and a bull, the first cattle to arrive in New England, and a good supply of clothing and other necessaries.

The Pilgrims' troubles were by no means over; but from now on it was not hunger or Indians that bothered them, but human folly.

FOOLS AND FROLICS

❮❖

MAD JACK OLDHAM

Although the food shortage was at an end and the Indians were chastened, the Colony had plenty of trouble during the next few years from factions within and troublemakers without.

As we have seen, the original Pilgrims of the *Mayflower* included several persons such as the Billington family who had nothing in common with them, but who were recruited by the London Adventurers to make up a full shipload. Next, the Adventurers began to send over "Particulars," as Bradford called them—men sent to work for their own profit instead of joining those who were obliged to labor for the community. And the Adventurers ordered the Colony to give these Particulars the same amount of land and the same rations as everyone else. Naturally this division made bad feeling among "the General," as the people were called who were obliged to pay off the debt. The General, however, outnumbered the Particulars and kept control of the Colony because the signers of the Mayflower Compact only admitted as Freemen or voters those who were sympathetic with their ideals and willing to pitch in for the common good.

In August 1623, there arrived at Plymouth the *Anne* and the *Little James*, which had been built by the London Adventurers expressly for the Colony to fish and trade along the coast. The two vessels brought about sixty passengers for the General, many of them wives or children of the Pilgrims, and also nine Particulars. One of these nine was John Oldham, who had an outfit for fur-trading and started right in on his own hook. The Particulars were discontented and wrote home to the Adventurers complaining against the Pilgrims and Plymouth. Some of their complaints were false, such as the statement that grass wouldn't grow in Plymouth or the fish "take salt"; and some were funny—the water was not "wholesome" and the mosquitoes were terrible. To which Bradford replied that the spring water at Plymouth was not so wholesome as beer or wine, but "as good as any in the world"; and that people who were too "delicate to . . . endure the biting of a mosquito" had better stay in England "till at least they be mosquito-proof." One can't help sympathizing with the newcomers about the mosquitoes, for they had no nets and the only protection at night was to close all doors and windows, unless you almost choked yourself with smoke.

One charge of the Particulars, however, went home—that

Plymouth had no sacraments, since there was no regular minister. It grieved the Pilgrims more than anything else that the Adventurers would not or could not send over their beloved pastor, the Rev. John Robinson. Instead, in the ship *Charity,* which arrived in the spring of 1624, they sent a clergyman who caused them no end of trouble.

LEWD JOHN LYFORD

◆§ THIS MAN, the Rev. John Lyford, appears to have ministered to an Episcopal parish in Ireland, whence he had been expelled for playing "wolf" with the girls of his congregation. Through friendship with one of the London Adventurers he was sent to Plymouth in the hope that he would do as their minister. He acted very sweet and humble, said he really was a Puritan at heart; and the Pilgrims, delighted to have a "Reverend" at last, gave him a house and double-rations for himself and his family of five. They would have elected him their pastor if he had not promptly got in cahoots with Oldham and started a faction to overthrow the Government.

The Colony, already, as we have seen, had a foreign policy and a defense force; now Governor Bradford organized a little F. B. I. of his own. Observing secret meetings and whisperings among the malcontents, who were writing long letters to be sent home in the *Charity,* Bradford and his friends went on board that ship the day she sailed, opened and read a batch of Lyford's letters, and kept some of the more damaging. They found plenty of evidence that the conspirators were about to pull off a revolution at Plymouth and were preparing the London Adventurers to accept it by telling a pack of lies about the Pilgrims.

Bradford and his Assistants (there were five of them now)

decided to let the conspiracy cook awhile, to see who was in it. Oldham became so violent and outrageous that he was known as "Mad Jack." He refused to perform military duty, pulled a knife on Captain Standish when ordered to turn out, and roared and cursed, "calling them all traitors and rebels." Lyford set up a separate church meeting on Sunday for the special benefit of his cronies. Things having come to that pass, the Governor summoned the Freemen of the Colony and preferred charges against the two conspirators. They denied everything. Lyford's letters were then produced and read. Oldham "began to rage furiously," calling on his confederates to "show their courage" and support him in overthrowing the Government; but "not a man answered." Lyford was asked what he had to say for himself. He broke down and confessed everything, and the Freemen sentenced him and Oldham to leave the Colony within six months.

Lyford now put on an act. He wept and wailed, confessed his sins, promised to be loyal; and he was forgiven and the sentence revoked. But he wrote another slanderous letter—which Bradford's F. B. I. intercepted—along the same lines as the others. Mrs. Lyford was so ashamed at this that she made a clean breast to the Assistants of all her husband's former evil doings; and Winslow, who had gone back to England in the *Charity*, obtained so much evidence of his bad record in Ireland that the London Adventurers decided to drop Lyford. He wandered north along the coast, preaching to fishermen, and ended up as Anglican minister of a parish in Virginia, where he died.

Oldham returned to Plymouth without permission in the spring of 1625, and soon resumed roaring and cursing at the authorities. The Pilgrims shut him up in the fort until he cooled off, and then sent him on board a boat after making *him* run the gantlet, Indian fashion, between two files of musketeers. Each man gave him "a thump on the breech with the butt end of his musket. Then they bid him go and mend his manners."

That, apparently, he did. On a winter voyage to Virginia in which his ship was almost cast away on Cape Cod, he confessed his sins before his shipmates and begged God to forgive him for what he had tried to do to the Pilgrims. "And in time afterwards," says Bradford, "Oldham carried himself fairly towards them," and often visited Plymouth on his trading voyages. Many years later, as we shall see, he was killed in a brawl with the Indians of Block Island.

GREEDY TOM

◆§ Thomas Weston, organizer of the London Adventurers, was one of those restless characters who go from one thing to another. Since the Council for New England had ordered him to keep away, he came over in a fishing vessel under a false name and disguised as a blacksmith, only to learn that his colony at Wessagusset had broken up. Shipwrecked on the shores of Ipswich Bay, he was robbed by the Indians of everything but his shirt, walked barefoot to the trading post at "Strawberry Bank" (Portsmouth, N. H.), borrowed a suit of clothes and a pair of shoes, and managed to get to Plymouth. There the Pilgrims, in spite of the hard usage they had had from Weston, "staked" him with supplies and lent him £100 worth of beaver. But he "never repaid them anything but reproaches and evil words." Using Virginia as a base, Weston made several trading voyages to the Maine coast. He was arrested a couple of times for breaking the laws of

Virginia, and finally returned to England where he died, heavily in debt. So much for Master Weston.

MERRY MORTON

IN THE MEANTIME small groups of people had come over to fish and trade at several points on the New England coast north of Plymouth. Besides the people at "Strawberry Bank" who had clothed the naked Weston, there was a group at "Cocheco" (Dover, N. H.), another on Cape Ann; the Rev. William Blackstone on Shawmut (later Boston); a couple of men at the site of Weston's Wessagusset, and Samuel Maver-

Oldham running the gantlet.

ick (ancestor of the Texas Mavericks) at Winnesimmet, the
site of the Naval Hospital in Chelsea. And the widow of
David Thompson, with a number of employees, had settled
on an island in Boston Harbor, still called Thompsons, and
where a famous school is located.

While these groups and individuals were rivals, all were
friendly and peaceable except Thomas Morton "of Merrymount," a jolly dog who made trouble for everyone, and
whose dealings with the Pilgrims are among the most amusing episodes in their early history.

Morton, formerly a lawyer in London, "left his country for
his country's good" and joined a small colony under a Captain Wollaston, which took over the deserted houses of Weston's colony. Wollaston did not like the place and moved to
Virginia, leaving Morton with a few boon companions and a
good supply of liquor, powder and shot, and trading truck.
Morton then established a sort of filling-station for Indians
and sailors on Mount Wollaston, which he renamed Merrymount, within the present city of Quincy.[1] Merrymount was
a great attraction for the Indians, whom Morton really seems
to have liked. He joined in their sports, gave them plenty of
liquor, and frolicked with the young squaws. Every May
Day he set up a Maypole on Merrymount around which he
and his friends and the Indian girls danced, "frisking together like so many fairies or furies, rather; and worse prac-
tices," wrote Bradford. Morton composed drinking songs
which he taught them to sing, and was so proud of one that
he had the words printed:

Make green garlands, bring bottles out,
And fill sweet Nectar freely about.

---

[1] The site, on Route 3 near the shore, is marked.

Uncover thy head and fear no harm,
For here's good liquor to keep it warm.

CHORUS

Then drink, and be merry, merry, merry boys,
Let all your delight be in the Hymen's joys;
Io! to Hymen, now the day is come,
About the merry Maypole take a room.

Give to the melancholy man
A cup or two of 't now and then;
This physic will soon revive his blood
And make him be of a merrier mood.

CHORUS

Then drink, and be merry, merry, merry boys,
Let all your delight be in the Hymen's joys;
Io! to Hymen, now the day is come,
About the merry Maypole take a room.

Give to the Nymph that's free from scorn
No Irish stuff nor Scotch over-worn.[2]
Lasses in beaver coats, come away,
Ye shall be welcome to us night and day.

CHORUS

Then drink, and be merry, merry, merry boys,
Let all your delight be in the Hymen's joys;
Io! to Hymen, now the day is come,
About the merry Maypole take a room.

The Pilgrims naturally did not like these goings-on, nor did any of the other white people along the coast. Trading-

---

[2] "Irish stuff" and "Scotch" were not whisky but woolens. Neither whisky nor rum had as yet appeared in New England; the only strong liquors known were aqua vitae and brandy.

ships bypassed Thompsons Island when they learned what a good time sailors could have at Merrymount; Indians would not bring furs to trading posts where they could get no liquor. But there was nothing that anyone could do about it until, after several years, they learned that Morton was selling muskets to the Indians and teaching them how to use them; even how to mold bullets. That was really serious. Indians still outnumbered whites at least ten to one in southern New England, and if they were furnished with firearms the English might as well pack up and go home.

Matters came to a head when word got around that Morton had sent for a whole shipload of arms to sell to the Indians. Chipping in a few shillings or pounds each, the white traders, from Portsmouth south, gave Plymouth, the most populous and the oldest colony, a mandate to put down Merrymount. Twice Governor Bradford sent messengers to order Morton in the King's name to stop this arms traffic which the King had expressly forbidden. Twice "insolently he persisted. Upon which they saw there was no way but to take him by force."

With a defense fund of £12 7s. in hand, Governor Bradford called for volunteers and offered them real money for "foreign service." Every able-bodied man wanted to go, for this expedition promised to be fun; but Myles Standish said twelve would be enough, and he picked out some of the young men, just turned sixteen, to give them a taste of fighting.

So, early in June 1628, the Pilgrims' "transport" (the shallop) landed Captain Standish and his "expeditionary force" on the shores of the present Weymouth Fore River. Marching to Merrymount, they found that Morton and his cronies had barred the doors of their house and "stood stiffly on defense."

Summoned to yield, they replied with a torrent of defiant oaths, scoffings, jeers, and foul language such as the Plymouth boys had not heard since Oldham's departure. Myles Standish, an old soldier, probably gave as good as he got. Fortunately for him, the Merrymount garrison had imbibed so much "Dutch courage" that the men were unable to hold their heavy matchlocks. Morton led a sortie, armed with a light carbine so choked with powder and shot that it would doubtless have exploded and killed everyone near by if he had pulled the trigger. But Standish knocked it away with his sword and collared Morton, and the rest surrendered. The only blood shed was from one of Morton's men

The fight at Merrymount.

who was so drunk that he ran his nose onto the point of the Captain's sword when he entered the house.

The Lord of Merrymount was shipped home to England (cursing and swearing as he was hoisted on board with block and tackle); and in England he avenged himself by writing an amusing book against the Puritans in general and Plymouth in particular. Twice he managed to return to New England, which he truly loved; and once the kindly people of Plymouth took him in. Always restless and "grown old in wickedness," he moved to Boston, got into serious trouble there, and finally died in jail.

It will be seen that the Pilgrims had a very Christian way of dealing with sedition-mongers and troublemakers, using force only when necessary; and it seemed to work. They always forgave the injury and recovered from the wound.

✤ XII ✤

THE TRANSITION
PERIOD, 1625–1630

(✦

THE COLONY IN 1625-27

I N JUNE 1625, shortly after Oldham and Lyford left, Bradford wrote to Robert Cushman in England that the people of Plymouth "never felt the sweetness of the country till
this year; and not only we but all planters in the land begin
to do it." They had really begun to love "thy rocks and rills,
thy woods and templed hills." After the harvest that fall
they had so much surplus corn that they tried a trading voyage to Maine. For, in the meantime, a really useful Particular, a ship carpenter who came over in the *Charity*, had built
them a couple of shallops. Fitting one of these with a half-
deck to keep the corn dry, Edward Winslow made a successful voyage to Maine and up the Kennebec River, exchanging

corn with the Abnaki Indians for 400 pounds' weight of beaver, and other furs as well.

The Colony was really getting on its feet when Bradford wrote about the "sweetness of the country." The first cattle and pigs had arrived; the first horses, "three or four jades" (what we should call "plugs") were imported in 1625. Cattle thrived on the lush grass of the Jones and Eel River meadows, the cows calved every spring, pigs picked up a good living from acorns in the oak forest behind the town. It was a healthy community, too. There had been only one death a year since the Great Sickness of 1621; and sixty-eight children had been born since Oceanus Hopkins increased the number of *Mayflower* passengers by one. By 1624 there were thirty-two houses for a total population of 180, and many more were built in the next few years, along the present Main Street and on both sides of the Town Brook. Isaack de Rasieres, the Dutch official who visited Plymouth in 1627, described it as follows:

> The houses are constructed of clapboards with gardens also enclosed behind and at the sides with clapboards, so that their houses and courtyards are arranged in very good order, with a stockade against sudden attack; and at the ends of the streets there are three wooden gates. In the center, on the cross street, stands the Governor's house, before which is a square stockade upon which four patereros are mounted,[1] so as to enfilade the streets. Upon the Hill they have a large square building with a flat roof, built of thick sawn planks stayed with oak beams, upon the top of which they have six cannon, which shoot iron balls of four

---

[1] A kind of cannon.

[OPPOSITE] *Marching to church at the fort meeting house.*

and five pounds, and command the surrounding country. The lower part they use for their church, where they preach on Sundays and the usual holidays. They assemble by beat of drum, each with his musket or firelock, in front of the captain's door; they have their cloaks on, and place themselves in order, three abreast, and are led by a sergeant without beat of drum. Behind comes the Governor in a long robe; beside him, on the right hand, comes the Preacher with his cloak on, and on the left hand the Captain with his sidearms and cloak on, and with a small cane in his hand; and so they march in good order, and each sets his arms down near him. Thus they are constantly on their guard night and day.

So the picture that we all know, is authentic. The armed Pilgrims in their best clothes really did march up the hill to church.

Food supply was vastly improved by the cattle and swine. Now a mother could get milk for her children, a family could slaughter and salt down a fat hog or an old cow for winter use, a housewife had tallow as well as bayberries to make candles, and the cobbler had leather to make and repair shoes. Poultry there had been since 1622, and before long someone learned how to tame wild turkey poults and raise those big and tasty birds. There were goats, too, which furnished an inferior mutton; and we soon hear of sheep, which made the Colony less dependent on England for woolen clothes. Sugar was wanting, and without it they could not preserve the wild strawberries, blueberries, raspberries, and blackberries that were abundant in summer; but fish, clams, and lobsters were always plentiful. For vegetables they had peas, beans, parsnips, turnips, and garden herbs grown from English seed, and abundant pumpkins grown in the cornfields; but no Irish potatoes until the end of the following century. What the people missed most, besides sweetening, was English beer. But as soon as the apple trees brought from England started to bear fruit, cider replaced the homemade beer of the ballad, made of "pumpkins and parsnips and walnut-tree chips."

THE WRECK OF THE *Sparrowhawk*

◄§ IN 1627, the Colony entertained visitors from abroad. A little Virginia-bound ketch named the *Sparrowhawk*, only forty-five feet long, but carrying twenty-five passengers and crew, came to grief on Cape Cod. After a rough voyage of six weeks, her master down with scurvy, and nothing left to drink but a few gallons of wine, she anchored off the shallow entrance—since closed up—to Pleasant Bay, in the present town of Orleans. An easterly gale drove the vessel onto the bar, to her great damage, and then across the bar and into the bay. There the people grounded her and carried their goods ashore. Some Nauset Indians soon arrived on the scene and offered to take a letter to Plymouth, and that was done.

Virginia, as we have seen, had more than once helped the Pilgrims with food. Now was their chance to repay. Although it was wild winter weather, Governor Bradford at once caused the shallop to be loaded with corn and other provisions, and pitch, oakum, and iron spikes to repair the ketch, and went in her himself. In order to avoid the rough trip around Cape Cod, he put in at Namskaket Creek[2] on the west side and helped his men carry the stuff overland to

---

[2] In the present Orleans. At one time in the eighteenth century the sea broke through some five miles north of Pleasant Bay and Capt. Cyprian Southack went through in a boat, but it soon closed up again.

Pleasant Bay, where the Indians conveyed it to the ship-wrecked people. But he had not long been back home when word came that another storm had driven the *Sparrowhawk* high onto the beach and so battered her that she was a total loss; and could her shipwrecked company spend the winter at Plymouth? So back went the shallop and brought all twenty-five people, with some cloth and shoes that they had salvaged, to Plymouth, where the local families took them in. Some were servants from Ireland, the first Irish the Pilgrims had seen. They probably more than paid for the hospitality they received by helping with household chores and telling the children tales of fairies and giants, and wars of long ago.

The Sparrowhawk *driving on the shoals.*

In the spring of 1628, the *Sparrowhawk* people were allotted fields to plant corn; and at the end of the summer, when a ship called, they went on to Virginia. Captain John Sibsey, the leader among the passengers, settled near Norfolk and became a councilor of that Colony; and "sundry of them," says Bradford, "have acknowledged their thankfulness since from Virginia."

Would you like to take a look at the *Sparrowhawk?* Well, you may! For her timbers, after being buried in Cape Cod sand for over two hundred years, were laid bare by a storm in the nineteenth century. And, carefully assembled by a naval architect, they are still displayed in Pilgrim Hall, Plymouth. These are the only remains in existence of a seventeenth-century emigrant vessel. Everyone who sees this hull of the *Sparrowhawk* is astonished at its tiny size. She was much smaller than the *Mayflower,* but of about the same burden as the *Fortune* and *Little James,* and typical of the hundreds of ships which brought thousands of English and other people to America in those early days.

THE CHURCH AND THE CLERGY

THE THING that bothered the Pilgrims more than anything else at this time was their want of a clergyman. Elder Brewster was a good preacher, but not qualified to baptize babies or administer Holy Communion. The Rev. John Robinson, the pastor at Leyden whom they had always hoped to bring over, died in 1625. What happened to the Rev. John Lyford we have already seen. In 1628, Allerton engaged a hopeful young parson named Rogers, but he turned out to be "crazed in his brain" and had to be sent home. Next year the Rev. Ralph Smith, a scholar of Christ's

College, Cambridge, was induced to come. He was ordained the first regular pastor of the Plymouth Church, "yet he proved but a poor help to them in that, being of very weak parts," and asked to be relieved after six years. Edward Winslow then engaged in England "a godly and worthy man," who promptly died. Next, he secured the Rev. John Norton who stayed in Plymouth only a year, and then accepted a call to Ipswich in the Bay Colony. At long last, in 1635, the Colony found a fairly satisfactory minister, the Rev. John Rayner, formerly of Magdalene College, Cambridge. Yet even he, owing to some "unhappy" rows with the Church, departed after twenty years.

In the meantime, since every Congregational church could use two clergymen, the Rev. Charles Chauncy, an eminent scholar from Cambridge, was procured as Mr. Rayner's colleague. Trouble with him began because he insisted that infants must be ducked all over to be properly baptized; which, as Bradford remarked, was "in this cold country not so convenient." Mr. Chauncy was stubborn, and so he moved to Scituate. There, too, he got in wrong; after immersing his own twin boys, which caused one of them to faint, an irate mother whose baby's turn came next grabbed the minister and tried to push him into the tank! Finally Chauncy was elected President of Harvard College, where he had no baptizing to do.

Plymouth Church held services in the fort until 1648, when the first meeting-house, a simple, square structure, was built fronting the Town Square at the corner of Leyden and Main streets. Like all Congregational meeting-houses, it was also used for other purposes, such as the General Courts or Assemblies of the Freemen, and for town meetings after the town and Colony governments were separated. That building lasted until 1683, when a "larger and handsomer one" was built on the same site.[3]

The First Church of Plymouth (the organization, not the building) has the distinction of being the oldest in New England. And it had the honor of showing the Puritans of Massachusetts Bay how to organize a Congregational church. The Plymouth people were able to do this because they were no longer Separatists. At Leyden, the Rev. John Robinson decided that rigid separation from all other Protestant churches was wrong, and converted his congregation to that point of view. Roger Williams, in fact, left Plymouth because its church was *not* Separatist. Thus the Pilgrims were in complete sympathy with the Puritans who came to Massachuestts Bay. They were glad to show the Bay people how to organize a Congregational church, and the people there were willing to learn.

Captain John Endecott had led a vanguard of the great Puritan migration to Salem. Some of the passengers died at sea from scurvy and "an infectious fever," and many were still very sick when they landed. Governor Bradford, to whom Endecott appealed for help, sent Dr. Samuel Fuller to Salem, and he cured many of the sick. While so doing he talked with the leading men about church organization, and they decided to form the First Church of Salem on the Plymouth model; and not only Congregational but Unitarian and Baptist ministers in the United States are still so ordained today. The Rev. Samuel Skelton and the Rev. Francis Higginson, who had been ministers in England, were questioned as to whether they had an "inward calling" to preach

---

[3] This meeting-house must have resembled the "Old Ship" Meeting-House at Hingham, Mass., which was built about the same time and is now the oldest standing in New England.

and teach. They allowed that they had. The congregation
then elected them Pastor and Teacher; and "three or four of
the gravest members of the church" laid hands on them, and
prayed. Skelton joined in the "laying on" of Higginson, and
Higginson in that of Skelton, so that there would be some
semblance of apostolic succession. Bradford and others
started for Salem to attend the ceremony, but were delayed
by contrary winds and missed it. Let us hope that they were
in time for the ordination feast that followed.

Things were now stirring in England. The great mass of
the Puritans who had been tolerated by King James became
the objects of persecution by King Charles I and Archbishop
Laud. And at the same time the King decided to dismiss
Parliament, in which there was a Puritan majority, and to
rule as an absolute monarch. Puritan leaders such as John
Winthrop, Thomas Dudley, and Sir Richard Saltonstall decided it was time to get out. Organizing the Massachusetts
Bay Company, they obtained a royal charter and, just as the
Pilgrims had done ten years earlier, sold property, chartered
shipping, bought supplies, and prepared to sail. Their emi-
gration was on a far greater scale than that of the *Mayflower*.
It was led by wealthy and prominent people, in contrast
to the simple Pilgrims. Governor John Winthrop in the *Ar-
bella* led a fleet of seventeen big ships which brought some
two thousand settlers to Massachusetts Bay before the year
1630 was out. This was the beginning of the "Great Puritan
Migration" which in ten years' time founded four more colonies in New England and made Boston the largest town in
America north of Mexico City.

❧ XIII ❧

FISHING AND FUR-TRADING

❧❧❧❧❧❧❧❧❧❧❧❧❧❧❧❧❧❧❧❧❧❧❧❧❧❧❧❧❧❧❧❧

COR-FISH AND POOR-JOHN

ALTHOUGH the Pilgrims always intended to make fish their "cash crop" for paying off debts to the Adventurers and buying supplies from England, they never had any luck; Bradford even called fishing "a thing fatal to this plantation." By fishing he did not mean catching cod and bass, eels and alewives, to eat at home; the Pilgrims always took enough of them after the first three years. Much less did he mean digging clams or picking up lobsters at low tide. He meant commercial fishing for European markets. That required a ship, a lot of gear, a supply of rock salt, and know-how.

Cod was the only fish wanted for market. It was the easiest to salt, and nobody then thought that haddock, hake, pollock, redfish, or flounder were fit to eat. (The Pilgrims once tried shipping a few barrels of pickled bass to Spain, but found no sale.) Forty or fifty English fishing vessels sailed to the Maine Coast every spring and fished for cod with hand lines on the many banks and shoals off shore. First, however, they landed some of their crew at a harbor that had good rocky ledges. Over these they built what was then (and in Nova Scotia still is) called a fishing stage—a wharf built of spruce trees, boards, and beach stones where the fish could be cleaned and cured. Every few days the ship, in order to prevent her catch from spoiling, sailed into the harbor and tossed the cod out onto the stage. There the shore crew gutted and split them, soaked them for a couple of days in brine, sprinkled the meat side with rock salt and then laid them out on "fish flakes"—a framework of split laths—to cure in the sun. If it rained or turned foggy, they had to be piled in heaps and covered with tarpaulins. This process was known as "making fish." Owing to refrigeration, it has become almost extinct in New England; but your author has done it himself on the coast of Maine, and he can tell you that homemade salt cod or pollock makes a mighty tasty dish, if cooked right.

Codfish thus "made" were of two qualities; the better, known as cor-fish, was caught close to shore, landed within a couple of days, and lightly salted and cured largely in the sun. There was a good market for this in England. The other kind, codfish caught on the Grand Bank of Newfoundland, had to lie in the ship's hold for a week or more before being landed, and so had to be very heavily salted to counteract the decay. It was known as dry fish or "poor-john," and could be sold only in Spain or southern France. There was also a "luxury" quality known as dun-fish, very large cod which were cured by being buried in hay, or, still better, in a heap of manure, which gave them a deep-brown color and a peculiar flavor. It is a tradition among the fishermen on the Isles of Shoals off New Hampshire that the King of Spain always insisted on one of their dun-fish for his Good Friday dinner. Your author has eaten dun-fish made in New Brunswick, and can testify that the King of Spain had very good taste.

In the fall, or as soon as the ship had a full load of "made" fish, she sailed for England if her cargo was cor-fish; or, if it was "poor-john," to one of the Catholic countries of southern Europe where the large number of fast days created a great demand for salt fish.

THE *Little James* AND *White Angel*

⚜ THE PILGRIMS had no success at this kind of fishing, even with the *Little James*, which the London Adventurers built especially for them. One August day in 1623, this pinnace[1] sailed into Plymouth Harbor, dressed with flags and pennants and colored "waist cloths" amidships, firing her cannon in salute. The children, who had never seen such a fine sight, laughed and clapped, and the big boys began to boast: "*I'm going fishing in her*"—"No, *I* am!" But the older men shook their heads and said: "How are we going to pay for this?"

The *Little James* had a very rowdy, mutinous crew who wanted to go privateering; the Colony had to raise their

---

[1] The term *pinnace* was then used for any small sailing vessel that was decked over. *Little James* was probably about forty-five feet long and had two masts, one rigged square and the other with a lateen sail like the *Mayflower's* mizzen.

wages right away, and no Plymouth boys were allowed to
ship in her. She first made an unsuccessful trading voyage
around Cape Cod, "having only a few beads and knives
which were there not much esteemed," and lost her mainmast in a gale. Refitted, she was sent on a fishing trip down
east. When at anchor off Damariscove Island in Maine, another gale of wind drove her onto the rocks, "which beat
such a hole in her bilge as a horse and cart might have gone
in," and her master was drowned. With the aid of friendly
fishermen the Pilgrims got her off, repaired her at great
expense, and sent her back to England where she was legally
taken over by the London Adventurers, and the Colony lost
its investment. Next year (1625) the Adventurers sent her
out again, together with a big ship, the *White Angel*, under
a good master with a crew of experienced fishermen.

The *White Angel* made a good haul of poor-john, which
would have been worth £1800 at Bilbao or San Sebastian in
Spain, says Bradford. But there was a rumor of war with
France, so the master dared not enter the Bay of Biscay and
sold his catch in Portsmouth, England, for less than the outlay. *Little James*, sailing home filled "with goodly cor-fish as
full as she could swim," together with 800 pounds' weight of
beaver, was captured in the English Channel by a Barbary
pirate and taken into Salé, Morocco, where the cargo was
confiscated and the master and men made slaves. The Plymouth boys who were mad with their fathers for refusing
to let them sail in this pinnace, now decided that the "old
man" had something!

The *Little James* had made her cor-fish at a stage in the
harbor of Gloucester, Massachusetts. The right to build
a stage there had been given to the Pilgrims by the Council
for New England, but in 1625 John Oldham and the Rev.

Mr. Lyford and some of their friends appropriated both stage and gear. Plymouth sent Myles Standish with armed men to recover the property, and they almost came to blows over it; but Roger Conant, boss of a third group of fishermen at Cape Ann, made peace on the basis of Oldham & Company helping them to build a second stage. The *White Angel* used it, too, to cure her cargo of poor-john.

In the light of these events, the Pilgrims concluded that God did not intend them to fish for profit, and that they had better confine themselves to fishing around Plymouth for their own consumption. So they turned to the fur trade although, as Bradford remarks, none of them had ever seen a beaver skin before they came to America. Squanto taught them the ins and outs of the business, and it proved to be their economic salvation.

THE BEAVER TRADE

⊷§ THERE WAS an immense demand in England for beaver and otter fur; mink, strange as it may seem, was worth no more than muskrat or rabbit. Fur was used not only to make coats for rich people but to make felt for the broadbrimmed hats worn by all men and women above the working class. Beaver fetched as much as one pound per pound weight in England for ten or twelve years; and some of the bigger skins —"coat beaver"—brought more. Otter skins were worth fourteen shillings to sixteen shillings apiece. In that era of low prices, with wages a shilling a day, this was big money. But you cannot buy a beaver coat for that price today!

All these furbearing animals were trapped by the Indians, who observed a closed season by general agreement, and knew how to cure the pelts so that they would last for years. And they soon learned that beaver was more valuable as an article of trade than to wear; the number of skins that would make a coat could be bartered for an English woolen "matchcoat" like the modern mackinaw jacket, a wool blanket or two, and some hardware to boot. Indians were eager to get English hoes, axes, knives, kettles, and other metal articles to substitute for their stone tools and wooden bowls. And those who lived in the future State of Maine—the Abnakis—preferred to swap beaver for corn rather than grow corn, or steal it from the Massachusetts.

From 1624 on, the Pilgrims had plenty of surplus corn, but they needed other trading truck as well, and that had to be bought from England. All such stuff should have been furnished by the London Adventurers; but they claimed that nothing was left over after furnishing the Colony with clothing, shoes, tools, pots and pans, cattle, medicaments, and English provisions such as flour and pickled beef. And the Pilgrims' efforts to "prime the pump" with beaver in the *Fortune* and *Little James* had been spoiled by pirates.

The London Adventurers, excepting Weston, were not a bad lot. Some of them, such as William Collier, a London brewer, and Timothy Hatherley, a London merchant, even emigrated to Plymouth; and others backed the later Massachusetts Bay settlements. But the Adventurers "had to live," and after four years of "losses and crosses at sea," with no dividends on their investment, they wrote to Governor Bradford in December 1624 that the partnership was dissolved. James Sherley, their treasurer, and forty-one others, bought up the shares of the rest, probably much below the par value of £10, and announced that the Colony still owed them £1400 for supplies over and above shipments received. Bradford remarks that they arrived at this figure by charging forty per cent profit on all the cattle and goods sent out, and taking thirty per cent commission on all the fur, fish, and clapboard sold—"a thing thought unreasonable by some." No wonder!

The Pilgrims could not simply say "Try to get it," however exorbitant the claim, because the forty-two partners had a legal lien on all the Colony's property until the agreed division in 1627. So they turned to and did their best to pay off the debt; and that they could only do by success in the fur trade. There was no other way, except the fishing, in which they had no luck, to make money in New England.

Myles Standish sailed to England in the fall of 1625 to seek financial help in the form of goods the Indians wanted, and the Pilgrims needed, to keep going. He arrived at the worst possible time. A severe plague was raging in London, most of the merchants had fled to the country, and no business was being done. Standish managed to borrow £150 at the exorbitant interest of fifty per cent, spent it on trading truck and necessary supplies, and returned as passenger on a fisherman. The following year, Isaac Allerton was sent to England to get more supplies. He borrowed £200 at thirty per cent and laid it out in goods. The same year, Bradford and Winslow sailed to Monhegan and bought half the stock of a trading company there which had failed. They also procured some goods from a French ship which was wrecked on the Maine coast. Shallops used in this coastwise sailing were manned by Plymouth boys, who got to know the Maine coast as well as Plymouth Bay.

NEW DEAL WITH THE ADVENTURERS

✤§ ALLERTON, in October 1626, made a "new deal" for the
Pilgrims with the forty-two remaining London partners.
In return for the promise to pay £1800, on the install-
ment plan, over a period of nine years, the Adventurers
gave up their claims to the real estate and property of the
Colony. "This agreement was very well liked of and approved by all the Plantation, and consented unto, though
they knew not well how to raise the payment and discharge
their other engagements and supply the yearly wants of the
Plantation," wrote Bradford.[2]

The way they arranged it was this. What was left of the
old "common course and condition" was abandoned. Every
single man or head of a family got twenty acres of land in
full ownership, and a house. The cattle were distributed at
the rate of one cow and two goats to every six persons.
Meadows were still the property of the Colony, but everyone
could cut hay on them, or graze cattle after the hay was har-
vested—and all near-by meadows, too, were divided up in
1633. Most important, the Colony organized a group called
the "Undertakers," consisting of eight leading men (Bradford, Brewster, Winslow, Allerton, Myles Standish, John
Howland, John Alden, and Thomas Prence). They undertook
to be responsible for the debt, in return for a six-year mo-

---

[2] They also owed £400 to Sherley and two others as their personal
account for supplies advanced. As a sample of the sort of thing they
had to import, Allerton brought them in 1628 a consignment of the
following articles, worth £232: shoes, leather, cloth, and Irish stockings; pitch, tar, ropes, and twine; knives and scissors; rugs (coarse,
thick woolen cloth); lead, shot, and powder; hatchets, hoes, axes,
scythes, reaphooks, shovels, spades, saws, files, nails, and iron pots;
drugs and spices.

nopoly of trade with the Indians, and the duty of procuring necessities from England. These, they agreed to sell to the people for corn at the rate of six shillings the bushel.

This was no charity scheme, since the London Adventurers would take a big commission on everything going and coming, but it would have been fair enough if the Adventurers had not cheated. James Sherley, whose letters were full of piety and good will, and Isaac Allerton, an original *Mayflower* passenger who acted as go-between, were the principal offenders. Allerton, the former tailor, was a real "go-getter." He showed such energy in the early years that he was elected the Governor's first Assistant; and, after his first wife died, he married Fear Brewster, daughter of the Elder. Always in search of new ways to make money, he took advantage of his position as the Colony's agent in England to invest £7000 from fur sales in trading and fishing ventures, instead of using it to pay off the debt or obtain supplies. After suffering from his spending habits for four or five years, the Undertakers dismissed him as their agent; he later went to New Haven, where he died "insolvent in reputation and estate."

James Sherley, by Bradford's account, received 12,120 pounds' weight of beaver and 1,156 otter skins from the Undertakers in five years, but cheated both his partners and them. So little of this went to pay off the debt that the more fur the Undertakers sent over, the more their debt increased. They were much too trusting in business matters. Josias Winslow, Edward's younger brother, who acted as accountant for the London partners, seems to have been unable to add or subtract. Twice a year the Undertakers called for accounts, but the creditors always had some good reason why they could not give one; and by taking excessive profits on the supplies they sent over, and heavy commissions on the fur they sold, they were always able to make a plausible case for piling it on. The Pilgrims were in the same position as a modern debtor in the hands of loan sharks. The more they paid back, the more (so their creditors claimed) they owed; and first and last they paid out some £20,000 worth of beaver and other goods to discharge the debt of £1800 agreed upon in 1626.

In 1642 Sherley claimed that the Undertakers still owed him £1200. He made a deal with a committee from Massachusetts (which was raising money for that Colony in England) by which the committee paid him £900 and undertook to collect from Plymouth—which the Bay Colony did, with interest. The other £300 was paid from a fur shipment. One Adventurer held out for £400 more; and the Undertakers did not get rid of his claims until 1648, when Winslow and Prence sold their houses, and the others sold some of their land to raise the money. Such was "the conclusion of that long and tedious business," as Bradford calls it. "Thus were they abused in their simplicity, and no better than bought and sold."

TRADE WITH THE DUTCH

Although the simple Pilgrims were no match for London financiers, or for "operators" like Allerton, they traded for furs with skill and success. Governor Winthrop of the Bay Colony complained, in 1634, that his people hadn't a chance; the Pilgrims had grabbed all the best places. And they made a good connection with the Dutch.

Men of that nation had been trading along the Hudson River and Long Island Sound for years before the Pilgrims arrived. New Amsterdam, the present New York, was founded in 1626. The following year, the Dutch Governor, Peter Minuit, sent a shallop to Buzzards Bay with a letter addressed in most flowery style to the "Noble, worshipful, wise, and prudent Lords, the Governor and Councillors residing in New Plymouth." He proposed to start trading, and the Pilgrims replied, in the Dutch language, that they would be very happy to do so.

Men of Plymouth had already noticed that Cape Cod was joined to the main part of New England by a narrow neck of land over which the Indians had a canoe carry. This enabled the redskins to get from Long Island Sound and Buzzards Bay to Cape Cod Bay without going around the Cape; a difficult voyage at best, dangerous for a canoe. So, in 1627, the Undertakers built a trading post at the head of navigation in Buzzards Bay and kept a pinnace there to trade with the Dutch. The site of their trading post, at a place called Aptucxet by the Indians, has been found, and the house reconstructed.[3]

That fall, the Secretary of New Netherland, Isaack de Rasieres, "accompanied by a noise of trumpeters," paid an official visit. He sailed to the Aptucxet trading post in a sloop, marched over the carry to the Scusset River, and there was met by a boat from Plymouth. Upon its arrival at the Rock, Myles Standish and his musketeers were drawn up to fire a salute, and two big boys beat lustily on drums while the Dutchman landed and trumpeters blared forth cheery music. Sugar and linen and woolen cloth he brought

---

[3] To visit this interesting reconstruction, follow Route 3 from Boston to Cape Cod; after crossing the Bourne Bridge over the Canal, turn sharp right; next, bear left at a fork and follow Shore Road to signs indicating the Post; turn right under the railroad bridge and follow a dirt road through woods to the Post.

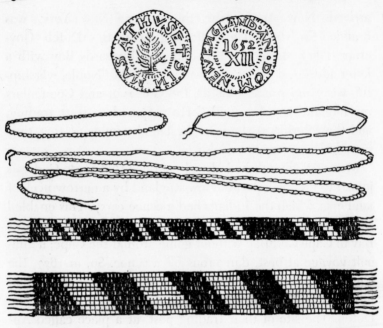

Massachusetts Pine Tree Shilling. Wampum. Treaty Belts.

as presents;[4] but the big transaction was to sell the Pilgrims
£50 worth of wampum.

Wampum was shell-money made by the Pequots and Narragansetts and the Indians of Long Island. It was manufac-
tured from parts of the quahaug or hard-shell clam, and
from sea-snails' shells, drilled and polished into little hollow
cylinders that could be strung together; several strings ar-

---

[4] Very likely the first sugar the Pilgrims had. Cushman, writing to
Bradford in 1624, said that owing to the high price of necessities,
"comfortable things such as sugar and butter" could not be provided
from England.

[OPPOSITE] *Governor Bradford welcomes Isaack de Rasieres
to Plymouth.*

ranged parallel to each other made a "belt." Wampum passed for currency among all the Eastern Indians, and even the English used it among themselves for small change. The Dutch were eager to sell it to the Pilgrims so that they would stay away from the source, and the Undertakers were glad to buy, as it meant one more article to barter for fur.

Relations between the two colonies continued to be pleasant and profitable for five years, until they fell out over rival trading posts on the Connecticut River.

TRADING POSTS IN MAINE AND CONNECTICUT

⇜ THE SECOND Pilgrim trading post was set up on the Kennebec River. The Undertakers, fearing that they would be squeezed out of the lucrative Indian trade there if they did not act quickly, instructed Allerton to obtain a patent from the Council for New England, which he did at considerable cost. It granted them the stretch of the Kennebec from the Nequamkick "rippling" down to the Cobbosseecontee Falls where the Androscoggin River enters, and the land fifteen miles on each side. The Undertakers put up a house on the site of Fort Western in the present city of Augusta, stocked it with trading goods, "and what they could not have out of England, they bought of the fishing ships." The Abnaki had developed an appetite for English food such as ship biscuit, peas, and dried prunes; and this post, in charge of John Howland, proved very profitable for several years.

In 1630, Allerton and four London Adventurers bought from the Council for New England a tract of land between Pemaquid Point and Cape Rosier in Maine. Within it they started a third trading post at a place called Pentagoët, at the site of Castine, on the Penobscot. After putting in charge of it a young man named Edward Ashley who had "lived among the Indians as a savage and went naked amongst them," these partners put the Plymouth Undertakers on a spot by writing, in effect: "Buy a piece of this—or else!" Fearing Penobscot competition to the Kennebec trading post, they accepted and sent down east one of the ablest young men of Plymouth, Thomas Willet,[5] with a stock of trading goods, to keep an eye on Ashley. However, Ashley, that "very profane young man," as Bradford calls him, "quickly gathered a good parcel of beaver," shipped it all to England where it was sold for the partners' account, and Plymouth got nothing.

Allerton not only paid no attention to the Undertakers' complaints; he even set up a fourth trading post, at Machias in eastern Maine, in which fortunately Plymouth was not involved.

Both of these down-east posts were broken up by the French. They took Machias first, killed two men who were in charge, and stole all the goods. Next, while Ashley and Willet were away in their boat to pick up supplies, a small French vessel cast anchor in Castine Harbor. The crew went ashore. "Many French compliments they used, and congees [deep bows] they made"; they picked up a couple of fire-arms in the trading house, pretending to admire them, and "stuck up" the three or four Englishmen in charge. The Frenchmen got away with three hundred pounds of bea-

---

[5] Willet, a member of the Leyden congregation, came over in 1629 at the age of twenty-four. He accompanied the English expeditionary force that wrested New Amsterdam from the Dutch in 1664, and was appointed by Gov. Nicolls the first English Mayor of New York. Returning to Plymouth Colony, he settled at Swansea and died, greatly respected, in 1674.

ver, and some £400 worth of trading truck. Two years later Charles d'Aunay, one of the French proprietors of Acadie (Nova Scotia), took complete possession of the post in the name of the King of France. The Undertakers chartered a large, well-armed ship, the *Great Hope,* and Myles Standish with twenty men accompanied her in the pinnace, hoping to wrest Pentagoët from the French. But the master of the *Great Hope* "began to shoot at a distance like a madman," and fired off all his powder before he got within range. "And this was the end of this business," says Bradford.

Not only the right kind of trading truck, but a good position on a long river, was the way to procure a substantial supply of furs from the Indians. That is one reason why the French at Quebec and Montreal were so successful. And in 1633 the Undertakers had an opportunity to get in first, or almost first, on the Connecticut.

The Dutch, who claimed that part of New England, invited the Pilgrims to go in with them on a fifty-fifty basis, fearing they were too weak to face the Indians alone. The Undertakers accepted. The Dutch then backed out and said: "Go it alone"; then changed their minds and founded Fort Good Hope, on the site of Hartford. It had just been set up when the Plymouth pinnace sailed up the river, carrying a sort of prefabricated trading house. The Good Hope garrison threatened to shoot, but hadn't the nerve; and the Pilgrims passed them and put up their house at a place called Matianuck (the site of Windsor, Connecticut), on a tract that they bought from the Indians. New Netherland "sent a band of about seventy men in warlike manner, with colours displayed, to assault them, but seeing them strengthened and that it would cost blood . . . returned in peace."

That was in 1633. Two years later some of the Puritan settlers of Massachusetts Bay began an overland trek to the Connecticut. Springfield was founded as a trading post; Hartford and Windsor as farming settlements. These newcomers allowed the Pilgrims to keep their trading post and a small part of the land they had bought from the Indians. But, with farmers all about and Springfield getting the best of the beaver, the Matianuck post ceased to pay and was abandoned.

The Undertakers were dissolved after the debt was paid off, but the fur trade never became free for all. The Colony "farmed it out," as the phrase was, to people who would pay a good fee for the privilege. The Kennebec land and trading post, for instance, was let to a partnership consisting of Bradford, Willet, Prence, and William Paddy. They did well with it for several years. Finally, in 1660, when the fur trade was declining, the Colony sold its entire tract on the Kennebec to a group of Boston merchants, for £400.

While the trade lasted, the Pilgrims were the best fur traders between the St. Lawrence and the Hudson. Despite the many "losses and crosses at sea," it was the redskins' beaver that got them out of the red.

PROSPERITY AND
EXPANSION

❮◆

THE NEW CATTLE INDUSTRY

WHAT DID little Plymouth think about the great Puritan migration that started in 1630? Her population was still only about three hundred; but instead of feeling envious, she was proud to have lit the candle that had lighted a thousand others, as Bradford put it. She was glad to have strong English neighbors, and Puritans at that, instead of being a lone and feeble colony with Dutch on one side, French on the other, and Indians all around. But the great migration did cause an upheaval in the life of the Colony.

It happened this way. Many of the emigrants to Massachusetts brought plenty of money and goods to buy corn, cattle, and other food until they could start farms of their own. Plymouth was the nearest place to get such things. All of a sudden, the Pilgrims found a market for all the corn and cattle they could grow, and at very attractive prices. Any day now, you could see men driving cows along the old Indian trail from Plymouth to Boston Harbor, or boating them in a shallop.

A few years earlier, the Colony had granted what were called "great lots," in the present towns of Kingston, Duxbury, and Marshfield, to people who wanted to raise cattle. The owners, however, were required to live in Plymouth and send a son or a servant up there to take care of the cows. Now these people said they must live on their great lots and have even more land to satisfy the demand at Boston. Plymouth began to be surrounded by veritable cattle ranches! Governor Bradford, Elder Brewster, and other *Mayflower* passengers were much distressed by this "progress." Their ideal always had been a compact settlement where everyone could attend divine service and lead a sociable life, as in Old England. Almost every English farmer lived in a village near the church, even though he had to ride or walk many miles to cultivate his fields.

EXPANSION NORTHWARD

◆§ BRADFORD and Brewster did not see how Puritan ideals of godliness and neighborly help could be kept up if people scattered up and down the coast to plant corn and raise cows. But they were unable to stop the movement. In 1632, John Alden, Myles Standish, Jonathan Brewster (the Elder's son), and Thomas Prence, who had great lots at Duxbury, asked to be dismissed from Plymouth Church and to form the First

Church of Duxbury, which was done. Even Elder Brewster and Stephen Hopkins moved to Duxbury, which in 1637 was recognized by the General Court as a town separate from Plymouth. Scituate had already been given the same privilege. Edward Winslow, who had married Susanna White when she was only seven weeks a widow, first sent Susanna's son Peregrine to take care of the cattle on his great lot in Marshfield—a big responsibility for a twelve-year-old boy—and moved there himself in 1636. Within a few years Marshfield (first called Rexham) had its own church and town meeting. That sort of thing, Bradford feared, would "be the ruin of New England, or at least of the churches of God there."

Actually, this sowing of the Pilgrim seed throughout the wilderness was the making of New England. But it was tough on Plymouth Town. Ships from England by-passed it now in favor of Boston. It had very little arable land except the Indian cornfields, and so many people left for other places that the population actually declined between 1630 and 1644. At that date there was serious talk in Plymouth of moving the whole town to Eastham on Cape Cod. "And thus was this poor church," wrote Bradford, "left like an ancient mother grown old and forsaken of her children."

Plymouth fell to so low a state around mid-century that when a noted privateer captain with two Spanish prizes was driven into the harbor by a northwest gale, Governor Winthrop considered it a special providence "for the comfort and help of that town, which was now almost deserted." For privateers, like pirates, are generous spenders.

Many families of the great Puritan migration, after arriving in Boston, took up land in Plymouth Colony and founded new settlements and towns. This movement was welcomed by the old settlers; they only objected to the town and church of Plymouth being broken up.

Scituate, first of these settlements made by "outsiders," was founded by six "men of Kent," who arrived in 1628. It was included in Plymouth Colony by the Warwick Patent because Timothy Hatherley and several other London Adventurers bought land there from the Indians. Scituate had a good harbor as a base for fishing, and some salt meadows, a continual bone of contention with Cohasset neighbors. More settlers arrived, and in 1637 they received permission from the General Court to organize a church and a town. Scituate people were quick to take advantage of several big brooks to furnish water power. Isaac Stedman, before 1640, built on Herring Brook the first sawmill in the Colony; James Torrey in 1653 built a fulling mill for finishing home-woven cloth, and a second sawmill was built in 1656. And on the banks of the North River, which flows between Scituate and Marshfield, shipbuilding began late in the century.

In spite of the fact that about half the population removed to Barnstable on Cape Cod in 1640, Scituate soon became, and long remained, the richest town in the Old Colony.

Bridgewater, which included not only the modern East, West, and North Bridgewaters, but Brockton and Abington, was originally an Indian purchase made by men of Duxbury from Massasoit, so as to have farms for their children. Their first settlement was made near Lake Nippenicket in what is now West Bridgewater, in 1656. A few years later they obtained as minister a young Scot named James Keith, educated in Aberdeen. Aldens, Ameses, Mitchells, Standishes, and Packards were among the first settlers.

The Marshfielders, too, showed a tendency to move elsewhere, which Bradford thought would "provoke the Lord's displeasure." Unknown to him, the American custom of moving on, if you don't like where you are, had started.

FIRST SETTLEMENTS ON CAPE COD

ᴥ§ so much for Plymouth's expansion northward to Duxbury, Marshfield, and Scituate.[1] The southward expansion, along the Bay side of Cape Cod, was equally important. For along that coast there were several small harbors, Nauset Indians had been friendly since the death of Aspinet, and the farming land was good. You must not suppose that Cape Cod contains nothing but sand; the soil in the western part of it, and in patches up through Wellfleet, is as good as any in New England. But Henry Thoreau wrote a century ago that he hadn't seen "enough black earth in Provincetown to fill a flower-pot, unless in the swamps."

Most of the first settlers on Cape Cod came there directly from England or from Massachusetts Bay; and the Cape Codders have always felt different from—even superior to—the people of Plymouth County.

Sandwich was the mother town of Cape Cod. The Pilgrims, on their boat journeys along shore, had noted a fine stand of oak which indicated rich soil, and extensive salt marshes where good hay for feeding cattle grew wild. A group of ten men drifted in there from Lynn in Massachusetts Bay, in 1637. A grant from the General Court of the Colony was obtained, and John Alden and Myles Standish went there early the next year to survey the boundaries. In 1639, the settlement was recognized as the Town of Sandwich. A church was organized, and the Rev. William

---

[1] This section of the Old Colony is now called the "South Shore," i.e., of Massachusetts Bay.

Leveridge, a graduate of Emmanuel College, Cambridge, was elected the first minister. Sandwich became the most prosperous farming town of Cape Cod; still standing are several houses built in the Pilgrim century.[2] Among the first settlers, Edmond Freeman, William Swift, Edward Dillingham, and Thomas Dexter founded famous families. And Almys, Nyes, and Hoxies were not far behind.

Barnstable early became a rival to Sandwich and is still the shire town of Barnstable County. The attractions here were a harbor deep enough for shallops and pinnaces, and the Great Salt Marshes, as they are still called. The Rev. John Lothrop, an alumnus of Christ Church, Oxford, came there in 1639 with a group of his followers, organized a town and church, and received recognition "for them" from the Colony.[3] The town was extended to the "back" (or ocean) side of Cape Cod in 1650 by purchase from Wianno, a Nauset sagamore. Barnstable became a happy and prosperous community, and among its first settlers attracted the founders of the Bacon, Bourne, Hinckley, Otis, Chipman, Crocker, and Allyn families.

Yarmouth, next east of Barnstable, is the parent town of Harwich, Chatham, Dennis, and Brewster. The attractions here were the little harbor (now Yarmouthport), the salt

---

[2] The Hoxie house, said to date from 1637 and, if so, the oldest on Cape Cod, is (1956) in a state of deplorable disrepair; the Wing house on Grove St., dating from 1641, is still lived in by his descendants; the Skiffe house on Route 6-A east of the town center is said to date from 1638; and the grist mill, next the Town Hall, is the original, although its waterwheel is a restoration.

[3] The site of their first meeting is marked on a rock monument on Route 6-A, about three quarters of a mile west of the cemetery where John Lothrop and other pioneers are buried. The First Church of Barnstable claims to be older than that of Plymouth since many of its members had belonged to a Congregational church in London under Lothrop as early as 1616.

marshes, and the good land. Within two years (in 1639) the
place had been recognized as a town, and a church was organized under the Rev. Marmaduke Matthews, formerly of
All Souls' College, Oxford. Pioneer families of Yarmouth,
such as the Sears and Howes, became famous in the annals
of American business and finance,[4] while the Thachers and
Lovells were eminent in the learned professions.[5]

---

[4] Richard Sears the pioneer was a surveyor. A tower has been built
on Scargo Hill, the highest point on Cape Cod, in the present town of
Dennis. From this hill Sears could look for miles around; on clear days
one can see both Plymouth and Provincetown from the tower. To
reach it, follow Route 6 north from Dennis, turning right on Scargo
Hill Road to a steep, unmarked road to the left which takes you to the
base of the tower.

[5] It was Anthony Thacher who, with Parson Avery, was wrecked on
Thacher's Island off Cape Ann in the hurricane of 1635, an incident
that inspired Whittier's poem, "The Swan Song of Parson Avery."
Bradford's account of this hurricane is so vivid and it so resembles the
hurricanes with which New England has been sadly familiar since
1938, that it is worth quoting:

> This year, the 14th or 15th of August (being Saturday) was
> such a mighty storm of wind and rain as none living in these
> parts, either English or Indians, ever saw. Being like, for the
> time it continued, to those hurricanes and typhoons that writers
> make mention of in the Indies. It began in the morning a little
> before day, and grew not by degrees but came with violence in
> the beginning, to the great amazement of many. It blew down
> sundry houses and uncovered others. Divers vessels were lost at
> sea and many more in extreme danger. It caused the sea to swell
> to the southward of this place above 20 foot right up and down,
> and made many of the Indians to climb into trees for their safety.
> It took off the boarded roof of a house which belonged to this
> Plantation at Manomet, and floated it to another place, the posts
> still standing in the ground. And if it had continued long with-
> out the shifting of the wind, it is like it would have drowned some
> part of the country. It blew down many hundred thousands of
> trees, turning up the stronger by the roots and breaking the higher
> pine trees off in the middle. And the tall young oaks and walnut
> trees of good bigness were wound like a withe, very strange and
> fearful to behold. It began in the southeast and parted toward

The only English settlement on the forearm of the Cape before 1660 was Eastham, the parent town of Orleans, Wellfleet, and Truro. This entire region was first called Nauset after the Indians, and became one of the Reserved Tracts deeded by the Colony to surviving *Mayflower* passengers in 1640. Four years later, when Plymouth was feeling deserted and discouraged, the town actually voted to remove both church and town to this "place called Nauset." A committee of the Church, sent to look it over, reported that there was not enough good land to warrant the move, nor so good a harbor as Plymouth's. So the plan was given up; but Thomas Prence, John Doane, Edward Bangs, and other leading Plymouth men purchased the land from the Indians, and enough of them moved there for it to be recognized as a town in 1651.

A good living was hard to get from the soil in Eastham; digging clams alongshore or dredging oysters from Wellfleet Harbor was found to be more profitable. Crows and blackbirds appear to have been more enterprising here than elsewhere, or else the Easthamites were poor shots; for the town voted in 1667 that every householder must kill at least three crows or twelve blackbirds per annum. This order was repeated annually, and toward the close of the century was reinforced by another, that each bachelor in town must kill at least six blackbirds or three crows per annum, and would not be allowed to marry until he had done his whack for the year!

---

the south and east, and veered sundry ways, but the greatest force of it here was from the former quarters. It continued not (in the extremity) above five or six hours but the violence began to abate. The signs and marks of it will remain this hundred years in these parts where it was sorest. The moon suffered a great eclipse the second night after it.

REHOBOTH

❧ SETTLEMENTS also started in the southwestern part of
the Colony, near Providence, Rhode Island. Edward Winslow and John Browne purchased from Massasoit the Seekonk plain, bordering on the Blackstone River, in 1641, for
one coat and twenty yards of wampum—quite a bargain!
They sold out to a group of people from Braintree and Hingham, Massachusetts, who began a settlement in 1643. Massachusetts Bay claimed this territory, but New Plymouth
appealed to the New England Confederation and won it. As
minister they obtained a distinguished Oxford graduate, the
Rev. Samuel Newman, at whose suggestion the Hebrew name
Rehoboth (meaning "roominess") was adopted.[6] It certainly
was appropriate. The Seekonk plain is a big one for New
England, and the towns of Seekonk, Swansea, and Attleboro
(Massachusetts) and Cumberland, Pawtucket, and most of
East Providence (Rhode Island), have been set off from the
original town. Rehoboth was admitted a town of Plymouth
Colony in 1645. The Paine, Peck, Bliss, and Fuller fam-
ilies were among the first settlers. They constantly traded
with Boston "by cart and horseback," said a visitor in 1660;
and also by water with Narragansett Bay.

Although the great Puritan migration forced Plymouth
Colony to expand, and changed its ways of making a living,
the character of the Colony did not change. The leaders of
the Bay Colony, and of Connecticut and New Haven too,
believed they had been chosen by God to set up a new world

---

[6] The meeting-house of the Newman Congregational Church, as it
is now called, is at the corner of Routes 1-A and 152, in East Providence, R. I. That was the center of the original Rehoboth settlement.

order, based on God's revealed Word. So, when anything went wrong, particularly after some years had elapsed and the younger generation was becoming bored with Puritan strictness, there was a great deal of beating the breast at Boston, Hartford, and New Haven. The ministers began to preach sermons along the line: "God hoped so much of us, but we have been so wicked that He has deserted us."

Now, there may have been that feeling in Plymouth Colony. We can't be sure there was not, because the clergy did not rush into print like other New England parsons, when they thought things were going wrong. But, if Bradford is a fair guide, the Pilgrims were content with a much more modest role in the world drama than those assumed by their sister colonies. They had no illusion that the eyes of the world were upon them, although they felt that God was watching them, as He did every other Christian. They did not expect to be a "city on a hill," as Governor Winthrop said the Bay Colony should be. All they wanted was freedom to worship God in their own way, to control their own government, and to make a fair living, so that they could dwell in friendship and affection with each other and with their neighbors. The most they expected was to set an example proving that it was possible to lead the New Testament life in New England; or, as Bradford put it, to be the candle from which thousands of other candles could be lit. And that they were.

Before continuing the story of the Plymouth Colony's expansion, we shall tell how the Pilgrim government developed from the simple Mayflower Compact to that of a full-fledged commonwealth. And we think that you would like to know about the houses and clothing, the manners and customs, the trade and business of the people.

XV

THE GOVERNMENT
OF NEW PLYMOUTH

THE FREEMEN

THE REV. SAMUEL STONE, one of the first ministers of Hartford, Connecticut, once described the government of the Congregational church as a "speaking aristocracy in the face of a silent democracy." That would do very well, too, for the government of Plymouth Colony. It was never a democracy in the modern sense, a government "of the people, by the people." But Plymouth Colony had a representative government, and a government under law.

It was always based on the consent of the Freemen, whom we would call the voters.[1] The first Freemen were the forty-

---

[1] We still use the term *franchise*, which comes from the same root as *freeman*, for the right to vote.

one signers to the Mayflower Compact, and those signers included every male among the passengers who was at least twenty-one years old, with the exception of a few servants, who were under bond to work for a certain master for a term of years.[2] But John Alden, the hired cooper, John Howland, who was Governor Carver's servant, Edward Doty and Edward Lester, who were Stephen Hopkins's, George Soule who was Winslow's, and a couple of other hired men signed and so were included among the original Freemen.

Every year more men were "admitted Freemen" by those who already were such. To be a Freeman you had to be at least twenty-one years old, of good reputation, not one of the Particulars, or a mere vistor. But the ex-Particulars who wished to stay were admitted in 1627. Each Freeman had to apply for the privilege. If approved, he was admitted at a formal court and took an oath to uphold the authorities and abide by the laws. After settlements were made outside Plymouth Town, a candidate for Freeman had to be passed upon first by his neighbors. In 1671, a property qualification of twenty pounds was set up, and testimony that the applicant was "sober and peaceable" and "orthodox in the fundamentals of religion," was required. That was meant to exclude Baptists and Quakers.

The Freemen were never even a majority of the menfolk. In 1643, for instance, there were 233 Freemen, as compared with 634 "males able to bear arms, from 16 years old to 60." In 1675, there were exactly 400 Freemen in the fourteen towns of the Colony, as compared with an estimated 800 to 900 heads of families. In other words, voting in the Old Col-

---

[2] "Servant," as used in the seventeenth century, meant any employee who was bound to work for a certain master for a definite term, as distinct from a person who worked for day wages.

ony was a privilege, not a right; and, once a Freeman, you had the duty to vote; if you failed to do so, you were fined ten shillings.

It was the Freemen who annually elected the Governor, the Deputy Governor (from 1680 on), the Assistants, and the Secretary. They met at least once a year as a "court" or assembly. During the early years the exact division of duties between them and their elected officials was vague. Governor Bradford wrote to the London Adventurers in 1623 that the "generality" were allowed to share in the government "only in some weighty maters, when we think good." Such weighty matters, for instance, were the expulsion of Lyford and Oldham and the new deal with the London Adventurers. Whether the Governor should do what he thought best in a given case, or take the advice of his Assistants, or submit the question to a General Court (as the full assembly of Freemen was called), depended on his own judgment and on circumstances. That informal system, suitable for a small, compact colony where everyone knew everybody else, went on for about ten years.

There was never a "separation of powers" in Plymouth. The Colony made no distinction between legislative, executive, and judicial business. Governor and Assistants sat with the Freemen in the General Court to pass laws; the Governor was charged with their execution; he and the Assistants formed the supreme judicial court, and until 1637 the Governor acted as Colony Treasurer.

Much business which we would call political was done by the Church, which included the women, and many men who were not Freemen. A minor offender might be ordered by the Assistants to be "admonished" by the Church, which usually meant being lectured to by Elder Brewster in his study;

but in bad cases it meant appearing in the meeting-house clad in the white robe of penitence, and confessing one's sins. "Juvenile delinquents" were attended to by their parents. The Pilgrims hated to put anyone in jail, even though the fort made a good one, because keeping a man in jail cost time and money. The usual punishments were fines, which could be paid in corn or worked off by labor; public whipping at the whipping post, or being put in the stocks.

Allotment of land remained in the hands of the "Old Comers," the *Mayflower* passengers, until 1640, when the whole body of Freemen took it over. But as each new town was created, the land there was granted by the General Court to a group of first settlers called the "Proprietors" who parceled out the lots.

The Council for New England, that organization of lords and gentlemen which received a royal charter to the entire region in 1620, always regarded the Pilgrims with respect and treated them generously. For their success in sticking it out at Plymouth was the best possible advertisement for New England as a place to live. The Patent of 1621 from this Council was the only authority the Pilgrims had for governing themselves, until 1630. But it must have given Governor Bradford and the Assistants great encouragement when, in 1624, the London Adventurers sent over a seal to be used on deeds and other legal documents; and the Adventurers must have had permission from the Council to do that. The design was four kneeling figures, each holding up something that looks like a bunch of tobacco leaves, surrounded by the inscription *Sigillum Societatis Plimoth Nova Anglia* (Seal of the Society of Plymouth in New England), and dated 1620. So strange a design for Puritans, who seldom knelt, and who grew only a little tobacco for their own use, suggests that the seal was originally made for their intended "Particular Plantation" in Virginia, and given a new inscription. Even though it does not say so on this seal, the Colony was always officially called the "Colony of New-Plymouth," probably to avoid confusion with Plymouth in England.

BILL OF RIGHTS AND REPRESENTATIVE GOVERNMENT

◖◗ THE GREAT Puritan migration, with consequent increase of population and spread of settlement, brought some changes in government. The old informal system was no longer suitable. Accordingly, in 1636, the Governor and Assistants, with the aid of four men from Plymouth, two from Duxbury, and two from Scituate, drafted a body of laws called the "General Fundamentals" which were adopted by the General Court of the Freemen. The Fundamentals were, in effect, a constitution for the Colony. They were equivalent to a Bill of Rights, and were the first Bill of Rights in America.

The preamble states that the Pilgrims came "hither as free-born subjects of the Kingdom of England," and claimed "all and singular privileges belonging to such." And here is the gist of the Fundamentals:

1. No laws may be made or taxes laid without the consent of the body of Freemen "or their representatives legally assembled."

2. There will be "a free election, annually," of the Governor and Assistants, by the Freemen.

3. Every person has a right to equal and impartial justice.

4. No one may be punished "in respect of life, limb, liberty, good name or estate" except by some express law of the

Colony, or by virtue of the English Common Law, if the case is not covered by the laws of Plymouth. And none shall suffer as aforesaid, without being brought to answer by due course and process of *Law*. (All that is derived from Magna Carta, the Great Charter of 1215. It is repeated by the "due process of law" clauses of the Fifth and Fourteenth Amendments to our Federal Constitution.)

5. All offenders are guaranteed a trial by jury "of twelve good and lawful men," and the defendant may challenge any of the jurors before the panel is made up. (This is repeated in the Sixth Amendment to our Federal Constitution.)

6. No person may be condemned or sentenced without the evidence of at least two witnesses, or sufficient circumstantial evidence.

7. All sane persons twenty-one years of age may dispose of their property by will.

8. The Congregational churches shall be protected and encouraged and all towns must provide for their ministers.

Thus, only sixteen years after their Colony began, the Pilgrims insisted on a "government of laws and not of men." Their political maturity is astonishing.

Owing to the founding of new settlements, the Freemen found it inconvenient to travel to Plymouth every time Court was held. So a representative system was established in 1639. Duxbury, Scituate, Barnstable, Sandwich, Yarmouth, and Taunton each sent two members, and the Town of Plymouth five, to the General Court. And as other settlements were established, they too were given representatives, who were called "deputies."

PATENTS AND BOUNDARIES

✍§ UNDER its patent of 1621, the Colony had no definite bounds; and this was a source of anxiety. In 1629, that clever fellow Isaac Allerton, then in England, "obtained the love and favor" of several big men on the Council for New England; and from them he obtained a new patent, dated 13 January 1630. This Warwick Patent, as it is called from its signer, the Earl of Warwick, assigned to the Colony definite boundaries between Cohasset River on the north, and Narragansett Bay on the south and west, including all Cape Cod and both sides of Buzzards Bay; and it also confirmed and enlarged their grant on the Kennebec River. All the land within these boundaries, as well as the right to govern the Colony, were conferred on William Bradford, his heirs and associates forever.

So Bradford, if he chose, could have become Lord and Proprietor of the Plymouth Colony, like William Penn of Pennsylvania or Lord Baltimore of Maryland, and nobody could have done anything about it. But he was too public-spirited to take advantage of this right. The Government went on as before, and Bradford, taking advantage of the word "associates," took in the Old Comers. They considered themselves trustees for the community.

But, by 1639, the Freemen were becoming uneasy about the power which Governor Bradford and the Old Comers held under the Warwick Patent, especially their monopoly of granting land, and began to grumble about the situation. As soon as they knew public opinion, the "privileged class" yielded gracefully. Bradford assigned to the "whole body of Freemen" all his governing rights under the Patent, and the

Old Comers did the same for the ungranted land. In return, the General Court voted £300 to the fifty-eight Old Comers and granted them three big tracts of land; one on Cape Cod embracing the present South Orleans and parts of Harwich and Brewster; one including the present Dartmouth, Fairhaven, and New Bedford; and a third which included Swansea, Rehoboth, and parts of Rhode Island.

The Warwick Patent, unfortunately, did not place the Plymouth Colony in a good position to contest boundary claims against Massachusetts Bay, because that colony had a royal charter granted a year earlier. Allerton did his best, in

Earl of Warwick signing the patent for Plymouth Colony at meeting of the Council for New England with Isaac Allerton in England.

1630, to obtain such a charter for New Plymouth; but as
Sherley wrote, there were too many locks to be "opened with
the silver, nay the golden key."

Massachusetts Bay would have been very glad of an excuse
to gobble up New Plymouth, and the authorities at Boston
were rather arrogant toward the older and smaller colony.
But they managed to agree on a boundary. The Royal
Charter of Massachusetts Bay gave that colony as a southern
boundary "three miles south of the Charles River." The
Charles is a very winding stream, and the Bay authorities declared that their southern boundary should be the
latitude of a place three miles south of the southernmost
tributary to the Charles, a brook that flows out of Lake
Pearl. That line, if extended to the ocean, would have given
Scituate, Marshfield, Duxbury, and Plymouth to Massachusetts! The Old Colony naturally would not agree. Commissioners were appointed by both sides, Bradford and
Winslow for Plymouth, Endecott and Stoughton for Massachusetts Bay. In 1642, they agreed on the eastern part of the
line, from Cohasset Harbor up Bound Brook to Accord
Pond—so called by reason of the agreement.[3] Over twenty
years later another board of commissioners agreed on the
"Angle Tree Bound" in the present town of Plainville as
"three miles south of the Charles," and ran a line northeast-
erly through the woods to Accord Pond. This "Old Colony
Line," which may be seen on our map, is still the principal
boundary between Norfolk County and the Counties of
Plymouth and Bristol.

Over the Council for New England was the Sovereign of
England. Plymouth Colony always remained officially loyal

---

[3] Hingham, however, has another explanation of the name; that it
was due to a successful conference with Indians on the ice.

to whomever was in power, whether James I, Charles I, the Commonwealth, Oliver Cromwell, or Charles II. Plymouth was more careful than the other New England colonies to do official business in the King's name, and to register wills by regnal years ("Ninth year of the reign of our Sovereign Lord Charles," etc.). The Colony never had any notion of going republican, or of attaining independence.

Nevertheless, except during the brief tyranny of Edmund Andros, the Old Colony was as good as independent of the Old Country. There was no royal official in the Colony. Laws of New Plymouth did not have to be sent to England for confirmation, as was the case with Virginia; and the Colony had too little commerce to be affected by the Navigation Acts.

UNITED NATIONS OF NEW ENGLAND

◆§ WHEN the Civil War broke out in England, the New England colonies knew that they would have to look to their own defense against Indians, French, and Dutch. To that end, representatives of Massachusetts Bay, New Plymouth, Connecticut, and New Haven organized, in 1643, a league officially called the United Colonies of New England and, unofficially, the New England Confederation. Each colony elected two commissioners to the Board, which met at the capitals of the several colonies in turn, and raised troops and money in proportion to population. For instance, when war with the Narragansetts was threatened, in 1645, the quota of troops was one hundred and ninety for Massachusetts Bay and forty for each of the other three colonies. Plymouth, therefore, was considered equal in manpower to Connecticut and New Haven. Its total population at that time cannot have been greater than 2,500. That was small; but we must remember that this was an era of small things. French Canada had a white population of only two hundred in 1640, and it rose only to 2,300 by 1663.

The New England Confederation was a force in colonial affairs for almost forty years. It held the Indians and Dutch in check. It settled colonial boundary disputes, supervised the conversion of Indians, provided for the return of runaway servants, and raised a scholarship fund for Harvard College by asking for voluntary contributions of a peck of corn a year, or a string of wampum, or a shilling, from each family in New England. When, in 1672, the Confederation asked everyone to chip in for a new building at Harvard, the General Court of New Plymouth invited the towns to take up a collection; and we have it on record that Eastham and Bridgewater, at least, did so.

Bradford and the other Plymouth authorities loyally supported the Confederation and took a leading part in its business.

LOCAL
GOVERNMENT
AND LAWS

❧❧❧❧❧❧❧❧❧❧❧❧❧❧❧❧❧❧❧❧❧❧❧❧❧❧❧❧❧❧❧

TOWNS AND TAXES

WHEN A NEW SETTLEMENT was recognized as a town, it not only sent representatives to the General Court at Plymouth, but enjoyed local self-government. The local Free-men, with other landowners, elected a board of select-men, one or more constables, surveyors of the highway, and other minor officials, subject to the approval of the General Court. Three counties were organized—Plymouth, Barnsta-ble, and Bristol—in 1685, so as to provide courts of justice

in three different centers. And each town had a selectmen's
court which settled cases of damage and the like where no
greater sum than forty shillings was involved.

Taxes in the Colony were incredibly light, according to
modern standards, because there was no great wealth and
the people did not expect much service from the government. Governor Bradford had no salary until 1639, when he
was voted twenty pounds a year; and for many years more
he had the privilege of dining the Assistants, when they
met for judicial business, at his own expense. Of the other
officials, only the town clerks, the Colony Secretary, who kept
the records (for thirty-eight years he was Nathaniel Morton), the Colony Treasurer (Myles Standish for twelve years;
then John Alden, Constant Southworth, and William Bradford, Jr.), were paid a salary. Every year the General Court
decided how much money was needed to run the government and apportioned it among the several towns, which
also raised local taxes for the church, the highways, and the
school, if there was a school. Taxes were levied on real and
personal estate, as today; and on "faculty," which meant a
man's earning power if he were a merchant or professional
man. Money was also raised by liquor licenses, after 1646.
There was no inheritance tax, sales tax, income tax, luxury
tax, or any other of the innumerable burdens that we bear
today. In time of great stress and expense, as in King Philip's
War, the General Court increased the levies on the towns by
several hundred per cent; but, unlike what happens today,
they went back to normal after the emergency.

CRIME AND PUNISHMENT

◦§ A STRICT Puritan Sabbath was maintained from sundown Saturday to sundown Sunday. Neither work, nor games, nor amusements were tolerated. Everyone had to attend divine worship morning and afternoon, and not go "sporting about the highways or fields." One Web Adey, for a second offense of working on the Sabbath, was "severely whipped" in 1638.

All games of chance, such as cards and dice, were forbidden. There was no prohibition of drinking, but drunkenness was prohibited. The penalty was five shillings fine, plus sitting one hour in the stocks for the first offense, double for the second, and triple for the third. And, lest there be any doubt about it, the law declared: "By drunkenness it is to be understood one that lisps or falters in his speech by reason of overmuch drink, or that staggers in his going, or that vomits."

There was little crime in Plymouth Colony; apart from petty offenses such as stealing, drunkenness, and idleness, it seems to have been a very law-abiding community. There were only five murders in the entire history of the Colony. John Billington, the persistent troublemaker among the *Mayflower* passengers, shot and killed a man in 1630 and was tried and sentenced to death. Governor Bradford, not sure that the Colony had the right to inflict capital punishment, consulted Governor Winthrop of Massachusetts Bay who said, in effect: "Go ahead and hang him"; and hanged he was. In 1642 there was an outbreak of sexual crime among recent emigrants from England, which greatly disturbed Bradford and the Assistants; they wondered how "it could happen here." Bradford pondered the matter and recorded in his History three probable reasons for this crime wave: 1. The devil was trying to shame a godly colony. 2. If streams are dammed up, they break forth with more violence; so here, "wickedness being here more stopped by strict laws . . . it searches everywhere and at last breaks out where it gets vent." 3. Plymouth is no worse than any other English-speaking community, but all evil doings are rooted out and brought to light.

Since the Colony had passed no law against the particularly nasty crimes that had been committed, Governor Bradford consulted three ministers of Plymouth and Duxbury, asking, among other things, whether torture could be applied to an arrested man to extort a confession. They replied that it couldn't be done, since it was a maxim of the English Common Law that "Nobody can be compelled to accuse himself." This is exactly the same civil right that has been placed in the famous Fifth Amendment to the Federal Constitution: "nor shall any person . . . be compelled in any criminal case to be a witness against himself." And Bradford followed the ministers' advice. Thus, an ancient liberty which has been sneered at and derided in the 1950's was respected in Plymouth over three hundred years earlier.

That case was unique; but, especially among the servant class, who were forbidden to marry until their terms of service were up, there were many violations of the Christian code of sex relations. The offenders were punished by fines and by whipping, and by being forced to wear the scarlet letter, as Hawthorne described in his great story of that name. Sometimes, however, these immoralities were treated with a certain sense of humor. For instance, a Scots servant employed by the Taunton iron works seduced a young Irish married woman when her husband was absent. The court found the pair guilty, and the husband too, for leaving his young wife alone and "exposing her to temptation." So all three, husband, wife, and lover, sat in the stocks side by side.

For humanity, the Colony of New Plymouth was well in advance of its era. It never used torture, or burned criminals alive, or punished an alleged witch, or applied any of the cruel punishments which were then common in civilized countries. In fact, the Pilgrims loved their land so much that the worst punishment they could think of, short of death, was to order a criminal to get out and stay out!

RELIGIOUS INTOLERANCE

⊷§ PLYMOUTH was no more tolerant of religious differences than the other European colonies in America. The famous Roger Williams, whom Bradford described as "a man godly and zealous, having many precious parts but very unsettled in judgment," spent a few months at Plymouth in 1633, joined the Church and was invited to preach; but he left voluntarily because the Church would not adopt his views. Bradford "blessed God" for having known Roger; but neither he nor the other Plymouth people wanted a piece of his "soul liberty." Samuel Gorton, who had the distinction of being expelled from four different colonies before founding his own at Warwick, Rhode Island, came to live with the Rev. Ralph Smith at Plymouth in 1638. After abusing his host and trying to start a revolt, he was deported.

In England during the 1640's the Puritans began to break up into several new sects, of which the most important were the Baptists and Quakers. Plymouth was not as much troubled by them as Massachusetts, because the ships from England discharged passengers at Boston. Its laws against religious dissenters were not nearly so severe as those of Massachusetts Bay. In 1649, the Bay Colony tried to prod Plymouth into cracking down on some Baptists in the town of Seekonk, but no action was taken. John Cooke, a *Mayflower* passenger, became a Baptist after he moved to Dartmouth in 1673; but he seems to have kept his standing as a local magistrate and deputy to the General Court.

Of all new sects, the Quakers were most offensive to regular Puritans, largely because a number of fanatics broke up divine service and "bawled out" ministers and magistrates in public. The first Quakers that appeared in the Colony stopped in at Sandwich. Two of them in 1657 were called before the General Court, then presided over by Governor Prence, and questioned. One shouted out: "Tom, thou liest!" and another: "Thomas, thou art a malicious man—thy clamorous tongue I regard no more than the dust beneath my feet." Both were whipped and banished to Rhode Island, whence they wrote abusive letters to the Governor and to John Alden, whom they called a "self-conceited fool." Either before or just after this incident, the General Court passed a law against Quakers entering the Colony, and disfranchised any Freeman who joined them or entertained them. And all Quaker literature was ordered to be collected and brought to the magistrates to be burned. About ten Quakers in all were deported from Plymouth and five of these were well whipped before they left; but none were hanged or mutilated, as in the Bay Colony and in England.

The Colony was no respecter of persons; the worst case of religious persecution was directed against one of its most prominent citizens. In 1668, James Cudworth of Scituate, a Freeman, Assistant, and captain of the local militia, was indicted for "entertaining of Quakers to meet in his house." He was deprived of his military office and, when elected to the General Court by his fellow townspeople, was not allowed to take his seat. The Court of Assistants, having obtained possession of a letter of Cudworth's (Bradford's old "F. B. I." still working!) which was disrespectful to the Government and encouraging to the Quakers, disfranchised him altogether. One is glad to note that Governor Josiah Winslow, in 1674, got Cudworth readmitted Freeman and reelected Assistant. And, being of a forgiving nature and no pacifist, Cudworth accepted a military command in King Philip's War when he was well over seventy years old.

For the most part, the "bark" of these anti-Quaker laws was worse than their "bite." As long as Quakers kept out of towns already settled, the authorities were satisfied; and by 1690 there were several Quaker Meetings (as their churches were called) along the Rhode Island border, at Rehoboth and Swansea, at Falmouth on Cape Cod, and at that part of Dartmouth which later became New Bedford.

Very few Anglicans emigrated to New Plymouth, and those that did worshipped in the Congregational churches and were admitted to the sacraments. There is no record of any Roman Catholic coming to the Colony to live, but in 1651 it entertained an important Catholic visitor, the Rev. Gabriel Druillettes, a Jesuit missionary priest from Canada. He came on a mission to New England in the hope of persuading the Confederation to declare war against the Mohawks. En route he called at the Plymouth Colony trading post on the Kennebec, then in charge of John Winslow, who had him as guest and treated him with respect and affection. Father Druillettes visited Boston and then went on to Plymouth, where he stayed with one of the leading citizens,

William Paddy. Governor Bradford received him graciously
and specially prepared for him a fish dinner on Friday, although Puritans rather made a point of *not* eating fish on
Friday. Thomas Willet, one of the five men who were then
running the fur trade on the Kennebec, spoke in favor of
the French efforts to convert the Abnaki Indians in Maine;
and as long as Plymouth Colony controlled the lower Kennebec, there were no clashes between French and English or
between Catholics and Protestants.

SPECIAL FEATURES OF THE LAWS

◄§ THE PILGRIMS were not political innovators, but we may
claim two "firsts" for them. In May 1621, when Edward
Winslow married the Widow White, they decided to adopt
the Dutch practice of civil marriage. Couples were joined in
wedlock by the Governor or one of the Assistants; never by
a clergyman. The other innovation, a useful one that has
spread throughout the United States, was to require that
every deed to real estate be registered. The first colony in
the New World to establish a registry of deeds was Plymouth, in 1636. And it was one of the first to require the
registry of births, marriages, and deaths, which some American communities even failed to do in the twentieth century.

The Plymouth government was definitely a government
under law. But there is little ground for reading into the
laws and customs of Plymouth Colony the so-called "American Way of Life" of free enterprise and individual liberty.
The Pilgrims were not interested in free enterprise; their
ideal was the New Testament life, as they understood it
from reading the Bible. Robert Cushman struck the keynote
for the Colony in a discourse he delivered at Plymouth in

1621. The text from I Corinthians 10:24, was, "Let no man seek his own, but . . . another's wealth." And, while he admitted that it was all right "for men to gather wealth," as Joseph did, a "godly and sincere Christian" should not do so at the expense of others.

Private property was indeed recognized and even encouraged, but its social duties and obligations were emphasized as they seldom were in the America of the nineteenth century.

Take, as an example, the grist mill, the first "public utility" of the Colony. A miller had to have a permit to set up a mill, since it affected other rights and properties such as the run of alewives. And when he had set it up, he was not allowed to charge "all the traffic would bear." Far from it! One "pottle" (two quarts) was the legal toll for grinding a bushel of corn.

And every other industry was regulated. John Jenney was given the right to make salt from sea water on Clark's Island in Plymouth Bay, but he was required to sell the salt for two shillings a bushel. Later, the Doty brothers and Thomas Hewes were given another "concession," to set up a fishing stage on Clark's Island. They could cut all the wood there that they needed, but they must not keep a dog, as the island was also being used as the town sheep pasture. Coopers were required to see that all barrels for salt meat, oil, beer, or cider had a capacity of thirty-one and a half gallons, and that tar barrels held fifteen gallons. The Pilgrims discovered early that tar for export could be made from knotty pine, not good enough for timber or firewood. And one year, after there had been overproduction, the General Court fixed a tar quota—no family could make over sixteen barrels of it that year.

Plymouth did not do much fixing of prices and wages, but those that it did fix were the maximum a man could take, not the minimum to which he was entitled. A man's wage was set at one shilling a day "and his dyett," or 1s. 6d. "without dyett," in 1638. Evidently this was found to be un-enforceable, as it was repealed the next year, and the courts contented themselves with cracking down on "extortion." For instance, in 1643, some men who had been mowing hay took "excessive wages, viz. three shillings per diem," and were told they would be fined if they didn't pay some of it back. Stephen Hopkins was fined for selling beer at two-pence the quart "that was not worth a penny," and for over-charging on wine.

Price regulation was important, because almost all busi-ness was transacted, and taxes were payable, in kind. For instance, in 1674, the price of wheat was fixed at 6s. per bushel; rye or barley, 3s. 6d.; corn 3s., and butter 4d. a pound, all delivered to the Treasurer, to pay taxes. Appar-ently eighteenpence (1s. 6d.) was considered the proper day's wage around mid-century. That was what soldiers were paid in King Philip's War.

A large part of the property now considered private be-longed to a town or to the Colony in the seventeenth century. The Freemen of each Plymouth Colony town, acting as a land company, allotted (not sold) land to approved new-comers or young men who needed farms. It did not occur to them to make money out of the land. The spring run of alewives belonged to the community—and still does, in the Old Colony and in certain Maine towns. At Plymouth, in 1663, William Wood and George Bonum were the committee in charge of "taking" the alewives when they swam up the brooks to the ponds. They must "let them go up on Friday

night, on Saturday night and on the Lord's day," so that
they would have a chance to spawn; and "take course for the
preventing of boys, swine and doggs from annoying them in
their coming up." They must distribute the catch equally
among the townspeople, and for that service they were paid
ninepence per thousand fish.

Cutting wood for winter fuel in the forest, which belonged to the town, was a community enterprise. Everyone
who owned an ox team and sled was called out, and the
men and big boys whose families had no oxen were allotted
to those who did. Each gang chopped enough wood for a
year's supply for all their families; and one gang who had

Catching alewives.

shirked the year before were told that they must cut double
this year. For it was a very serious thing for a family to run
out of fuel during a New England winter.

Freedom of movement, too, was restricted. Nobody could
leave town, buy land, and settle elsewhere in the Colony
without permission from the authorities. A newcomer was
on probation, as it were, for a year, before he could be admitted as an "inhabitant," and if he misbehaved during that
year he was "warned out." In 1656, one Joseph Ramsden
who "hath lived long in the woods, in an uncivil way, with
his wife alone," was ordered to move to "some neighborhood"
within four months; and if he did not comply, his house in
the woods should be pulled down. For the Pilgrim ideal was
that everyone should live in a village where the parson and
constable could check up on sinners.

In Puritan ethics, the "waste of precious time" was a sin;
one of their divines wrote: "An hour's idleness is as bad as
an hour's drunkenness." This life was short; God had given
every man just so much time, and he should "improve" it to
his family's or the community's advantage. Massachusetts
Bay, for instance, passed a law against "common coasters and
unprofitable fowlers." There was no objection to real sports-
men shooting ducks, but the Colony did not want beachcombers and bad shots wasting time and powder, and scaring
the wild fowl. For the same reason, Stephen Hopkins of
Plymouth was fined forty shillings "for suffering servants
and others to sit drinking in his house and to play at shuffle
board." A servant's time belonged to his master; he of all
people had no right to be idle.

The Plymouth Colony law on idleness provided that the
grand-jurymen of every town must "take a speciall view and
notice" of all people "that have smale meanes to mayntaine

them and are suspected to live idely and loosely, and to require an account of them how they live." And, if they think proper, to present these idlers to the Court of Assistants, "that such course may be taken with them as in the wisdom of the Government shall be adjudged just and equal." And it was later enacted that these unprofitable citizens should be punished by "stocking and whipping."

THE CHARACTER OF THE COLONY

IT CANNOT be denied that Plymouth Colony had a "nosey," interfering sort of government that did its best to make everyone conform to what the Freemen conceived to be the New Testament way of life. Nothing like it is tolerated today, outside the totalitarian countries. But, unlike the situation in those countries, the laws of Plymouth were adopted by the body of the people, not imposed by a self-appointed governing class. And this was not exceptional for that era. We find the same sort of thing in the other New England colonies and in Virginia; and, except for the great stress on "no idleness," in French Canada, and in England itself.

Plymouth was not a democracy, in any modern sense. The Freemen were a minority of the men. The ex-servants who did well were often elected to town offices, or as deputies to the General Court; but almost never to high office. The principal exceptions were John Alden, the cooper, John Howland, who had been Governor Carver's servant, and Thomas Prence, son of a London coachmaker, who came over in the *Fortune* in 1622 at the age of twenty-one. The two Johns were included in the "Undertakers" in 1627 and elected Assistants a few years later. Tom Prence showed a

genius for marrying the right girl. His first wife was Patience
Brewster, and his second the daughter of wealthy William
Collier. That probably explains why Prence, rather than Alden, was chosen Governor for two years in the 1630's when
Bradford refused to stand. And he filled the place well; it
was said that he "had a countenance full of majesty, and
therein as well as likewise was a terror to evil doers." After
Bradford's death he was annually re-elected until his death
in 1673, when he was succeeded by old Governor Winslow's
son Josiah.

Josiah Winslow was in every respect a remarkable man.
Born at Plymouth in 1629, he entered Harvard College, but
did not graduate, probably because his father wished to send

The Mason children—David, Joanna and Abigail.

him on a voyage to England. His portrait, painted there in 1651, shows a sensitive and studious face; but he later showed the finest leadership in peace and in war. And he brought away from Cambridge something better than a diploma—the beautiful Penelope Pelham, daughter of the college treasurer.[1] An heiress, too, she made "Careswell," the Winslow mansion at Marshfield, a center of hospitality and culture. The Freemen, far from being jealous of all this, were delighted with the Winslows, approved their way of life, and annually re-elected Josiah their Governor until his death in 1680. He was succeeded by Thomas Hinckley of Barnstable, who had been an Assistant for many years.

Thus, New Plymouth had only six Governors, including Carver, during the seventy-two years of its existence. And although between seven and ten Assistants were annually elected after 1634, only twenty new names appear on the list in over fifty years!

What if the Old Colony wasn't democratic? It had self-government, and government under law, which are far more important. The Bradfords, Winslows, Standishes, Aldens, Prences, Colliers, Hatherleys, Southworths, Brownes, and Hinckleys were a ruling class, an aristocracy in the real sense of that word; but they held office by the will of the Freemen. These men showed a judgment rare even among statesmen of great countries, when dealing with external enemies, internal sedition, and powerful neighbors of their own nation. The Freemen were very wise to elect them and re-elect them as long as they would serve.

---

[1] She was also great-niece to the Lord de la Warr (usually spelled Delaware) who was an early Governor of Virginia, and for whom the the bay, the river, and the state are named. "Careswell" is still standing.

HOUSES AND
CLOTHING

❧❧❧❧❧❧❧❧❧❧❧❧❧❧❧❧❧❧❧❧❧❧❧❧❧❧❧❧❧❧❧❧

A DWELLING-HOUSE AND ITS
FURNISHINGS

AROUND 1630, even before prosperity set in, the Pilgrims began to replace their early houses with more substantial structures. Thatched roofs were forbidden after 1628; and for the same reason—the fire risk—brick chimneys were substituted for the old ones of wood and clay. Brick, at first imported as ballast in ships, within a few years was being made at Plymouth.

The typical Plymouth Colony house from 1630 on was built of oak and pine around the great central chimney, and allowed to weather dark gray or brown—no paint was used outside, and little inside. The ground floor had two rooms, the "hall" (sometimes called parlor), which did duty as living-room, dining-room, and spare bedroom; and the kitchen. Each was warmed by a great open fireplace and was built low-studded to conserve heat in winter.[1] Up a small winding staircase were two "chambers," each with its open fireplace; and over them was the loft. The second story protruded over the first or ground story, not in order to pour boiling water on attacking Indians (as the myth runs), but because that was the English fashion of the day. The outside was covered with split cedar clapboard, and the inside sheathed with the same. Eel-grass, marsh-grass, or brick and mortar were packed between sheathing and clapboard, as an insulator. For windows, the oiled paper of the early days was now discarded in favor of imported casements with small, leaded, diamond-shaped panes. Heavy wool curtains were drawn over these windows to help keep out the cold. No square-paned sash windows were used in the seventeenth century. The floors, of wide pine boards, were scrubbed clean with beach sand. There were no rugs or carpets except a few bulrush mats made by the Indians. If anyone owned a "Turkey carpet," it was too valuable to throw on the floor, and was used as a table cover.

Every house had near it a barn and one or more sheds for keeping cattle, storing corn and hay, and for poultry or pigs. There was, of course, no plumbing, but every house had its own well; some wells had a long well-sweep (as may be seen

---

[1] The Sparrow House on Summer Street, Plymouth, now headquarters of the Plymouth Potters, has a "hall" which well preserves the seventeenth-century atmosphere. And the Howland house is particularly interesting, since one half was built in the seventeenth and the other in the eighteenth century, illustrating the difference between the two manners of building.

at the "Old Oaken Bucket" house in Scituate); others had just a rope and bucket.

These houses were very sparsely furnished. Chairs, other than simple rush-bottomed ones without arms, were rare, and none were upholstered. Children seldom had a chance to sit on anything better than a stool or bench. There was always an oak or pine table in the hall, and a big one in the kitchen. Linen tablecloths were fairly common. Each fireplace had a pair of andirons; and the great one in the kitchen, on which all the cooking was done, was provided with a variety of cranes, brass and iron pots, pot-hooks, kettles, and skillets. Clothes were commonly kept in homemade pine chests. Only the wealthy had "court cupboards" of oak, which, in the next century, gave place to "chests of drawers."

Bedsteads were generally rough, homemade four-posters; only the wealthy had curtains and valances around them to keep out the night air. The Pilgrim who wanted "beauty rest" had no better spring than a laced cord which was always going slack and had to be taken up. The most valuable possession in many families was a featherbed. This was a big linen bag stuffed with goose feathers that could be used either as a mattress or a blanket. Poorer people had what was called a flock bed, in which the stuffing was woolen rags and remnants; or a cat-tail bed. Most people had plenty of "ruggs" or woolen blankets, colored white, gray, blue, or green; and linen sheets, some white, some of brown "Hollands," and others colored. Everyone had pillows and linen pillowcases, which they called "pillowbeers."

Many of the dishes were wooden plates and platters, called "trenchers," but pewter ones were common, and a few people had some earthenware. Wooden and pewter spoons were used, and there is occasional mention of an iron fork. That was probably for toasting, as table forks were very rare in the seventeenth century. You grabbed your meat with one hand, cut off morsels with your own knife, and ate with your fingers, wiping them, if you were very nice, on a linen napkin. Some families had pewter porringers for cooked cereals and soup. Very few—only six people who left wills before 1650—left silver, and that generally in the form of spoons, worth five shillings each. Bottles were usually of leather or pewter rather than glass, which was somewhat more rare in the Colony than silver. Every family had a big wooden "bucking tub" for laundry. Washing clothes was called bucking because the women slapped the soaking garments with

Interior of Sparrow House—Plymouth.

wooden paddles. (Remember how the Merry Wives of
Windsor hid John Falstaff in a buck basket?) Many families
also had a "powdering tub" for salting down meat.

Every man owned several weapons, usually a musket and
a fowling or "byrding" piece, a sword or a "cuttle-axe" (cutlass), and sometimes a rapier or a "culleever" (cleaver, or
broadsword). Corslets (steel breastplates) and headpieces
(helmets) are frequently mentioned.

THE WELL-DRESSED PILGRIM AND INDIAN

◆§ THESE DETAILS are taken from inventories attached to
wills prior to 1650. From the same reliable source we can
confirm what we said earlier, that the Pilgrims wore colorful
clothes. How the notion arose that the men of Plymouth
Colony always wore black suits and steeple-crowned black
hats and carried a bell-mouthed blunderbuss that couldn't
have hit an elephant at fifty yards' range, I do not know.
Anyway, it is false. Puritans dressed like everyone else of
their social class in England. Mostly middle-class people, they
did not go in for the elaborate slashed breeches, fancy buttons, lace coats, and funny hats such as you see in portraits of
Charles I and his courtiers. In any case, they could not afford
them. But they wore no odd or peculiar garb, as the Quakers
did. The only Pilgrim whose inventory shows many black
clothes was Elder Brewster; and even he had a violet cloak,
a blue cloth suit, a pair of green drawers, a lace cap, a red
cap, a green waistcoat, and two green "ruggs."

Richard Langford, who died in 1633, had a complete suit
of doublet, breeches, and cloak, a satin suit, a canvas suit
(for working outdoors), a complete black suit, a red woolen

lining for a doublet, a black hat and a white hat, a Monmouth cap (the usual stocking-cap headgear) and a "cap with silver lace on it," besides a pair of sky-blue garters and one silk garter. Will Wright, who died the same year, left a black coat, a blue coat, four waistcoats (one white cotton, one dimity, and two red), two silk caps, and one "sad colored" suit and cloak. These "sad colored" articles are perhaps what led people to suppose that all Pilgrims looked drab; but "sad," as they used it, meant simply a deep color. For instance, a "murrey" (mulberry-colored) red was sad; Navy blue and forest green were sad, as were nut-brown and orange yellow as distinct from pale brown and canary yellow.

The breeches worn by the Pilgrims were cut full, somewhat like the "plus fours" that golfers used to wear, and were fastened below the knee by garters which had long tags called "points." They wore plain knitted stockings, or Irish stockings, which were really knitted leggings, having no foot but coming up over the thigh. Their shoes and boots were either of natural-colored tanned leather, or black. Popular illustrators always place silver buckles on their shoes and hats; but not one is mentioned in a Plymouth Colony inventory.

A few Pilgrims, around 1630, still wore on dress occasions the stiff, starched neck ruffs that went out with King James; but most of them wore a "band," a large white linen collar that lay flat over the coat collar. All wore long-sleeved linen shirts, colored white, blue, brown, or green. Undershirts were then unknown; and though "drawers" figure in the inventories, they were probably light summer breeches rather than underwear. Cotton cloth came from India and was very expensive; only two or three women owned any.

The woman's or girl's dress of the period was an ankle-length gown, the bodice shaped to the figure and the skirt cut full. Under the laced bodice a "stomacher" was worn to provide a contrast in color or material; and sometimes a waistcoat over that for warmth. These waistcoats were usually red. For headwear women wore the coif, a white linen cap which came down over the ears, or a beaver felt hat similar to the men's; and, outdoors, a cloak with a hood. Their only underclothing was a petticoat, and a linen smock which fell below the knees.

The women's dress was even brighter than the men's. A widow named Mary Ring, who died at Plymouth in 1631, shortly after her arrival from England, left a bewildering array of clothes and household utensils. She owned seven smocks; one red, one violet, and one "mingled-colored" petti-coat; one white and two violet waistcoats; four stomachers; one black, one murrey, two white, and three blue aprons; white and blue stockings. She owned only two gowns, one of them black; but she left a large number of "peeces" of black, gray, red, and blue cloth, indicating that she was about to make up some new ones. Mrs. Ann Atwood, who died at Taunton about twenty years later, left a collection of six colored petticoats valued at £7 3s. 8d.; four of them were red, one of silk, and a green one made of a then fashionable silk-and-wool material called philip-and-cheney.

Children's clothes were of the same cut as those of grown-ups, except that small boys wore a long dress, called a coat, until about six years old. After that they dressed like little men.

Not much change in clothing was made for different seasons. People in those days expected to be cold in winter and hot in summer, and to get wet if they went out in rain or snow, for waterproof clothing and shoes had not been invented. All children, and many grownups too, went barefoot in summer.

A word, too, on what the well-dressed Indian wore. He has suffered as much as the Pilgrims themselves at the hands of careless illustrators. Dear to the illustrators as the Pilgrim's black suit and plug hat is the full-feathered Sioux war-bonnet (never worn east of the Mississippi), and a colored blanket draped like that of a football player on the sidelines. Actually the Wampanoags, and all Indian men with whom the Plymouth Colony came in contact, wore their hair in a sort of roach or crest from forehead to rear, and stuck in it a single, jaunty eagle feather. They wore a breech-clout of deerskin with a sort of square tail falling down behind; sometimes deerskin leggings, and moccasins on their feet.[1] In other words, they went almost naked except in cold weather, when they put on a mantle of deerskin to protect their chests. After they had been trading with the English, a woolen "matchcoat" resembling the modern mackinaw jacket, was substituted for the deerskin. Women dressed their hair in various ways, and wore, as their principal garment, a deerskin draped about their waists like a Scots kilt, but coming below the knees. Young girls wore a jaunty little beaver coat, such as those which aroused Squanto's cupidity; older squaws had to make-do with deerskin. Both men and women, especially if people of rank, wore belts of wampum or of dyed porcupine quills, as ornaments.

---

[1] Cyrus E. Dallin's statue of Massasoit at Plymouth and Charles Hoffbauer's painting of Samoset appearing among the Pilgrims, at the hall of the New England Mutual Insurance Company on Boylston Street, Boston, are correct in every detail.

XVIII

MANNERS AND CUSTOMS

・・・・・・・・・・・・・・・・・・・・・・・・・・

THE PILGRIM FAMILY

THE SAME SOCIAL DISTINCTIONS that were observed in England and in other English colonies were followed at Plymouth. There was an upper class or gentry, a middle class, and a lower class of servants. Those who had been considered gentlemen and ladies in the Old World kept that status in Plymouth, and everyone elected Governor or Assistant, as well as the ministers and the better merchants, were regarded as members of that class. They were addressed as "Mister" or "Master" and "Mistress" so-and-so. Ordinary respectable folk were called "Goodman" this and "Goodwife" or "Goody" that; and servants were called by their first names, like children. The Pilgrims usually gave their children ordinary Christian names like John, William, James, Charles, Edward, Richard, Thomas, and Henry; and Mary, Ann, Ellen, Elizabeth, Alice, and Priscilla.[1] Old Testament names like Samuel and Ichabod were fairly common, but only a few parents followed the lead of extreme Puritans in England in giving such names as Desire, Resolved, Constant, Consider, Comfort, and Humility. Elder Brewster's two sons were named Love and Wrestling; the latter, generally pronounced "Rassle," probably earned its bearer a lot of fights. And we may be sure that Oceanus Hopkins and Peregrine White wished that their parents had been more considerate!

The family was the social unit in Plymouth Colony, as in England; and since there was always a shortage of women in the Colony, widows did not long stay single, and girls were married young. It was then unheard of, among respectable people, for the young to make their own matches. A law of the Colony made it a penal offense for a young man to propose to a girl or a maidservant without first obtaining the consent of her father or master. Arthur Howland, who found Elizabeth Prence fair to look upon, proposed and was accepted without asking her papa. He was haled before the Court of Assistants and fined five pounds for "disorderly and unrighteously endeavoring to obtain the affections" of Elizabeth. He had to promise "solemnly and seriously" that he would let her alone in future. We are pleased to relate that her father, the Governor, relented, and that the couple were married and "lived happily ever after."

---

[1] A poor man of Scituate, William Dennis, left three daughters named Remember, Dependence, and Experience. They had to split his only cow three ways. Mrs. Thomas Hinckley gave birth to a daughter who was baptized the very day that her father, the future Governor, was fighting the Narraganset Indians; she was named Reliance.

Although some marriages were arranged by the parents,
in most cases the young people fell in love and then did their
best to get papa's consent. The marriage ceremony was very
simple, without wedding dress, bridesmaids, or music. The
Governor or an Assistant merely joined the couple's hands,
asked if they took each other freely for wedded wife and
husband, asked the parents if they approved, and then
pronounced them man and wife.

No doubt there was plenty of romance in the Old Colony,
but not much of that sort of thing gets into cold records.
Everybody knows about the Courtship of Myles Standish,
but few have heard of the courtship of John Saffin. John
came over from England in 1644, at the age of twelve, as a
ward of Governor Edward Winslow, in whose house he grew
up. At the age of twenty-one or -two, he fell in love with
Martha Willet, who "in splendid beauty did much excell,"
as he wrote in one of his poems. She was a daughter of
Thomas Willet the fur-trader, who by this time had become an Assistant of the Colony. Mr. Willet gave consent to
the match on condition that John make some money first;
and to help him, arranged that he should go to Virginia as a
merchant.

Upon departing, John went to the Willet house to say
good-by to his fiancée, but found her asleep and kissed her
without awaking her. So, en route to Virginia, he wrote a
poem to Martha, of which these are a few of the lines:

> *Sweetly, my Dearest, I left thee asleep,*
> *Which silent parting made my heart to weep;*
> *Fain would I wake her, but Love did reply*
> *O wake her not, so sweetly let her lie.*
> *Thus in sad silence, I alone and mute,*

My lips bade thee farewell with a salute,
And so went from thee. Turning back again
I thought one kiss too little, then stole twain
—And then another!

John and Martha remained true to each other during his four-year absence in Virginia. Then, having made a modest fortune, he sailed home in one of those small two-masted vessels called a pinnace, to claim his bride. And, on the voyage, he wrote a charming poem, "To Her, Coming Home," of which the chorus runs:

Sail, gentle pinnace; Zepherus doth not fail
With prosperous gales; sail, gentle pinnace, sail!

Who could resist a young man who wrote such flattering love poetry? Anyway, Martha could not. They were married shortly after his return, and he continued to write poetry to her during the twenty years of their happy married life.

Most of these marriages were very fruitful; families of fourteen and more were common. And there are many tributes of affection in the wills. One Goodman Wright, who died at Plymouth in 1633, wrote in his will: "Whereas God of his great mercy and goodness . . . hath given me a faithful and loving wife which hath lived with me to the present time to our mutual joy and comfort; therefore my will is, and hereby I do freely give and bequeath to Priscilla Wright my loving and lawful wife, all real estate, livestock, goods and chattels." He asks her to give a ewe lamb to the Church within a year of his death, and to Elder Brewster a cloth suit which he had from Dr. Fuller, and five shillings to Governor Bradford for serving as the supervisor of his will. Priscilla is appointed his "full and sole executrix."

William Palmer of "Ducksburrow" had children living

from his first marriage when he died in 1637, and little grandchildren too; but in his will he said: "Whereas I have married a young woman who is dear unto me I desire my executors to deal well with her," to give her one third at least of his estate, and one third more, if she is with child when he dies. This second wife, Elizabeth, had evidently been a servant, because her husband expressed a wish that she "should be ruled by her ancient master Edward Winslow in her marriage." And within a year she married John Willis.

William Gilson of Scituate, on his deathbed, told Edward Foster that he wished his wife Frances to be his sole executrix "and to take all that he hath and to pay all his debts." And when Foster suggested that he leave "something more" to his cousin and servant John Damon than his "land on the Third Cliff" which he had willed to him, he said no; wife Frances should have everything except that land; his aunt could look after John. Foster himself died three years later, leaving everything to his "loving wife Lettice." John Atwood, dying at Plymouth in 1644, gave everything including "all those debts which be due to me in Old England and Virginia" to his "loving wife Anne"; and though he would like to give something to his "little kinsman William Crowe" and his nephews and nieces, he leaves them "to the will of my wife to deal with them as shall seem good to her."

A custom that seems odd to us, though then common in England, was to swap children for a year or more. The Whites would send Johnny and Mary to live with the Browns for a year, who sent their Dick and Ann to live with the Whites; and sometimes these families lived at great distances from each other. Dr. Fuller, for instance, had a child from Lynn and another from Salem living with him at Plymouth when he died, but his daughter was in another family elsewhere. Apparently the motive for this exchange was partly social, and partly the notion that children would learn better manners and discipline away from their fond parents.

THE DAY'S ROUTINE

✌§ NOW, let us follow the day's routine for a typical Plymouth family. The master and mistress, in their forties, by this time have ten children aged from a few months to eighteen years, and a young servant. The day starts by one of the big boys or the servant raking out the wood fire which was banked with ashes the night before, building it up again with pine kindling and hardwood logs, and bringing in buckets of water from the well. The mother, after dressing (and possibly washing) her littlest ones, comes down to cook breakfast. The favorite breakfast dish was hasty pudding (what we call corn-meal mush), boiled in a big iron pot and served with milk or molasses. The breakfast drink is cider, or milk for the children; no tea, coffee, or cocoa reached the Colony until the very end of the century. Breakfast is served at sunrise, or earlier in winter. The master of the house, after feeding the livestock, reads a chapter of the Bible and asks a blessing, before anyone sits down.

Breakfast over, the mistress or one of the girls milks the cows; for it was assumed in the seventeenth century that cows would not "give" for men. The womenfolk also feed the chickens and cultivate the little kitchen garden of herbs and "sallets" next the house. The master and the big boys go afield to plow, sow, cultivate, or reap; or, if it is winter, to the forest to cut wood or hunt deer. One boy has to lead the family's cattle to pasture (which is mostly woods), and to look out for the herd all day. Perhaps two of the boys are allowed to take the family boat and go fishing. Almost every family who lived on the coast went out after cod in the fall and "made" a quantity of dried fish.

Baking in the earliest days was done in outdoor ovens; but by 1660 most chimneys were built with a brick oven attached. This was filled with hot embers from the fire. After it was well heated the coals were raked out and the bread, pudding, or pot of beans was baked by the heat of the bricks. The common bread, called "rye and Injun," was baked from a mixture of corn meal, barley, and rye flour; for wheat never grew well in Plymouth. "Rye and Injun" resembled the brown bread which New England Yankees still like to serve with baked beans; but it was not so sweet, and more nutritious.

Dinner, between eleven o'clock and noon, starts with another blessing, followed by more hasty pudding. The main course is fresh or salt fish, beef or pork or mutton roasted on a spit before the open fire or made into a stew. Another mainstay was succotash, which the Indians taught the colonists to make. Colonial succotash was not the pallid side-dish of canned corn and lima beans that is served under that name today, but was a meal in itself.[2]

For vegetables there were peas (picked ripe, not green), turnips, parsnips, onions, squash, and pumpkin. The pump-

---

[2] The recipe furnished by an aged member of the Old Colony Historical Society calls for 2 lb. round steak cubed and boiled; 1 boiled chicken, 2 cups pea beans parboiled; 3 pints hulled corn cooked for 2 hours with the beans; 4 big potatoes diced and cooked with one diced turnip. Then you throw everything together, including the liquor in which the ingredients were boiled, and cook very slowly until blended.

kin, celebrated in the ballad of the early days that we have
quoted, was stewed and served as a sauce, not made into
pumpkin pie; the Pilgrims' only pies were meat pies. For
dessert there would be an "Injun pudding" made of corn
meal sweetened with molasses. And in season there were
wild strawberries, blueberries, raspberries, and blackberries;
but the Pilgrims seem never to have used the cranberry, cul-
tivation of which is now a leading industry in the Old Colony.
The women knew how to preserve fresh fruit with sugar,
in earthenware crocks sealed with wax; but sugar was so
scarce and dear in those days that only the wealthier people
could afford it. Molasses imported from the West Indies was

Clamming

the principal sweetening; maple sugar and honey were used, too. Nathaniel Tilden of Scituate left "10 stocks and swarms of bees" worth ten pounds, in 1641.

Dinner over, the men go out to the fields again or, if it is fall and the harvest has been gathered, to shoot wild fowl. The women and girls now set to churning the morning's cream into butter, or to spinning and weaving. As early as 1639 every householder was required to sow at least one square rod (a rod is sixteen and a half feet) of hemp or flax, from which yarn could be spun to make shirts and sheets. Wool was carded and spun into yarn from which stockings were knitted and cloth woven, if the family had a loom.[3] Dyestuffs were made from native plants or from imported materials such as indigo and cochineal. Some families evidently made cheese, as they had "cheesefatts," the wooden molds in which the curds were pressed.

Toward sundown the menfolk return, hungry for supper; but first father must hear the younger children recite their A B C's and catechism. Supper is largely a repetition of breakfast, together with leftovers warmed up from dinner. A big pot of beans, first baked for Saturday-night supper, will do for Sunday as well. It is against Puritan principles to cook hot meals on the Sabbath or to do any work except to water and feed the stock; for Jesus Himself had said that that was all right (Luke 13:15).

---

[3] This homespun and home-woven cloth was sleazy and stretched badly unless it was fulled, or finished, at a fulling mill. There the cloth was pounded with big hammers to a uniform thickness, and shrunk. A kind of clay called fuller's earth was applied to soak up the grease in the wool, and the nap was trimmed by big shears. James Torrey had a fulling mill at Scituate in 1653, and one was built on the Town Brook at Plymouth within twenty years. At the Harlow house in Plymouth, visitors can see the spinning and weaving on the old wheels and looms, done by an expert.

Supper cleared away, a tallow candle is lighted and the master, mistress, and big boys and girls take long clay "churchwarden" pipes to "drink tobacco," as smoking was then called.[4] Maybe the master casts up accounts in a big book, writing with ink made of oak-galls and a quill pen that was once a goose feather. Tales are told of the early days of hardship, of Indians, and old wars. Members of other families drop in to exchange local gossip and retail such news as trickles through from the outside world; for there are no newspapers. Finally the master opens his great Bible, reads a chapter, and prays that God will protect them all from the "perils and dangers of the night." And so to bed. Father, Mother, and one or two small children pile into the big four-poster; a little "truckle-bed" is pulled out from underneath for other small fry; there is a cradle for the baby; the big boys and girls and servants spread pallets of corn-husk mattresses on the floors of the other rooms.

CHOICE OF A "CALLING"

⋘ BY THE TIME a boy was ten years old he had decided, with the help of his parents and older brothers, what his "calling" or business should be. If he seemed a likely "scoller," he was sent to the local minister for instruction and, in rare cases, went to college. William Bradford, Jr., Josiah Winslow, and Thomas Prence, Jr. entered Harvard in the 1640's —the first native-born Americans to enroll in the college—

---

[4] There is plenty of evidence that New England women smoked in the seventeenth century. For instance, there is a letter from the very respectable James Cudworth of Scituate stating that his wife was so feeble that "when she is up she cannot light a pipe of tobacco, but it must be lighted for her; and until she has taken two or three pipes, for want of breath she is not able to stir."

but none of the three managed to graduate. Isaac Allerton, Jr. did graduate in 1650, but he went to live in Virginia, where he became a great swell. Very few Plymouth Colony boys, except ministers' sons who could be prepared at home by their fathers, went to college in the seventeenth century.

Many boys decided to stay at home and help their father until they married. Others hired themselves out in order to get a little money to stock a farm of their own; and in a new settlement they could usually get fifty acres from the town, free. A boy handy with tools, or with a mechanical turn of mind, would be apprenticed at about the age of fourteen to a bricklayer, a carpenter, ship- or boat-builder, or keeper of a grist mill or sawmill. He went to live with his master and worked for him without wages for seven years. Boys who yearned to go to sea would be taken as cabin boy or cook on a fishing vessel, coaster or West Indies trader.

The girls were kept busy helping their mother in her household tasks, and learning to spin and weave and make butter and cheese. When they reached the age of eighteen they could choose between hiring out as a servant to another family or getting married. The only occupation other than housewife open to women was that of midwife, to bring babies into the world. Elderly dames sometimes learned enough of the use of herbs and simple medicaments to become "herb doctors." They were called in whenever a child was sick, to administer a soothing draft of sassafras tea or maybe a purge. Practicing physicians were rare in the Colony, and medicine at best was so primitive in the seventeenth century that dozens of little children died of complaints that are easily cured today.

SERVANTS AND THE POOR

◆§ SERVANTS were the only people who owned no property. They were regarded as much members of the family as children. Often they were young relations sent out from England. Masters of families were required to feed, clothe, and shelter servants properly; the records are full of cases in which masters were punished for failure to do so, or for abusing a servant, such as requiring one "to bring a log beyond his strength." The head of a family was responsible for teaching his servants as well as his children to read, and for giving them elementary religious instruction out of the Westminster Shorter Catechism—fifty pages short!

Servants sometimes quarreled—Ned Doty and Ned Lester, servants of Stephen Hopkins, fought the only duel on record in the Colony. But in many families the servants felt brotherly affection for each other. John Cole, an ex-servant of William Collier, had very little to leave when he died. He bequeathed his bedding, clothes, and a sow to his brother; one sheep to his sister; half a crown (2s. 6d.) each "unto Master Collier's men, namely Edward, Joseph, Arthur, Ralph and John," and five shillings to his master's daughter Elizabeth. The Colliers must indeed have been a happy family.

Menservants who had behaved themselves were always given a tract of land by a town when their terms of service expired. Many servants, however, were unruly and lazy, and such young men would be "warned out" of town instead of being invited to stay and acquire a farm. I have been unable to find record of anyone in the Colony having owned a Negro slave, although every other New England colony had a few, and Rhode Island became active in the slave trade.

It may seem strange that in this land of plain living and hard work there should be any poor people. But it was as true of Plymouth as of Palestine: ". . . ye have the poor always with you." Children were left orphans, houses burned down, some men were shiftless and some women were slatterns, and many a family faced winter without food or fuel or even shelter. So, as Jesus taught Christians to feed the hungry and clothe the naked, the Plymouth people did their best.

Taking care of the poor was a job for the town, not the Colony. In Plymouth, for instance, when the first board of selectmen was elected in 1649, they were given power to inquire into "the state and condition of the poor," to see "that the poor be comfortably provided for," and that their provisions "be not unnecessarily embezzled, misspent and made away in the summer season before the winter and time of hard things come." And if the selectmen found any aged or crippled poor who could not work, they were empowered to raise taxes for their relief.

Plymouth Town was fortunate in having a special donation for this purpose. James Sherley, the London Adventurer who was such a cheat in big matters, sent out a heifer in 1624 for the use of the poor. This heifer, bred to the town bull, throve to such good purpose that by 1638 she had twelve descendants, which were lent to poor people who couldn't afford to buy a cow; and other calves of hers were sold to add to the poor fund. Bradford, Prence, Willet, and other leading men were a committee of the town to handle "the poor's stock"; and, for a quarter-century after her arrival, Sherley's heifer's offspring were being distributed annually.

In those small communities, private and neighborly charity took care of most cases of misfortune, but the towns often made contributions of food and fuel to the needy. Children left orphans were added to some other family, in the same status as servants. This system was far more humane than the later one of herding the poor into orphan asylums and "poor farms."

Readers may regard the life we have described as a very drab one for young people. They had no modern forms of amusement or methods of transportation, and were forbidden to "date" without father's or master's permission. Actually it was a very full and interesting life, because there was something for every child to do from the time he could walk; he had his place in the family team. For amusement, he whittled toys out of wood, made dolls out of rags, and played a game called stool-ball with a leather ball stuffed with feathers. In winter, he coasted on a homemade sled, skated on homemade skates, walked over deep snow on "rackets" (snowshoes) that the Indians taught him to make and use; or fished for pickerel through the ice on the big ponds. In summer, he went fishing and swimming when father could spare him from the cornfields—but never on Sunday! Best of all, from the modern point of view, he had a minimum of book learning. His education was finished as soon as he could do a little simple arithmetic, write his name, and read the Bible; and there was not much but the Bible to read. He learned by doing, from his elders; and he learned self-control by having to handle and tame a variety of animals, and to row and sail a boat. His father taught him to fear God and honor the King and the Governor; he took pride in being an English subject, and looked forward to becoming a Freeman of the oldest Colony in New England. And, strict though the Puritan religion was, it taught him that he was a child of God, and that God had brought him into the world for a definite purpose; that if he believed in God and obeyed His commandments so far as human nature would permit, he would enjoy eternal life.

There is no need to pity the Pilgrim boys and girls. They really enjoyed the life that they led, and they envied nobody.

FARMING, TRADE, AND BUSINESS

●◆|◆●|◆●|◆●|◆●|◆●|◆●|◆●|◆●|◆●|◆●|◆●|◆●|◆●|◆●|◆●|◆●|◆●|◆●|◆●|◆●|◆●|◆●|◆●|◆●|◆●|◆●|◆

CATTLE AND CORN

THE PRICES that Plymouth obtained for cattle and hogs in
the 1630's are astonishing, in comparison with the value
of other things. William Wright's house and garden, for instance, were valued only at ten pounds, and seldom was any
house valued at more than twice that; but his "1 cow and 1
steer calf" were worth twenty pounds. Francis Eaton, a
Plymouth carpenter, left a cow worth twenty pounds, and a
"cow calfe" worth twelve pounds; but his best suit of clothes
was valued at only one pound and his chest of carpenter's
tools added up to only a little more.[1] And a day's wages was

---

1 We remind the reader here that one pound (£1) was roughly
five dollars; one shilling (1s.) twenty-five cents.

only a shilling or eighteenpence. If Mr. Sherley's heifer hadn't done so well, the poor would have been unable to own a cow.

Yet even when the price fell, their cattle were the most valuable possessions of the Plymouth colonists. A cow was a part of the family. As proof of it, although dogs and horses are never mentioned by name in Plymouth Colony wills, the names of the cattle often are. It may amuse you to know some of these names:

Of oxen, always in pairs: Buck and Duke, Spark and Swad, Quick and Benbo, Duke and Butler.

Of cows and heifers: Motley, Symkins, Damson, Prosper, Thrivewell, Cherry, Colley, Brown, Gentle, Moose, Blacking, Nubbin, Pretty, Daisy, Bunny, and Traveler. Perhaps Traveler came over from England; but I suspect that she was a leaper of fences.

Cattle were as important to a Plymouth family as a donkey to a Sicilian or Greek peasant. They furnished milk, veal, beef, and hides for clothing and shoes. All plowing, pulling up stumps, and transport by two-wheeled cart was done by ox-power. Horses were rare in the Colony before 1650, but later the breeding of them became general.

Farming was so taken for granted as the main business of everyone in the Old Colony that we have very little information about it. We do know, however, that the principal crop through the length and breadth of the Colony was Indian corn. And we are fortunate to have a detailed account, from the pen of Governor Winthrop of Connecticut, as to how it was cultivated in 1660.

The corn of that period was just as it had come from the Indians; rather small, nubbly ears, the kernels colored not only yellow but red, blue, green, and black. The ground was prepared by plows and harrows, or even with hoes alone, Indian fashion. Corn hills were laid out six feet apart. In each hill four or five kernels were planted, together with two or three fish to "nourish" the corn, as the Governor put it. If alewives were not available, any fish offal would do.

After the green blades appeared, furrows were dug crisscross by a plow or hoe, and the earth hilled up so that the cornfield presented a checkerboard appearance with a hill in the middle of each square. Beans were often planted in the same hill as the corn, using the cornstalks as poles. In the intersections of the furrows, squashes and pumpkins were planted; and their vines, spreading all around, served

Planting corn.

to keep the weeds down. Some farmers, however, did not believe in this, and used the spaces between the hills to plant turnips or parsnips.

Corn was used in a variety of ways for man and beast. It was eaten green as "roasting ears"; parched so that the kernel was partly cooked and became easily digested; pounded in a mortar or ground in a grist mill to make bread, hasty pudding, and Indian pudding; treated with lye to make samp or hominy. Beer was often made out of it, for lack of wheat malt. The stalks were left on the ground as winter fodder for cattle, and the grain was also used to fatten cattle and swine. Corn was the greatest gift from the red man to the white.

Many kinds of apples, pears, plums, and quinces were planted in the orchards of the Old Colony, apples predominating. As most of the varieties that they had were soft summer apples, and as the colonists always shook them off the trees, they did not keep well and had to be cut up and sun-dried for winter use. But a large proportion of the apples went into cider, the favorite drink of the Old Colony farmer.

Owing to the habit of cows and other animals of breaking into cornfields or orchards and raising havoc, the Colony and the towns were always fussing about fences. The common fence in most parts of the Colony was a loose stone wall; but on Cape Cod and in other regions, where stone was scarce, fences of split chestnut or round cedar were built. All had to be "ox-strong" and "hog-tight." Pigs were so clever at worming through a fence and rooting up crops that they had to be yoked and ringed, except in winter.[2]

---

[2] The hog yoke was a sort of wooden frame in the form of the letter A, which was fastened around the pig's neck. The ring, inserted in piggy's nose, prevented him from rooting.

The keeping up of fences was very important. Robert Frost's poem "Mending Wall" tells of a custom that started very early in the Old Colony: neighbors walking along a stone wall in early spring, to pick up and replace the stones that winter frost or animals had thrown down. Then, as now, "good fences make good neighbors."

The wave of prosperity based on cattle-raising came to an abrupt halt in 1641, because civil war had broken out in England and Puritans had stopped emigrating. Corn now "would buy nothing," wrote Governor Winthrop. The price of a cow fell off to four or five pounds. Many a good bossy was now slaughtered and eaten because there was no market for her. As a Boston poet put it, in an early almanac:

That since the mighty Cow her crown hath lost
In every place she's made to rule the roast.

And Winthrop adds, the depression caused the New England people to concentrate on "making" fish and cutting lumber products for export to the West Indies.

This "fall of cow," as it was called in New England—and we may fairly call it the earliest crash in the stock market —affected Plymouth even more than the Bay Colony. For Plymouth had gone in heavily for raising cattle and corn for the Boston market, and by this time the fur trade had declined. The Old Colony tried the same remedy as the Bay. Already she had some experience in building small vessels; a pinnace with a ketch rig, about forty feet long, was built at Duxbury in 1640 for forty pounds. Next year, the leading men of Plymouth chipped in £200 or more to build a "barque" of forty to fifty tons for the West Indies trade. But what became of her we do not know.

THE WEST INDIES TRADE

◆§ TRADE with the West Indies was the economic salvation
of New England. Planters in the English, French, and Dutch
islands from Barbados to St. Croix preferred to employ
their labor in growing tobacco or sugar cane, and to import
all luxuries, and many necessities. New England found the
islands a wonderful market for corn, salt fish, pickled beef
and pork, oak pipe staves to make hogsheads, and shooks to
make boxes, lumber to build houses. Even horses were ex-
ported to provide power for the (literally) one-horse sugar
mills of that era, and also live cattle, and poultry. As our
almanac poet wrote:

> That heaps of wheat, pork, bisket, beef, and beer,
> Masts, pipestaves, fish, should store both far and near,
> Which fetch in wines, cloth, sweets, and good tobac—
> O be contented, then, you cannot lack.

Plymouth Colony ports seldom entered this trade directly;
they were feeders to Boston, Salem, Newport, or New London. Sloops and shallops carried local products to one of
those larger ports, where they were trans-shipped, and
brought back West India goods, and clothing, tools, and
luxuries which the merchants had imported from England.
The great demand for fish in the West Indies made it worth
while for the towns from Scituate to Eastham to "make fish"
for the foreign market. And many Plymouth boys "shipped
foreign" in Boston vessels.

The West Indies in the seventeenth century were very
much wealthier than the mainland colonies, and a winter
spent in a voyage down there was lots of fun, and profitable,

too. Big boys came back home with pockets full of Spanish dollars ("pieces of eight") and boasting that they had seen "mountains of sugar, rivers of rum, and fish that fly in the air." One Pilgrim mother said she could believe the first two, but flying fish she could not swallow, and scolded her sailor son for telling such a whopping lie!

How did the New Englanders, who had no previous experience in seafaring, find their way to the West Indies? It was not too difficult. As one old sea captain put it: "Sail south till your butter melts, then west!" The little ketches and barks, making a wide sweep outside Cape Cod, Nantucket Shoals, and Bermuda, sailed south until the skipper saw by the altitude of the North Star that he was about on the latitude of Barbados, and then turned west. The time to start was in the late fall, when the hurricane season was over and you could count on the tradewinds to take you easily from island to island.

This trade had grown to such an extent in 1662 that the old Colony laid export taxes on boards and planks, barrel staves and headings, tar, iron bars—and oysters! The last item is surprising; apparently the West India planters were demanding Wellfleet pickled oysters.

MARKETS

◄§ LITTLE actual money reached Plymouth Colony; most of the imported silver dollars were spent in Boston, and many a boy grew to manhood without seeing any bigger coin than a Massachusetts pine-tree shilling. It was a barter economy. Everyone kept accounts in pounds, shillings, and pence but little money changed hands; and there was nothing in the entire Colony like a modern shop or store. But that seemed strange to nobody, because in England at that time there were no shops except in London and the shire towns. Plymouth Colony followed the English practice of doing most of its trading at markets or fairs. Plymouth Town had a market every Thursday, and a May fair; Duxbury had an October fair; almost every other settlement had a market day, and the larger ones held annual fairs. On market days everyone who had something to sell or who wanted to buy, and many who just wanted to talk, came to the village green or town square. A fisherman with an extra barrel or two of pickled mackerel might sell some of it to a farmer in exchange for salt beef or a live hog. Chickens, eggs, butter, and all manner of farm produce were traded; much of it to a local merchant who sold it in Boston.

The annual fair brought lots of people by boat or trail from the other towns; it was the time for visiting friends and relatives as well as for trading. Indians brought great heaps of baskets, brooms, and wooden ware; peddlers in sloops from Boston or Newport spread out a tempting array of knives and cutlery, pins and needles, combs and brushes, and all manner of small wares, and were ready to take country produce in exchange, or salt fish, tar, and barrel staves. Fur-traders from the Kennebec and local trappers had attractive parcels of beaver, otter, and musquash for sale—even a few mink, then esteemed only a little better than tabby-cat. Flocks of sheep, herds of cattle, coops of poultry, and even a few horses were driven in for sale, and the usually quiet green or square resounded with moos, baas, neighs, barks, clucks, and the hissing of indignant geese.

The constable strode about with his brass-tipped black rod

[OPPOSITE] *Pilgrim fair.*

of office, to see that the Indians got no liquor and that nobody got drunk; but, all the same, everyone had a gay time chaffering, swapping, and gossiping. The young men showed off the paces of colts they had raised, and bought ribbons for their girls; young matrons exchanged cow "Daisy" or heifer "Bunny" for a dress straight from London; men talked crops and discussed the likelihood of war with France or Spain or the Dutch, and wondered what effect it would have on the price of corn and beef.

The nearest thing to a permanent store in the Colony was the warehouse of a merchant who collected the products of farm, fishery, and forest for export, and brought in molasses, wines and liquors, clothing, hardware, and various English and West Indies goods. Rum came in about 1670, and was at first frowned upon as a disreputable sailor's drink.

THE TAUNTON IRON WORKS

THE MOST modern business established in Plymouth Colony was the iron industry. Throughout eastern New England there was a fair amount of iron ore in swamps and on the bottoms of ponds; the problem was how to smelt it. Around 1643, two groups of English capitalists set up iron works at Saugus and at Braintree in the Bay Colony. With imported Scots labor—prisoners taken by Cromwell in the English Civil War—they set up a furnace or "bloomery" where the ore was melted by roaring fires of oak wood, flowing out red-hot into sand molds where it cooled off and became iron "pigs." The pig-iron was beaten by a trip-hammer run by water power until impurities were expelled, and it became wrought- or bar-iron; and this iron was fashioned into nails, spikes, kettles, skillets, anchors, chains, and other useful articles. The old iron works at Saugus, lately restored, are the best example anywhere of an American colonial factory.

The seat of this industry in Plymouth Colony was at Taunton, at the head of navigation on the Taunton River which flows into Narragansett Bay. That settlement was founded by English emigrants in 1630 who purchased land from Massasoit at two shillings an acre. In 1637 the population was increased by the arrival of 48-year-old Elizabeth Pole, described by Governor Winthrop as "a gentlewoman, an ancient maid" of Taunton in Old England. She walked through the woods from Boston, driving her cattle and accompanied by her brother William and sundry servants. After purchasing another tract of land from the Indians, she persuaded the people to name the place Taunton, and Taunton was shortly after given representation to the General Court.[3] Members of the Cobb, Morton, Deane, and Macy families were already there, or came shortly after. Iron ore was discovered on the banks of Two-Mile River; a stock company with capital of £600 was organized, Elizabeth Pole being a prominent stockholder. The Leonard brothers and Ralph Russell, former officers of the Braintree iron works, were invited to come, and in 1656 the Taunton Iron Works opened. They were so successful that iron bars became currency in Taunton; taxes and the schoolteacher's salary were paid in this "iron money," and the town became the most prosperous in the Colony. A visitor, in 1660, described it as "a pleasant place, seated among the windings and turnings of a handsome river, and hath good conveyance to

---

[3] So much land was acquired by the early settlers of Taunton that at one time it covered an area greater than the present District of Columbia. In due course it was cut up into the present city of Taunton and the towns of Norton, Easton, Mansfield, Raynham, Dighton, and Berkley, which were called "Taunton and her six daughters."

Boston by cart." The Taunton Iron Works were operated until 1876.[4]

Apart from these iron works there was nothing you could call an organized industry in Plymouth Colony. Almost every town had a few simple specialists such as carpenters, boat builders, bricklayers, blacksmiths, millers, brewers, and cobblers. Every town had a minister and some had a physician; but even these professional gentlemen owned farms and grew most of the food for their families. There were no such extremes of wealth as in Virginia, New York, or Massachusetts Bay; everyone worked at something, and almost everyone made a fair living.

Altogether it was a simple society with a primitive economy and a static social system. There was no printing press or silversmith as in Boston, there were few schools and little evidence of intellectual life. Apart from the poems of John Saffin that we have quoted, Governor Bradford's noble History, and Nathaniel Morton's *New England's Memoriall* (which is largely a poor paraphrase of Bradford), Plymouth Colony produced no literature. In this, as in foreign trade, the Colony was a backwater, sheltered from the main currents of New England life.

But whenever there was trouble with the Indians, Plymouth men were up in front, shooting!

---

[4] The actual site of the iron works is on Route 104 in Raynham, two miles from the center of Taunton. Elizabeth Pole died in 1654 and is buried in the Plain Cemetery; her family, still prominent in England, have to this day kept up their connection with Taunton.

❧ XX ❧

PEQUOTS AND NARRAGANSETTS

❮❮❮❮❮❮❮❮❮❮❮❮❮❮❮❮❮❮❮❮❮❮❮❮❮❮❮❮❮❮❮❮

SASSACUS AND THE PEQUOTS
DESTROYED

A NATURAL RESULT of the great increase of English population in New England after 1630 was trouble with the
Indians. Massasoit stood firm as the ally of Plymouth, and
the Massachusetts were allied with the colony named after
them; but Connecticut, though friendly with the Mohegans,
became embroiled with the Pequots.

That warlike nation occupied the territory between the
Narragansetts and the Connecticut River, and farther west.
Sassacus, a great Pequot sachem, had brought under his
sway most of the Indians between Point Judith, Rhode Island, and the Hudson River.

An English trader from Virginia named John Stone, while sailing up the Connecticut River, was killed by the Pequots, together with the entire crew of his pinnace. A few months later, in the spring of 1635, Sassacus sent an "embassy" to Boston to make a treaty with the Bay Colony, as he wanted help against his enemies the Narragansetts. Governor Winthrop consented, on condition that the murderers of Captain Stone and his men be delivered for trial and punishment. The Governor sent a pinnace to get the culprits, but Sassacus refused to surrender them, claiming that they were only trying to rescue two of their fellows whom Stone had kidnapped to pilot him up the river. Their story was probably true, since Stone had a bad reputation for that sort of thing; but the Bay authorities felt that there should be a trial.

Shortly after this, our old friend "Mad Jack" Oldham, now trading out of Boston, was "knocked on the head by a hatchet" at Block Island, and his Indian murderers took refuge with the Pequots. Again Sassacus refused to give them up. Winthrop fully agreed with Bradford's principle, that Indians who killed Englishmen must be surrendered for trial. He could not overlook these murders. So Captain Endecott and some forty armed men were sent on a punitive expedition, by sea.

Endecott, who, unlike Myles Standish, had no experience in fighting Indians, landed on the banks of the Connecticut, burned a lot of Pequot lodges, and accomplished nothing except to stir up the entire tribe.

Early in 1637, the Pequots began to take revenge on English settlements along the Connecticut, killing men and women working in the fields and even assaulting the fort at Saybrook. Connecticut appealed to Massachusetts for help, and the Bay asked Plymouth to join in. Governor Bradford consented reluctantly, since, as he pointed out, the war was the result of Endecott's folly; but he realized that all English colonists must stand by each other. The General Court of Plymouth authorized him to send Lieutenants William Holmes and Thomas Prence, with forty-two armed men, to help Connecticut and Massachusetts. Contrary winds delayed their voyage around Cape Cod and they arrived too late for the war.

Fortunately for the English, the Narragansetts joined them and led them to the Pequots' stronghold near the mouth of the Mystic River. The Bay force of forty under Captain John Underhill, joining with the Connecticut contingent of ninety under Captain John Mason, surrounded a rude fort where hundreds of Indians had gathered and built strong defenses. But they were armed only with bows and arrows. The English assaulted the fort and set fire to the Indian lodges, destroying more by fire than by gunshot. "It was a fearful sight," wrote Bradford, "to see them thus frying in the fire and the streams of blood quenching the same, and horrible was the stink and scent thereof; but the victory seemed a sweet sacrifice." Sassacus with his "treasury" of wampum escaped to the Mohawks, who murdered him. Pequot prisoners were distributed between Massachusetts Bay and Connecticut and enslaved. Those who escaped death or capture joined the Narragansetts or the Mohegans, and lost their land.

"From savage violence the land had rest for nigh forty year," wrote an early chronicler. But conflicts with the Narragansetts were very narrowly avoided.

UNCAS AND MIANTONOMO

⚬§ THE FIRST disturbing event was the reprehensible murder and robbery of a peaceful Narragansett by a Plymouth veteran of the Pequot War, Arthur Peach. Being "out of means and loath to work," and also having got a maidservant into trouble, he decided to seek his fortune at New Amsterdam. He enticed three menservants to flee from their masters and go with him. While on their way, in the present town of Seekonk, they met an Indian named Penowayanquis who was returning from a trading trip to Boston, carrying wampum and woolen cloth to make matchcoats. Peach and his pals, after sitting down and smoking with the Indian, ran him through the body with a rapier, robbed him of his wampum and cloth, and went their way, leaving him for dead. But Penowayanquis was tough. He managed to crawl to the nearest village where he told his story before he died.

This cold-blooded murder aroused the Narragansetts to fury. A body of them came to Providence, told their friend Roger Williams all about it, and threatened to go on the warpath unless justice was done, and quickly. Williams, after checking on the story from Penowayanquis himself just before he died, caught the four culprits and turned them over to the New Plymouth authorities. One escaped, but Peach and the other two were tried for murder by a jury at Plymouth, found guilty, and hanged. Some Narragansetts were present at the hanging, "which gave them and all the country good satisfaction," says Bradford; but "some of the rude and ignorant sort" among the whites "murmured that any English should be put to death for the Indians."

More trouble arose in 1643. Miantonomo, nephew of Canonicus who had sent the rattlesnake-skin challenge to the Pilgrims, was now sachem of the Narragansetts. He was furious because his chief rival, Uncas, sachem of the Mohegans, had been allowed to incorporate large numbers of the surviving Pequots into that tribe. His entire force—almost a thousand pinses (warriors)—made a surprise attack on the Mohegans. They were badly beaten and Miantonomo was taken prisoner.

The usual Indian action in such a case was to torture the prisoner with exquisite cruelty until he died. Uncas, fearing Narragansett revenge if he did that, put the case into the hands of the New England Confederation. They knew that if Miantonomo was not killed he would escape, and that Uncas, as faithful an ally of the English as Massasoit, would never be safe while Miantonomo lived. So they advised him to put Miantonomo to death without torture. Uncas's brother did so, with a hatchet.

NARRAGANSETTS PACIFIED

❧ THE NARRAGANSETTS now complained to the New England Confederation that they had paid Uncas a ransom for Miantonomo, and demanded permission to take revenge. The Confederation (with Edward Winslow and William Collier representing Plymouth) heard both sides, decided that this story was false, and ordered the Narragansetts to keep the peace. Nevertheless, Pessacus, Miantonomo's brother and heir, defied them, attacked the Mohegans "and slew many," besides capturing a lot of muskets which Connecticut had given to her ally. Roger Williams warned his

English friends that unless they acted quickly, "the whole country would be all of a flame."

The New England Confederation prepared for an Indian War. Massachusetts was to raise 190 soldiers, Plymouth, Connecticut, and New Haven forty each. Messengers from the Confederation to Pessacus were received "with scorn and contempt." He even threatened to draw in the dreaded Mohawks from New York as allies and wipe out the English colonies. Myles Standish and the Plymouth contingent marched to Seekonk, ready for action; and it looked as if a general war was inevitable.

And there would have been one, too, but for a dispute within the United Nations of New England. The General Court of Massachusetts said they had not been consulted, and demanded that one more effort be made to keep the peace. Messengers were sent to Pessacus to tell him that if he and some of his sagamores would come to Boston to talk peace, they would be guaranteed safe conduct. They came, and in August 1645 concluded a treaty with the United Colonies. They promised to pay four thousand yards of white wampum, to restore all Mohegan captives to Uncas, to keep the peace with him and Massasoit and all the Indian tribes of New England, and to give hostages for good conduct.

"And thus was the war at this time stayed and prevented," concludes Bradford. Peace with the Narragansetts lasted thirty years.

❧ XXI ❧

THE PASSING OF
THE ELDER
STATESMEN

❧❧❧❧❧❧❧❧❧❧❧❧❧❧❧❧❧❧❧❧❧❧❧❧❧❧❧❧❧❧

ELDER BREWSTER

SINCE the Great Sickness of 1621, and a smaller epidemic which occurred in 1633, the members of Plymouth Colony had been remarkably healthy, and many lived to a good old age. Bradford marveled that it should be so, since "it is found in experience that change of air, famine or unwholesome food, much drinking of water, sorrows and troubles, etc. are enemies to health . . . and shorteners of life." Possibly the death of Dr. Fuller in 1633 had something to do with the Pilgrims' longevity, since drugs administered by seventeenth-century physicians were more apt to kill than to cure.

First of the leaders to die was Elder Brewster, in 1643, at the age of eighty. Bradford tells how wonderfully this gentleman and scholar had borne the hardships of early days, working in the fields with the rest of them as long as he had strength, preaching two sermons every Sunday until they obtained a regular minister, and giving everyone spiritual as well as practical advice. And all that, having "nothing but water" to drink until he was seventy-five years old. He was "of a very cheerful spirit, very sociable and pleasant . . . tenderhearted and compassionate of such as were in misery," but scornful of people who had got rich in the rising stock market and put on airs. The Elder's sons, Love and Jonathan, carried on; and today there are plenty of Brewsters in Plymouth, and elsewhere.

EDWARD WINSLOW

◄§ EDWARD WINSLOW was lost to Plymouth Colony in 1646, when Massachusetts sent him to London to defend it against various complaints. He found conditions under Oliver Cromwell so pleasant that he stayed on, greatly to Bradford's displeasure. The Lord Protector was asked by the Barbadians to appoint Winslow their Governor; but Cromwell had already selected him to be his No. 1 civil commissioner to accompany an English force under Admiral Penn, sent to capture Hispaniola. His salary was £1000, about fifty times that of a Governor of New Plymouth. After being beaten by the Spaniards near Santo Domingo, Admiral Penn decided to have a try at Jamaica. Before reaching it, Winslow sickened and quickly died of a tropical fever. As one of the ship's company wrote:—

The eighth of May, west from Spaniola shore,
God took from us our grand Commissioner,
WINSLOW *by name—a man of cheerful trust*
Whose life was sweet and conversation just.

His son Josiah, as we have seen, inherited the family estate "Careswell" at Marshfield, and became Governor of the Colony in 1673, the first native-born governor in America. His wife Susanna lived to a great age, dying in 1680.

MYLES STANDISH

MYLES STANDISH died in 1656, at the age of seventy-two. Standish served the Old Colony well, not only as a brave and skillful captain and interpreter to the Indians, whose language he learned, but as surveyor and colony treasurer. And he did well, too. His armory comprised a fowling piece, a sword, a cutlass, three muskets, four carbines, two small guns, and three cartridge belts or bandoliers. His house and land were valued at £140—the highest in the Colony to that date; his stock amounted to four oxen, five of horse-kind, and 14 swine. Although Myles never became a full communicant of the Pilgrim Church, he certainly shared their faith; for most of his books were of Puritan divinity, and he left a legacy to "Mercy Robinson, whom I tenderly love for her grandfather's sake." Her grandfather was the Rev. John Robinson of Leyden. Besides the religious books, he owned Caesar's *Commentaries*, and *The Swedish Intelligencer*. So we may picture the Captain in his old age, seated by his Duxbury fireside, studying the campaigns of Julius

Caesar and Gustavus Adolphus. After his death his position as commander-in-chief of the Colony stood vacant for three years, when Josiah Winslow was appointed to succeed him. He is commemorated by a great monument on Captain's Hill, Duxbury, which he owned.

WILLIAM BRADFORD

WILLIAM BRADFORD died in 1657, at the age of sixty-seven, a few days after his thirtieth term of office as Governor had expired. Since the Undertakers had wound up their affairs, he had been one of the group that hired the right to trade on the Kennebec, and had done fairly well in that declining business. He left a house at Plymouth valued at forty-five pounds; another at Jones River (the future Kingston), and many parcels of land; the whole estate being valued at £900. Among his possessions were a "great beer bowle" and two smaller ones; ten good chairs, a court cupboard, and a large quantity of linen; five dozen pewter dishes and vessels, thirteen silver spoons, and some Venetian glass; a red cloak and waistcoat, a violet-colored cloak, a "lead-colored" suit with silver buttons, and a black and a colored hat. His library of English, Dutch, French, and Latin books was second only to Brewster's in the Colony. Alice, his second wife, survived him by many years, living to see their son, William, Jr., become major of militia and an Assistant of the Colony. And their descendants are legion.

To no one among the original Pilgrims did the Colony owe so much as to Bradford; and of America's colonial founders, only John Winthrop, William Penn, Captain John Smith, and Lord Baltimore can be mentioned in the same breath. In the early years he had almost complete power; he was at once Governor, overseer of the workers, constable, and judge. Yet Bradford was one whom power did not corrupt; gladly he surrendered it to others as soon as they were willing to share his burdens. In his Indian and domestic policy, in his organization of the fur trade, and as representative of Plymouth in the New England Confederation he showed the genius of a statesman, even though his sphere was small. Although born a poor farmer's son, he educated himself, learned to speak Dutch, French, and Latin, and was able to meet sophisticated gentlemen like Governor Winthrop on equal terms. He was also capable of writing virile, expressive English; his History *Of Plymouth Plantation,* from which we have constantly quoted, is one of the really great books of the seventeenth century. At the age of sixty Bradford began to teach himself Hebrew, having "a longing desire to see with my own eyes something of that most ancient language and holy tongue in which God and the Angels spoke to the holy patriarchs of old time." And he always had before him the Pilgrim ideal of leading the New Testament way of life, of which he was a living example to the Colony.

Now the "big four" of the *Mayflower* Pilgrims were gone. Thomas Prence became Governor, and new faces appeared among the Assistants: James Cudworth of Scituate, Josiah Winslow, Thomas Southworth (Bradford's stepson), William Bradford, Jr., and Thomas Hinckley of Barnstable, destined to be the last Governor of New Plymouth. These men were annually re-elected until they died or resigned; nobody, unless it was the deputy of a town, was ever defeated at the polls.

THE ALDENS

◄§ BRADFORD's remarks on the long lives of the Pilgrim Fathers are well borne out by the facts. In 1690, seventy years after the voyage of the *Mayflower,* three of her passengers were still living in the Colony. These were Resolved, son of William White, John, son of Francis Cooke, and Mary Allerton, the wife of Elder Thomas Cushman. Mary died in 1699 at the age of eighty-three, last survivor of the *Mayflower* passengers. But Resolved White's younger brother, Peregrine, born on board ship but not counted as a passenger, outlived Mary Cushman five years, dying in 1704.

The Alden family were famous for their longevity. John died at the age of eighty-seven and Priscilla survived him several years. Their daughter Elizabeth married William Paybody. He died in 1707, shortly after they had celebrated their sixty-third wedding anniversary; and she died at the age of ninety-three, a three-times-great grandmother. When her first great-great-great-grandchild was born, the old lady composed this couplet:

> *Rise, daughter, to thy daughter run;*
> *Her daughter's daughter hath a son!*

Samuel Alden, a grandson of John, lived to be ninety-three, and Sam's son John died in 1821 at the age of one hundred and two. And his funeral was attended by one hundred and seventy-three of his descendants.

But the Methuselah of Plymouth Colony was Deacon John Doane, an early settler of Eastham, who died in 1707 at the age of one hundred and ten.

Governor Bradford, pondering the long lives of several

Pilgrim Fathers besides Brewster, quoted the words of Paul the Apostle in II Corinthians 11:26-27: ". . . in perils by the heathen . . . in perils in the wilderness, in perils in the sea, in perils among false brethren; In weariness and painfulness, in watchings often, in hunger and thirst, in fastings often, in cold and nakedness." He concluded: "It is not by good and dainty fare, by peace and rest and heart's ease in enjoying the contentments and good things of this world only that preserves health and prolongs life. . . . It was God's visitation that preserved their spirits."

EXPANSION
AFTER
1660

❧ ❧

THE COLONY AND THE KING

IN 1661, after hearing that Charles II had been restored to the throne of his fathers, Plymouth Colony publicly proclaimed her allegiance and consumed a whole barrel of powder in firing salutes. Three years later a royal commission arrived to look into the New England colonies. It met with a very hostile reception in Boston, but a most friendly one at Plymouth. The commissioners, after questioning Governor Prence and reading some of the records, said that everything in the Old Colony seemed to be all right. The only changes they demanded were that all men of "competent estate and civil conversation" be admitted Freemen; that all Christians be given baptism and admitted to the Lord's Supper in the Congregational churches, or else be allowed to set up churches of their own; and that all householders take an oath of allegiance to the King. The Colony accepted these conditions and was praised for its loyalty by Charles II. "Your carriage," he wrote, "seems set off with the more lustre, by the contrary deportment of the Colony of the Massachusetts." Someone now suggested that Plymouth cash in on this royal favor by applying for a charter; but as that might mean having a royal governor placed over them, the Freemen decided that they "preferred to remain as they were."

That was a bad decision which the Colony later regretted. Charles II gave charters to Rhode Island and Connecticut, which allowed their freemen to elect governors and all other officials. Plymouth could have had a similar charter, if she had been willing to spend a little money in the right places at court, at the right time.

New Plymouth may have been the most loyal of the New England Colonies, but she was also the poorest. The total population of the twelve towns that had been organized by 1664, and whose founding we have briefly described, was around three thousand.[1] The royal commissioners observed that the Colony had no big river, no good harbor like Bos-

---

[1] R. L. Bowen's estimate is 2,520 in 1653, 4,884 in 1675. Comparable estimates for Connecticut (including New Haven) are about twice that; for Massachusetts Bay, between three and four times that of New Plymouth. Even Rhode Island probably had more people than did Plymouth by 1660. But, in my opinion, the New Plymouth population was nearer 7,000 than 5,000 in 1675.

ton or Newport, and only one sawmill; and the people were
so poor that they were unable to pay competent ministers.[2]
Twelve years later Edward Randolph, whom Charles II sent
over to report on New England, stated that Plymouth Colony had very few merchants and no big ships in foreign
trade, only "small ketches and barks, to trade along the
coasts and take fish." The shore towns from Scituate to
Plymouth, and all the Cape settlements, were feeders to Boston, while the Buzzards Bay and Narragansett Bay villages
traded largely through Newport, Rhode Island.

FISHING, SCHOOLS, AND HIGHWAYS

GOVERNOR PRENCE, who owned land at Eastham, organized the first profitable fishing from Cape Cod. At the same
time the seining of bass and herring in the brooks and along
the beaches of the Cape was declared a Colony monopoly
and was leased to fishermen at so much a year. To conserve
the slippery and valuable mackerel, it was forbidden to take
them between January and July, or at any time with a net or
seine. Another source of wealth along the Cape was the occasional big whale or school of blackfish, stranded when chas-
ing small fish close to shore. (Remember how the men on
the exploring expedition in 1620 saw Indians cutting up a
blackfish?) Both kinds yielded good oil. The Colony declared that they should belong to the town on whose beach
they were stranded, and that the town should pay one barrel
of oil from each whale as a tax to the "country." [3]

---

[2] This, as we have seen, was not true of the Cape towns or of
Duxbury, Scituate, and Rehoboth; but Plymouth had no settled
minister in 1664. The Colony actually had two sawmills—at Scituate,
and Sandwich.

[3] In Thoreau's *Cape Cod* there is a description of a community

Harpooning a whale in Plymouth harbor.

Live whaling started from the Cape villages at this time.
A company of young men would build a whaleboat and buy
harpoons and other necessary gear. When anyone ashore
sighted a whale the cry "Thar she blows!" went up; the crew
launched their boat, and, if skillful and lucky, killed the
whale and towed it ashore. The whole village turned out to
cut the blubber off the whale's back and try out the oil in big
iron kettles on the beach, while the gulls and crows took care
of the meat. Whale oil and whalebone were valuable articles
of export, so the capture of a whale or two meant a great

cutting-up of blackfish in 1855 that might have happened almost two
centuries earlier.

deal to the people of Sandwich, Barnstable, Yarmouth, and Eastham.

It also made a difference to the schools of the Colony, because the General Court in 1670 appropriated the whale-oil tax and the fishing-license fees toward free schools "for the training up of youth in literature for the good and benefit of posterity." The first school in Plymouth was established soon after. In 1677, the Colony voted to distribute the fishing-license money among all towns which would set up grammar schools, at the rate of five pounds to each, provided it would raise the rest itself. Duxbury and Taunton qualified the same year, and Rehoboth the next. Taunton, whose schoolmaster was paid in iron bars, had eighty boys at school in 1685. Swansea anticipated the five-pound encouragement by setting up a complete grammar school in 1673 where Latin, Greek, and Hebrew were taught, "and also to read English and to write." Swansea's enterprise was due to the local Baptist minister, the Rev. John Myles, who doubled as schoolmaster.

The Town of Plymouth, so depressed in the 1640's, was still half deserted in 1660, "the people being removed into farms in the country," as a visitor then described it. But soon it began to pick up. The Plymouth Church, which had got along for years with just an elder (Thomas Cushman) to preach, in 1667 obtained a minister fresh out of Harvard, the Rev. John Cotton, Jr., and he stayed with them for thirty years. A good preacher was one of the best attractions to settlers in those days, and Mr. Cotton, by all accounts, was one of the best. But Plymouth Town never became "the place it was" until the following century. Although it included the territory of the future towns of Kingston, Carver, and Plympton and parts of Halifax and Wareham, the value of its real and personal property remained less than that of four or five other towns in the Colony. Scituate was the richest and paid the highest tax. Barnstable, Yarmouth, and Taunton were wealthier than old Plymouth.

Within the existing limits of the Colony, population continued to increase. Nemasket, the Indian village nearest to Plymouth, was purchased in 1661 by Captain Thomas Southworth and twenty-five others from Josiah Wampatuck, Indian sagamore, for seventy pounds. Nemasket became the Town of Middleborough in 1669. Its center was near the old "Wading Place" on the Nemasket River, through which all traffic between Plymouth and Massasoit's country had to pass. There were sixteen English families in Middleborough in 1675, when King Philip's War broke out.

Such traffic as there was between Plymouth and Boston or Cape Cod or Narragansett Bay went mostly by foot or horseback. These highways at first were mere trails, but by 1660 they could be used by two-wheeled ox-carts. Lack of big rivers saved the Colony from having to spend much money on bridges; there was one over Jones River quite early, and a few elsewhere; but wherever there was a ford that a horse or ox could splash across, no bridge was built. The North River, between Marshfield and Scituate on the main road to Boston, was crossed by a ferry. There was never much of a traffic problem on the roads of the Old Colony, because it was much easier to get about by boat, and most people who had to travel went by sea.

HORSE RAISING

HORSE RAISING now became as important as cattle raising, if not more so, because a market for work and saddle horses had opened in the West Indies and the Southern colonies.

The horses were kept in barns during the winter and the mares bred so that they would foal in the spring. Mares and their foals, and all horses not being used by the family, were then turned out to pasture in the common lands of each township. Every town had to have a distinctive brand for its horses, and every owner a distinctive mark, usually some sort of slit in one ear. Fences now had to be made "horse-high" as well as "ox-strong" and "hog-tight," so that the horses would not desert the woody pastures for luscious fields of green corn, or meadows where the hay had to be saved for winter fodder.

In the early fall there was a round-up, which must have been great fun for the young men and boys. All the horses they could catch were collected in the town pound, or some other enclosure, and sorted out according to brand and mark. Each owner then decided which ones he wished to sell, and one or more young men undertook to drive the town's collection to Boston. Plymouth Town became so much annoyed by herds of Boston-bound horses from the Cape being driven along Main Street and lunching off the flower and vegetable gardens, that the constables were ordered to take special measures for protection of property.

The Colony itself made the rules about branding and marking, and regulated horse raising. Unmarked stray horses that were picked up had to be "cryed" (advertised) at two sessions of a court; and if not claimed within a year, could be kept by the finder. Horses running in from the Bay Colony or Rhode Island, "causing damage and annoyance to English and Indians alike," were to be treated as strays; the "foreign" owner could get them back only if he paid damages. And, in order to keep up the breed of Old Colony horses and eliminate runts, no stallions under thirteen hands high and over two years old were permitted to run free during the summer.

Naturally the young men took to racing their horses along the highways, and this became such a traffic menace that it had to be forbidden. But it was very fortunate that New England had plenty of horses when King Philip's War broke out, and that every young man knew how to ride; for by mounting the troops they were able to catch up with fast-moving Indians.

HOUSES AND POSSESSIONS

❧ THE ENTIRE Colony was more prosperous after 1660 than before. It was a poor farmer indeed who did not leave his family a good house and a hundred acres of land, as well as cattle, sheep, and horses. For instance, Samuel Hinckley, the Governor's father, leaves three mares worth thirty-six pounds in his will, besides two colts and a two-year-old. William Carpenter gives his son the choice of taking the "young gray mare," or two yearlings with "5 lbs. in sugar or wampum" to boot. James Parsivall of Falmouth leaves his black mare to daughter Elizabeth, gray mare to his wife, "and to my son John, I give the mare that he usually rides and calls *his* mare." Just like a modern young man with Dad's second car! Mares were used within the Colony for breeding or riding, and the geldings were sold for export; I have not found one mention of a horse-cart or carriage in the records. Oxen did all the plowing and hauling.

The style of houses did not change between 1650 and 1690; they were still of wood, two stories and a loft, unpainted, and with leaded casement windows. But they were usually larger than those of the early days.

For this period we have a few family portraits, made by an unknown artist, possibly when the subject visited Boston. They indicate that the wealthier people in the Old Colony were dressing in the latest London fashions. The portrait of Penelope Winslow, wife of Governor Josiah Winslow, confirms the tradition of her beauty. She wears her chestnut hair in the ringlets that were fashionable at the court of Charles II; and she drapes a red silk scarf over a simple brown dress with a rather low neckline. The portrait of Elizabeth Wensley, daughter of William Paddy, shows the full dress of the latter part of Charles's reign. She wears an elaborate gown of brown and green material with rose lining, bodice trimmed with lace and red silk, a red and green underskirt, red and white striped sash, puffed sleeves, and a white muslin or silk hood tied under her chin. And she is wearing four rings.

Farmers and fishermen probably still dressed about as they had in 1630—linen shirts, leather or wool breeches, and a wool or deerskin jacket, knitted woolen stockings, and cowhide boots. The Colony made strict regulations for the tanning of leather to keep up the quality of footwear. Every town had a couple of "sealers" (inspectors) of leather, and shoemakers were not allowed to use any skins not passed upon by them.

In the inventories of furnishings we find more pewter,

brass, and bell-metal utensils than before; and a few pieces of silver and a gold ring or two are not unusual. The most surprising list of possessions is that of Captain Matthew Fuller of Barnstable, in 1678. His inventory included silver money valued just short of £100—pieces of eight, presumably—almost six pounds in "old England silver money," and "perle, precious stones and Diamonds, at a gesse £200." Had Captain Fuller been a-pirating?

NEW SETTLEMENTS ON BUZZARDS BAY AND THE CAPE

◆§ THE PRINCIPAL new area opened to settlement after 1664 was the northern side of Buzzards Bay. Land at Sippican Harbor had been granted much earlier to Plymouth Town "for the keeping of their cattle . . . and never to be alienated to any other use." After the "fall of cow" in 1641, the salt meadows there became less valuable, and people in Scituate, Marshfield, and Sandwich wished to move in. The General Court gave them permission, in 1661, and settlements were made on Wareham, Sippican, and Mattapoisett Harbors shortly after. The whole area was recognized as the Town of Rochester in 1686.[4]

Adjoining Rochester on the west was an extensive Reserved Tract, one of those granted to the Old Comers when they gave up their right to the rest of the land in the Colony. It extended from Nasketucket Bay and Sconticut Point on the east, past Westport and the Hen and Chickens ledge, around Sakonnet Point, and up Narragansett Bay to the pres-

---

[4] Wareham in part, Marion, and Mattapoisett were originally a part of Rochester.

ent Fall River. The Old Comer grantees, Bradford, Standish, Winslow, Thomas Southworth, and John Cooke, in 1652, paid Massasoit for his title to this tract of some two hundred square miles, thirty yards of cloth, fifteen axes, fifteen hoes, fifteen pairs of breeches, eight pairs of shoes and stockings, one cloak, eight blankets, eight moose skins, two pounds of wampum, one iron pot, and ten shillings' worth of other goods. King Philip later disputed the title but was satisfied by a payment in money. Dartmouth, recognized as a town in 1664, was settled in part by younger-generation Pilgrims (Cookes, Delanos, Howlands, Soules, and Spooners), partly by Baptists and Quakers who objected to paying taxes to support the Congregational ministry in other towns. They guessed that after the Colony had been warned by the royal commissioners to be tolerant they would be left alone; and they guessed right. From Acushnet, the eastern section of the town, were later set off New Bedford, the famous whaling city, and its opposite neighbor, Fairhaven. South Dartmouth, Apponagansett, Padanaram, and Nonquit are all in the eastern half of this tract.

The western half of it, bordering on Narragansett Bay, was first used for land grants to servants in the Town of Plymouth whose terms were up, and for whom no meadow land was left in the old town. They found the salt meadows and long necks of land, easily fenced off, to be best for raising horses; as the name Horse Neck Beach in Westport recalls. Awashonks, the squaw sachem of Sakonnet, was willing to sell part of that peninsula. Among those who moved in were Benjamin Church, and the Paybodies, Almys, and Richmonds. After King Philip's War, in which Awashonks took the Indian side, the rest of her land was confiscated and

Little Compton was admitted as a town of New Plymouth in 1682.

A number of settlers in Rehoboth who had organized a Baptist church under the Rev. John Myles from Swansea in Wales, asked to be set off as a separate town. Admitted as Swansea in 1667, it had the sad distinction of meeting the first attack by King Philip's warriors from Mt. Hope, across the Kickemuit River.

Falmouth, on the other side of Buzzards Bay from Rochester and Dartmouth, was an offshoot of Barnstable. Isaac Robinson, son of the Rev. John Robinson of Leyden, was one of the earliest settlers. As a Quaker sympathizer he was forced to leave Barnstable, with Consider Hatch and a number of likeminded Friends. They intended to go to the Quaker refuge on Martha's Vineyard, but took a fancy to the land facing Vineyard Sound and decided to stay. A tract, from Woods Hole to Five-Mile River, extending inland four or five miles, was purchased from the natives in 1661 and later confirmed by "Job Notantico, Indian of Suckanesset." Falmouth is more thickly studded with Indian names than any other part of the Cape—Teaticket, Acapesket, and Waquoit on the Sound side; Quisset, Sippowisset, Wepecket, Chapoquoit, and Megansett on the Bay side; and inland Coonamessett. Settlement increased very slowly, and Falmouth was not recognized as a town until 1686.

Except there, and around Woods Hole and at Nickerson Neck on Pleasant Bay, there seem to have been no English settlements on the "back side"—the ocean side—of the Cape. The future towns and villages of Cotuit, Osterville, Hyannis, South Yarmouth, Dennis, Harwich, Chatham, Orleans, and Nauset were inhabited only by Indians before 1690.

When the Plymouth committee bought Nauset (Eastham) from the Indians in 1640, they inquired of the sagamores as to who claimed Billingsgate, the land north of Eastham. The Indians answered "Not any." "Then," said the committee, "that land is ours"; and "the Indians answered, that it was." To quote Henry Thoreau, from whom we have the story: "This was a remarkable assertion and admission. The Pilgrims appear to have regarded themselves as Not Any's representatives. . . . But history says, that when the Pilgrims had held the lands of Billingsgate many years, at length 'appeared an Indian, who styled himself Lieutenant Anthony, who laid claim to them, and of him they bought them.' "

From Eastham onward, Cape Cod grows wilder and bleaker; it is "the forecastle of New England," a high ridge of sand with one stratum of clay—the Clay Pounds—running across it. On the Bay side are sheltered beaches and the shallow Wellfleet Harbor; on the back side, the Highlands of Truro, constantly being eaten away by the Atlantic surges.

Wellfleet and Truro were not settled during the life of Plymouth Colony; and, at the site where the Pilgrims first landed, no houses were built before the following century. The "Not Any" lands became the property of the Province of Massachusetts Bay when it absorbed Plymouth Colony; hence they were called the Province Lands, and the village, Provincetown. The tip of the Cape, behind Race Point, is still "Province Lands" today; the State must see that they are kept well planted with beach grass and dwarf pines so that they will not blow away. Here, if you wish, you may see the rosy dawn over the Atlantic as if you were in a ship at sea; and at evening, in old Homer's words, observe the sun's shining torch sink below the Ocean's rim.

All Cape Cod, and all Plymouth Colony, once belonged to the Indians; and if the claim of "Lieutenant Anthony" was somewhat belated, nobody could contest it. So, before we get on with the story of the Old Colony, let us see how they got on with the original owners.

☙ XXIII ☙

INDIAN PROBLEMS

᚛᚛᚛᚛᚛᚛᚛᚛᚛᚛᚛᚛᚛᚛᚛᚛᚛᚛᚛᚛᚛᚛᚛᚛᚛

THE COLONY'S LAND POLICY

DURING the last one hundred years, the American treatment of Indians and Negroes has lain heavily on the national conscience, since so much of it has been contrary to the principles of liberty, equality, and justice that Americans profess to uphold. And new myths and slogans have arisen about it. "The Indians were cheated out of their land by getting them drunk"; "The Indians were exterminated," and the like offset the old white pioneer myths: "Indians are nomads, hunters; they have no right to the land"; "All Indians are cruel and treacherous"; "A good Indian is a dead Indian." [1]

---

[1] For instance, William Maxwell Evarts said: "The pious ones of Plymouth . . . reaching the Rock, first fell upon their own knees and then upon the aborigines."

The basic fact was the sudden clash of a civilized race with a backward one. That has always been unfortunate if not fatal to the backward peoples—the Australian aborigines, the Polynesians, and many African Negroes are examples. Scientists who have made a study of backward races tell us that they ought to be let alone to keep their religion and their tribal customs. That has never happened. The conquering race (and this is as true of the Moslems and Hindus as of Christians) always feels duty-bound to impose its religion and culture upon the native. The American Indian could not be fitted to live under English law, to absorb English culture, or to embrace English forms of Christianity until he had had a chance to get used to the English; and the process was so painful as to be a calamity. He was glad to get the white man's tools, guns, and liquor, but the Englishman expected him to take the whole of his culture, including Puritan theology, in one package. That was like expecting a stone-age savage to be at home in a modern skyscraper apartment. New Plymouth tried hard to be fair and just to the natives; but its best was not good enough to absorb them without a conflict.

At any time down to, say, 1680, the Indians could have thrown the English out of North America if they had been able to unite. But they were in a chronic state of intertribal warfare when the white man arrived; and, wherever he landed, he was welcomed as an ally. The Algonkins used the French against the Mohawks; New York depended on the Mohawks to protect them from the French; and Massasoit welcomed the Pilgrims as protection against the Narragansetts. Half a century passed, and the Indians of southern New England did unite under Massasoit's son Metacom, better known as King Philip. How that came about, the causes of the most colorful, tragic, and hard-fought war in colonial history, is the subject of this chapter.

Josiah Winslow, Governor of Plymouth Colony when that war broke out, once declared: "I think I can clearly say that the English did not possess one foot of land in this Colony but what was fairly obtained by honest purchase of the Indian proprietors. We first made a law that none should purchase or receive of gift any land of the Indians without the knowledge of our Court. And lest they be straitened, we ordered that Mount Hope, Pocasset, and several other necks of the best land in the Colony, because more suitable and convenient for them, should never be bought out of their hands."

This was almost literally true. The Pilgrims did not buy their original site at Plymouth, because no Patuxet was alive to sell—except Squanto, who, had he but known, might have got a good price and retired. All other land in the Colony was bought from the Indian owners or claimants before settlement, unless there was "not any," as at Billingsgate. Whenever a claimant did turn up, he was paid. There is even an instance of an Indian making good a claim and collecting the money twenty-two years after the English had settled on a piece of unoccupied land. Governor and Assistants insisted that even before bargaining started, the Englishmen must have a permit from them to buy, and they confirmed no lands to white settlers until they had good evidence that the Indian owners and claimants had been satisfied. William Nickerson, a Freeman of Yarmouth, for "buying of land of the Indians contrary to order of Court, and for not appearing when summoned," was fined and even disfranchised. If the natives refused to part with their land, the government told would-be settlers to go elsewhere. And certain tracts, as Governor Winslow said, such as King Philip's headquarters at Mt. Hope, were made permanent reservations, not subject to sale or purchase.

Whether the prices paid were fair is another question. Most of the purchases, in terms of matchcoats, axes, and wampum, seem absurdly low to us; but it must be remembered that the Indian wanted these things as much as or more than the white man wanted land. Moreover, these transactions were not regarded by the Indians as final. They or other members of the tribe usually came back for more within a few years, and got it, too. King Philip himself not only sold land for a good price in money (£190 for a four-mile tract to Taunton in 1672), but asked and received money for confirming some of his father's bargain sales.

It was always illegal to give or sell the Indians alcoholic liquors; and there is no recorded example in Old Colony history of that familiar picture in American mythology, the redskin bartering his ancestral hunting grounds for a jug of firewater labeled "XXX."

THE INDIAN "D. P.'S"

◄§ MOST of the land that the Indians sold was not village sites or cornfields, but hunting ground. In some cases, however, they did sell their home sites. The problem then arose of what to do about what we might call "displaced Indians." Many did not understand what selling land meant—they looked on it simply as allowing the English to move in, not as an agreement to vacate. Often they solved the problem by

moving into some corner of land near by, building new wigwams, and continuing to hunt and fish and gather basket
materials on the land they had sold to the English.[2] Although
this was usually tolerated, the colonists, especially the common people, did not like to have Indians living near by.
Their habits were filthy and unpleasant; they seldom would
work for wages, and they were a bad example of idleness—
"waste of precious time." When two sachems who came before the General Court of Massachusetts were told: "You
are not to do unnecessary work on the Sabbath"; they replied: "That will be easy: we haven't much to do any day,
and can well take our ease on the Sabbath!"

Plymouth legislation marked the Indians as a subject race.
They could own a horse but not a mare—probably to prevent them from breeding low-grade horses—and they could
not own a boat bigger than a canoe—probably to prevent
piracy—or be given alcoholic liquor. There was a five-pound
fine for any white man who broke this law. Until 1665 they
were not allowed to buy or own firearms. The prohibition
was then lifted at the Indians' request because game was
becoming so scarce that they could no longer get their meat
with bow and arrow. But it was revived whenever there appeared to be danger of war. An Indian could earn a bounty
of twelve shillings or a coat of "duffels"—a coarse woolen
cloth—for killing a wolf, and he hadn't much chance of getting a wolf without a gun.

The most frequent complaint by friendly Indians against
Englishmen was about cattle. Cows, pigs, and horses would
break into the Indian cornfields and destroy their corn. The
town of Rehoboth, adjoining the Wampanoag country, was

---

[2] In Middleborough, for instance, the Indians after selling out retired to "Betty's Neck" and about forty were still living there in 1794.

the most frequent offender. Year after year we find the Plymouth Government fining Rehoboth, ordering the town to build fences around Indian cornfields at its own expense, and to construct a "pound" where Indians could leave stray animals until the owner claimed them and paid damages. Nothing seemed to stop Rehoboth cows; they would even swim across Taunton River to get at the corn.

On the other side, the most common charge of colonists against Indians was theft; for if an Indian found an ax, hoe, or other article that he wanted, he was apt to pick it up. Pigs, too, were a great temptation; the Indians caught them in the woods and cut off their ears to remove the owners' marks; so it became a serious offense to own an earless pig. Plymouth law required fourfold restitution of the value of goods stolen by Indians; and if they could not pay, they had to work it out. One such, an "incorrigible thief" who had escaped from jail where he was serving a term for burglary, then stole a horse and was still "shirking and lurking about." He was sentenced to be sold as a slave to Barbados, both to satisfy his debts "and to free the collonie from soe ill a member." But the very same day, Captain William Macomber, for "abusing two old Indians" and on the Sabbath at that, was fined forty shillings and given a public whipping.

As the latter case shows, Plymouth courts treated English offenders against Indians as severely as the Indians were punished the other way round. We have already told how the Peach gang was hanged for murdering Penowayanquis. Indians haled into Plymouth courts were not bound by English rules of giving testimony on oath, or subject to the penalty of perjury if they lied. Indians sometimes served on juries that tried members of their own race. And allowances were made for the Indians' ignorance. The penalty for rape in Plymouth Colony was death; but "Sam the Indian," who confessed to raping Sarah Freeman, got off with a whipping and an order to leave the Colony, "considering he was but an Indian and therefore in an incapacity to know the horribleness of the wickedness of this abominable act."

CONVERSION OF THE INDIANS

WHEN the Rev. John Robinson at Leyden heard about Myles Standish's exploit at Wessagussett, he wrote to Governor Bradford: "Concerning the killing of those poor Indians, Oh, how happy a thing had it been, if you had converted some before you had killed any!" The Pilgrims took this to heart; but how to begin? They had no organized church behind them to supply missionaries, as the French and Spaniards had. Their own ministers were few, and very busy trying to keep young Pilgrims on the straight and narrow path. Nevertheless, they did a great deal to convert the natives to Christianity.

Massasoit, shrewdly suspecting that missionaries would undermine his authority, would have none of them. But as early as 1641, Richard Bourne, a merchant of Sandwich, and Captain Thomas Tupper, a farmer and soldier of the same town, began to try and convert the Nausets of Cape Cod. That was five years before the Rev. John Eliot started his famous mission in Massachusetts. The "Apostle Eliot" himself preached to the Nausets who lived near Yarmouth, in their own language, in 1648.

The Pilgrims' problem was made easier in 1649 when Parliament, at the instance of Governor Winslow, chartered the Society for the Propagation of the Gospel in New England.

This society not only supported Eliot's efforts, which included translating and printing the entire Bible in the Algonkian language, but supported missions in the Old Colony. Richard Bourne was appointed superintendent of Praying Indians by the Colony in 1665. Five years later he was ordained pastor of the first Indian Congregational church, in the present town of Mashpee. From the Colony he obtained a grant of land which extended five miles one way and ten the other, for his converts, who were settled in eight or nine different villages, but with one church. These efforts have lasted to this day, as the Town and First Church of Mashpee. The minister there still receives a small addition to his salary from Harvard College, as interest on a sum left to Harvard for that purpose in 1697 by the Honorable Robert Boyle, the celebrated Irish chemist and philanthropist.

The Rev. Samuel Treat of Eastham and the Rev. John Cotton of Plymouth also learned the Indian language and took great pains to preach in their villages and make converts. By 1674 there were "Praying Indian" villages, not only in Mashpee, but along Cape Cod from Barnstable to Truro, at Middleborough, and at Wareham on Buzzards Bay.[3] Thomas Hinckley was appointed a sort of roving judge to visit these towns, hold court, and help the Indians to govern themselves. The Colony then contained over a thousand converted Indians. One hundred and forty-two of them had been taught to read their own language, as

---

[3] Richard Bourne's Report of 1674 to Daniel Gookin names the following settlements of Praying Indians in the Old Colony: Meeshawn and Punonakit in Truro and Wellfleet; Potanumaquut in Eastham; Manamoyik in Chatham; Sawkattuket (Harwich), Nobsquassit (Yarmouth), and Matakees in Yarmouthport; Cheehwacket in Barnstable; Satuit, Cotuit, and six other villages in Mashpee; Pispogutt and Wawagontat in Wareham; Succonussett in Falmouth; Titicut and Assowamset in Middleborough.

printed in the Rev. John Eliot's *Up-Biblum God,* printed at Cambridge in 1663.

The number had risen to 1,439 in 1685.[4] And, without exception, these Praying Indians remained loyal to the Colony during the desperate war started by Philip of Pokanoket.

THE COLONY'S ARMY

෴ ALTHOUGH Plymouth Colony had never yet fought in a real war, and was not well prepared for this one, the martial spirit of Myles Standish and the early Pilgrims had not disappeared. The Colony required every able-bodied man between the ages of sixteen and sixty, ministers and schoolmasters alone exempted, to be enrolled in the militia, which drilled on the village green several times a year.

Every militiaman had to provide himself with a musket, a sword or cutlass, bandolier and knapsack, and an initial supply of powder, bullets, and match. The heavy matchlock musket with its rest was now giving way to the lighter and more efficient flintlock. Men who could not afford a musket carried a long pike. Pikemen were supposed to protect musketeers from an enemy charge while they were reloading. This militia army was divided into companies of about forty-five officers and men each, the men electing their company officers. There was no bigger "brass" in the Colony than a major, who was appointed by the General Court. Plymouth Colony had no such thing as field artillery, and but one cavalry troop. Nobody had anything even slightly resembling a uniform, except that an officer might sport his father's old corslet and helmet, if he had one. A buff or

---

[4] These figures do not include children under twelve.

"russet" long-skirted woolen coat was the favorite garment, because troops usually had to sleep outdoors without a blanket.

Wars were not fought by the entire militia. Only young and active men were of any use in fighting Indians; the rest served as home guards. When a campaign was about to start, the General Court decided on the number of men to be raised by each town, and if enough did not volunteer, they were "pressed," that is, drafted. Any draftee who chose could hire a substitute to take his place. The wartime pay scale ranged from a shilling and sixpence a day for a private to five shillings a day for a captain. The troops were never paid promptly, because responsibility for their pay rested on the towns, not the Colony; those who turned out to defend Swansea in the summer of 1675 were still unpaid a year later.

As the Colony had plenty of warning that there might be trouble, certain strongly built houses in each settlement were designated garrison houses. Loopholes were pierced in their thick wooden walls, arms, munitions, and supplies were stored in the cellars and garrets, and what we would call a quartering bill was drawn up, stating which families would pile into what garrison house when an alarm of Indians was given.[5] But for this garrison house and militia system, most of the Plymouth population west of Cape Cod would have been wiped out in King Philip's War.

---

[5] A good example of these garrison houses was Russell's Garrison in the Padanaram section of South Dartmouth. Its foundations have been restored and marked.

❧ XXIV ❧

PHILIP
OF
POKANOKET

᚛◆

THE WAMPANOAGS

WHO WAS this Philip? What dreams and devils haunted his imagination? Did he aim to build a native empire on the ashes of Puritan New England? Or was he just a poor underdog, so often kicked that he finally went mad? Or something else again?

Massasoit, sachem of the Wampanoags or Pokanokets, always a faithful friend to the English, died in 1661, leaving two sons named Wamsutta and Metacom. Neither became a Christian; but Wamsutta, when visiting Plymouth to

"make his number," declared that he and his brother
wanted English names. So the General Court, prompted by
some member who had read Greek history, named them Alexander and Philip. Alexander's reign was brief. He caught
a fever while staying at the Winslows' "Careswell" and died
shortly after reaching home. His widow Weetamoe, and his
brother, always believed that he had been poisoned.

In 1662, Philip succeeded to the "throne" of Massasoit
at what is now Mt. Hope, a beautiful hill on a peninsula
that extends into the Taunton River.[1] His "kingdom" extended north into Massachusetts and, in theory, covered
all the Indians of Plymouth Colony. But, unlike his father,
he had no authority outside Pokanoket (the present town of
Bristol, R. I.) and the eastern shore of Narragansett Bay.
The present towns of Tiverton and Little Compton were
ruled by his lady lieutenants, Weetamoe and Awashonks, the
squaw sachem of Sakonnet. His own subjects, by 1674, were
estimated to be only a thousand in number. On their western
border the Wampanoags were hemmed in by the Providence
Plantations of Roger Williams, and by the Narragansetts.
Philip brooded over what his father had once been—lord of
all southeastern New England; and what he was, ruler over a
few thousand acres, crowded by the English and Narragansetts. And he was a proud young prince.

Immediately after his accession Philip was summoned to
Plymouth and questioned about an alleged conspiracy between the Wampanoags and Narragansetts. He denied it and
offered to leave a younger brother as hostage. The Court,

---

[1] Mt. Hope is plainly visible on the right as you cross Mt. Hope
toll bridge from Newport to Bristol. Mr. Haffenreffer, who now owns
the property, has an interesting museum of local Indian antiquities;
and Philip's alleged "throne," carved out of rock, can be seen.

evidently satisfied, declined to accept the hostage, renewed the treaty of 1621 and offered to give Philip any friendly assistance he and his people needed.

Nothing happened for several years. In the meantime, Philip, who is described by one who knew him as "exceedingly fond of elegant apparel," was selling more land to the English in order to pay his tailor's bills in Boston. And there was almost continual trouble between the Wampanoags and the towns of Rehoboth, Taunton, and Swansea about trespassing cattle. Several unpleasant incidents occurred. Ninigret, sachem of the Niantic tribe in eastern Connecticut and a rival of Philip, accused him in 1667 of plotting to join the French and Dutch against the English. The Plymouth Government sent Josiah Winslow to investigate, and held a hearing on the subject at Rehoboth, which ended in giving Philip a clean bill of health. But it did not change his ways.

In 1671, rumors again reached Plymouth of a conspiracy headed by Philip. Again he was summoned to a conference, this time on Taunton Green. According to English accounts, the sachem confessed that he had "through indiscretion and the naughtiness of his heart" taken up arms with intent to attack his English friends, but he now repented and wished to renew the treaty. He promised to deposit all his firearms as security for good behavior, and was dismissed.

Two months later, in June, the General Court met at Plymouth. Governor Prence's intelligence service reported that Philip still had plenty of firearms, and that he was trying to make Plymouth "odious to the neighbor colony." The General Court then declared forfeit the weapons that Philip had deposited, and distributed them among the towns. It appointed a Council of War, consisting of the Governor and Assistants and eight representatives, and

sent delegates along Cape Cod to receive promises of friendship and loyalty from the sagamores in that region.

Philip refused to give up any more arms; he claimed that
he had agreed at Taunton only to deposit those that
his men brought with them. He now appealed his case to
the Government of Massachusetts Bay, which wrote to Governor Prence that it thought Plymouth was treating
Philip too harshly, and offered to mediate the quarrel. The
Colony accepted this offer, and Philip, when assured that
Massachusetts would be represented, came to Plymouth
Town in September 1671. Governor Leverett of the Bay Colony was there, and Governor John Winthrop, Jr., of Connecticut. Philip had his day in court, admitted that he had done
wrong, and was advised by this informal council of the three
colonies "to humble himself unto the Magistrates and to
amend his ways if he expected peace; and that, if he went
on, he must expect to smart for it." Again he made his submission, acknowledged that he was subject to the Government of New Plymouth, and as a sign of loyalty promised
to pay an annual tribute of five wolves' heads and a fine of
£100 within three years. Philip and five sagamores signed
a paper to that effect, Philip signing with his usual big capital P, as befitted a king. And at the same time he agreed to
sell no more land without the Colony's permission.

MURDER OF SASSAMON

⁕ THERE was no more trouble for three years, and in
1674 the Plymouth Government again permitted the sale of
firearms to the natives. Then everything boiled up with the
murder of John Sassamon. That converted Indian, a
protégé of the Rev. John Eliot, attended Harvard College,

acted for a time as Philip's secretary and interpreter, and
then qualified as preacher to one of the Praying Indian towns.
When visiting his former employer he picked up so many
alarming rumors and so much evidence that Philip was plotting with other tribes to attack the English, that he went
straight to Plymouth to tell Governor Winslow, and begged
him to keep this intelligence secret. But someone blabbed
and the word reached Philip. Three of his men, including
two of his intimate counselors with the fearful names Poggapanoffoo and Mattashannamoo, waylaid Sassamon on the
way home, killed him, and shoved his body under the ice of
Assawompsett Pond in Middleborough.

A friendly Indian named Patuckson happened to see the
murder from a near-by hill, identified the murderers, and
helped the authorities to track them down and bring them to
justice. They were tried by a regular jury augmented by six
of the "most gravest and sage Indians," who fully concurred
in the verdict of guilty. Poggapanoffoo and Mattashannamoo
were executed on 8 June 1675 and the third was shot within
the month.

That was the final humiliation for Philip.

Even before Sassamon's murderers were executed, Englishmen living across Taunton River from Philip's seat on
Mt. Hope could hear him mustering and drilling his warriors, with drums beating and trumpets blaring martial airs.
Important Indians from other nations were seen passing
along the trails, and some of them boasted that they were
about to join the Wampanoags in war. And Philip sent his
womenfolk across the Bay to the Narragansett country—an
ominous sign.

The Plymouth Council of War set a twenty-four-hour
watch in the towns next the Wampanoag country; and on

14 June sent a messenger to Philip with a friendly message advising him to dismiss his "foreign" friends, and assuring him that Plymouth "intended him no wrong nor hurt." No answer was returned.

A last attempt to prevent the war was made by some leading Quakers of Rhode Island. At a conference with Philip at Tripp's ferry, where the Mt. Hope bridge now crosses Narragansett Bay, the sachem spoke his grievances—his loss of land, the hanging of his two friends, English cattle trampling his people's corn, and unscrupulous traders making his subjects drunk. The Quakers proposed that these grievances be arbitrated by some neutral person such as the Governor of New York, but Philip would have none of it. And within a week the war began.

WAR BREAKS OUT

◄§ SWANSEA was the nearest English settlement to Philip, just across the Kickemuit River from Mt. Hope. The people there had been on friendly terms with the Wampanoags, but signs of war were so ominous that in June several left their homes and took refuge on the island of Aquidneck. On Sunday, 20 June, a party of Indians burned two houses at Swansea while the rest of the people were at church. William Salisbury and his son John then returned to look after their property. They saw three Indians running out of their house, and young John shot one of them dead. That proved to be the first shot of King Philip's War.

Next day, 24 June, the Indians returned in force, killed both Salisburys (and cut off their heads and mutilated their bodies), besides killing a number of other inhabitants. The tragic tale of what happened to Mrs. Rachel Mann and her

baby, at the hands of an Indian whom she had nursed
through an illness, is told in a poem written at the time by
Philip Walker, the bard of Rehoboth. These things are not
nice reading; but you must know about them in order to
understand the bitterness and horror of King Philip's War.

The impious acts of these infernal beasts
Acted abroad, and in their hellish nests
Would swell a volume to a magnitude;
One hideous act near us I here include.

A serious, modest well disposéd woman,
Well spoke of all, and ill bespoke of no man,
That oft relieved a sordid, cruel brute
That like a beggar to her oft made suit,
That many years had kept this rogue alive
And in a sickness had the best contrived
To do what in her lay, the best and all
For food, and matters metaphysical;
Yet when surprised upon the Sabbath day
With stretched-out hands did supplicate and pray
This impious beast to stay his fatal stroke
A little time, that she might God invoke,
'Tis like, for pardon for sin, in Christ her Saviour;
This cruel rogue dispatched and would not leave her,
Dash'd out her brains, as he had done before
Her sucking infant, tumbling in its gore,
Firing the houses and killing seven more.[2]

---

[2] A slight error here by the bard. It was not Sunday but Thursday,
and most of the people were in the meeting-house keeping a solemn
day of fast and humiliation as decreed by the General Court. Rachel
Mann had stayed at home because her baby was ailing. The whole of
this long poem is printed in Richard LeBaron Bowen's *Early Rehoboth*,
III, 40-50.

The war had begun. And who was responsible?

Evidence that Philip did try to organize an alliance to attack "Apaum" (as the Indians called Plymouth Colony) and
rub it out, is overwhelming. But it is equally certain that,
like Hitler in 1939, he was unprepared for war when it
came, since he had not yet completed his Indian "axis." Im-
patient young warriors had forced his hand by attacking
Swansea. And what of Plymouth's policy? The discussion as
to whether the Colony did right or wrong reminds one of
the arguments about who was responsible for World War II.
On the one hand, Plymouth is accused of "warmongering"

Indian attack on Salisbury home.

—of hounding Philip into a position where he had no choice but to fight. On the other hand, Governors Prence and Winslow are accused of "appeasement." Some of the Quakers in Rhode Island accused Plymouth of starting the whole thing in order to grab the Wampanoags' land; but of that there is not a shred of evidence. Maybe the Plymouth authorities were not very tactful with Philip—as the pacifists accuse us of not being polite to Hitler and the Japanese—but it is clear enough that nobody wanted war with Philip, that war was postponed as long as possible by diplomacy. The English of New Plymouth were perfectly willing to live and let live. But Philip felt stifled, "encircled," in little Pokanoket. That this was largely his own fault, in selling land, and that New Plymouth had ordered him to stop it, did not occur to him; none of this would have happened if the English had not come to his father's kingdom. He couldn't get out of his head how great Massasoit had been, when the English numbered less than a hundred; and how weak he had become. Perhaps it was not too late to get rid of these Englishmen. Anyway, Philip of Pokanoket would try, or die in the attempt.

And don't suppose that he had no chance. Plymouth Colony's total population is variously estimated between 4,800 and 7,000 in 1675. But Philip could command several hundred warriors right from the start, and he counted on his northern allies to keep Massachusetts Bay busy while he snuffed out the Plymouth settlements one by one. The terrain was all in his favor. If you had been able to fly over the Old Colony in 1675, you would have found it mostly forest and stream. Here and there, at long distances apart, would appear village greens surrounded by wooden houses and a perimeter of cleared cornfields, with meadows along the streams. It was easy for Indians to slip through the woods unseen and jump on a settlement, and very hard to prevent them. People could not always be a hundred per cent alert; farmers had to plow, sow, and reap and feed their stock; women had to cook and tend children and milk cows, in order to live. Total war was impossible for a simple farming and fishing colony that had no support from outside. But it was not impossible for the Indians. Total war was in the Indian tradition, and they knew very well how to wage it.

❧ XXV ❧

KING PHILIP'S
WAR
(1)

◄◄◄◄◄◄◄◄◄◄◄◄◄◄◄◄◄◄◄◄◄◄◄◄◄◄◄◄◄◄◄◄◄◄◄◄◄◄◄

THE OPENING PHASE

Plymouth Colony never forgot that June of 1675, when mothers dared not let children out of their sight, fishermen stayed at home to protect their families, farmers could hoe corn only if someone protected them with a gun, and most of the young men marched off to war.

Philip hoped to localize the war—to make "Apaum" his Poland—but he soon learned his mistake. Governor Winslow heard of the first raid on Swansea at Marshfield on the night of 20-21 June, and promptly sent a messenger to Boston. Governor Leverett received the word at 4.00 P.M. on the 21st, summoned his council promptly, and decided to help the Old Colony. Within a couple of days, troopers and foot soldiers from the Bay Colony were tramping down the old road to Providence, via Dedham, Wrentham, and Rehoboth, followed by two-wheeled ox-carts bearing provisions and ammunition. And at the same time troops from Plymouth Colony took the old Indian trail that passed through Middleborough, Bridgewater, and Taunton.

By 28 June, there had converged on Swansea a company of foot soldiers under Captain William Bradford of Plymouth, a second company under 77-year-old Captain James Cudworth of Scituate, a Massachusetts mounted company under Captain Daniel Henchman, a troop of Bay cavalry under Captain Thomas Prentice, and a volunteer company from Boston under Captain Samuel Mosely. The last-named was a privateer captain just returned from Jamaica, "an excellent soldier and of undaunted spirit," who recruited his company from sailors and others not liable to military service, with a sprinkling of pirates whom the captain had just captured in the West Indies. These were released from jail on condition that they fight Indians.

The Bay troopers first made contact with Philip's men, who surprised them and drove them back in disorder. Next, Mosely's company almost trapped the sachem's force. Philip cleverly got out of the trap by embarking his men in canoes and crossing the bay to Pocasset (Tiverton, Rhode Island). The English had no navy, not so much as a boat patrol, to stop him. Major Thomas Savage soon arrived at Swansea with reinforcements from Massachusetts, bringing the total up to 500, and took command as the senior officer present.

He led the English force into Philip's now deserted territory, the Pokanoket peninsula. On the way they found the heads of eight Englishmen stuck up on poles, a display that Philip had specially arranged to terrify them.

Major Savage foolishly took time out to throw up earthworks on Mt. Hope, and then made an armed demonstration in the Narrangansett country, which was completely useless. If he had only acted in concert with the Plymouth troops who were trying to surround Philip in Pocasset, the sachem and his army might have been bagged. And the aged Captain Cudworth was not too bright, either. On the excuse that supplies had given out and the army had to eat, he led a

King Philip escapes.

large part of the Plymouth force home, leaving only a small number at Pocasset to watch Philip. The Plymouth authorities ordered him to turn right around and march back.

During his absence Captain Matthew Fuller, with about forty Plymouth men, attempted an amphibious raid on Pocasset from Aquidneck Island. Landing on the shore of Punkatees Neck, just west of Tiverton Four Corners, they marched into a pea-field, but did not get far. On the nearby hillside were a multitude of Indians, "their bright guns glittering in the sun," and all running like the devil in order to surround the English. Fuller's men formed a defense perimeter on the beach and managed to hold off the Indians until a sloop sailed over from the Rhode Island shore and evacuated them.

In the meantime, Philip was free to raid deep into New Plymouth territory. At Dartmouth all the village houses, some thirty in number, were burned, and many of the inhabitants—most of them Quakers—were slaughtered. The Indians tortured some by skinning them while they were still alive.

In the attack on Dartmouth, the garrison houses held out; and 160 Indians, upon assurance of being treated as prisoners of war, surrendered to Captains Eels and Earle, who had come to the town's assistance. But so great was the fury and fear aroused by recent attacks that these promises were repudiated by the General Court and the whole lot were shipped to Spain, to be sold as slaves.

Middleborough was devastated on 9 July, but everyone living there escaped to Plymouth and saved their necks. Things looked bad even for Plymouth Town. But Indians, fortunately, never followed up a victory. They stayed around the spot looting, feasting on the cattle and pigs that they had killed, and mutilating the bodies of the slain. So there was time to put the militia of the other towns into a warlike posture.

The war should have ended at Pocasset. Major Savage, upon his return from the Narragansett country on 19 July, led an advance into the cedar swamp where Philip had his headquarters.[1] This foray was a complete failure. The Indians, nimble as fleas, always kept one jump ahead of the English, whose plight was described by one of them thus:— "eyes muffled with the leaves, arms pinioned with the thick boughs of the trees, as their feet were continually shackled with the roots spreading every way in these boggy woods." Yet an Indian prisoner said later that if the English had been a little more resolute, they could have caught Philip.

Believing that he had the sachem bottled up, Savage marched most of his force back to Boston, leaving only Henchman's and Cudworth's companies to keep the cork closed; and the Plymouth company marched off on 29 July to garrison Dartmouth. That was the greatest blunder of the war. The crafty Philip, after seeing Cudworth's men march away, broke out of his retreat on 30 July, crossed the Taunton River again in canoes, and, tardily pursued by Henchman, marched up the Blackstone Valley to join forces with his fellow redskins in central Massachusetts.

This Mt. Hope campaign, as they called it, was a complete failure. Now the war would spread, but how far? Might not even the dreaded Mohawks get into it? If they did—good-by New England!

---

[1] Still called Pocasset Cedar Swamp. It is in Tiverton, R. I., adjoining the Fall River city line.

THE NIPMUKS JOIN PHILIP

~§ Philip's first allies were the Nipmuks, who spoke the same language and fought as fiercely. They occupied most of the land between upper Narragansett Bay, the Merrimac, and the Connecticut. The Bay Colony, relying on Nipmuk friendship, had imprudently allowed isolated settlements to be made at Worcester and Brookfield on the old "Bay Path" to Springfield. These Nipmuks were much more numerous than the Wampanoags, but not so well organized. They were under several independent sachems or sagamores, of which the most powerful were Monoco or One-eyed John, Matoonas, Shoshanim or Sagamore Sam, and Muttaump.

These sachems may have been in cahoots with Philip from the first, but they were not prepared to strike when his men attacked Swansea. They watched how the war went in Plymouth Colony before deciding. Matoonas's men attacked Mendon in the upper Blackstone Valley on 16 July, but this seems to have been another case of "heady young warriors" jumping the gun. In any case, Philip's arrival in the Nipmuk camp on 1 August ended all hesitation. On the very next day a troop of horsemen sent from Boston to parley with Monoco were ambushed by his Indians, and eight English were killed. Next, Muttaump's warriors besieged the garrison house at Brookfield in which the entire population of that frontier settlement had taken refuge. The garrison put up a stout resistance, and the siege was raised on 4 August by the arrival of Major Simon Willard and a cavalry troop. But all the dwelling-houses in Brookfield had been destroyed, and the town was now abandoned.

It is hard for us to imagine the horror of these Indian raids on New England villages. If the people were warned in time they crowded into the garrison houses, and the men took pot shots at any Indian that came within range. In the meantime, the redskins, whooping and yelling hideously, were plundering and burning every dwelling-house and barn, digging up corn or valuables that had been hastily buried, killing or mutilating all the cattle, swine, and horses that they could not use, destroying the mills, and even breaking up the millstones so that the people could not grind corn. Shrieks of tortured animals and sometimes of tortured people were mingled with war-whoops; flames and smoke and the stench of burning flesh were everywhere. When the Indians retired, or were driven away by the arrival of a troop of horse, there was nothing for the people to do but take refuge in some other settlement until the war was over.

The Indian allies, after attacking Lancaster, turned west against the scattered settlements along the Connecticut River. In late August and September, Deerfield, Hadley, Hatfield, Springfield, and Northfield were attacked. Captain Lothrop, ambushed at the Bloody Brook near Deerfield on 18 September, lost two thirds of his force of ninety men, "the very flower of the county of Essex." Deerfield had to be abandoned, Northfield was wiped out, and all except the garrison houses in Springfield were burned. Every town in the valley was threatened, and it looked as if all Massachusetts west of Sudbury would have to be abandoned to the enemy.

By October it seemed that the Indians were winning the war. North of Massachusetts, the Abnaki began to attack English settlements along the Maine coast. And the Mohawks had not yet been heard from; Philip was known to have crossed the Berkshire Hills on a "diplomatic mission" to obtain their alliance. The New England Confederation begged Governor Andros of New York to keep them quiet. He managed to do so, but was unable to prevent the Dutch traders of Albany from selling muskets and ammunition to Philip's men. Fortunately the Mohawks regarded Philip and his people with contempt, which they expressed by killing and scalping a few members of the royal suite.

The New England Confederation met in Boston on 9 September and voted unanimously that the war was just and necessary and that it ought to be paid for by the United Colonies. But no commander-in-chief was appointed, except for specific expeditions. Governor Leverett continued to command the Massachusetts forces, Governor John Winthrop, Jr., those of Connecticut, and Governor Winslow, those of Plymouth.

THE NARRAGANSETTS AND THE GREAT SWAMP FIGHT

◆§ SO FAR, only the Wampanoags, Nipmuks, and Abnakis were fighting. What if the Narragansetts should join King Philip's "axis"? They had as many warriors as the other three allies together, and their country adjoined that of the Nipmuks on the north.

Canonchet, son of Miantonomo, was summoned to Boston, where he promised the Confederation to keep the peace and to surrender enemy Indians who had taken refuge in his country, by 28 October. That day passed, and none were given up; according to the best intelligence that reached Boston, Canonchet had decided that the redskins were winning the war and that he had better join if he wanted any of the loot. But he intended to wait until spring, when the new foliage would afford his warriors good cover for surprise attacks.

The United Colonies decided that the Narragansetts "doe but juggle with us"; that they must be destroyed, or the Narragansetts would destroy them. On 12 November 1675 the Confederation voted to raise a thousand men for an expeditionary force, of which forty-six-year-old Governor Josiah Winslow of Plymouth was appointed commander in chief. Massachusetts contributed 540 troops, commanded by Major Appleton; Connecticut sent 315, together with 150 Mohegan Indians; and Plymouth contributed 158 men, led by Captain William Bradford.

Canonchet was delivered an ultimatum: if he did not give hostages for peace within a week, he could expect the worst.

On Thursday, December 2, a day of solemn fast was held throughout New England. The inhabitants gathered in their meeting-houses and listened tensely as their ministers exhorted them to be firm and courageous, and invoked the blessing of the Lord of Hosts on their enterprise. Four days later, when the Plymouth contingent was ready to march, the War Council of the Colony issued this address to the militia:

GENTLEMEN SOLDIERS:

The providence of God so disposing that we are still exercised under the calamity of a war, and the Councils and Authority of the several Colonies resolving that there is a necessity of sending forth a considerable force, with all possible speed; it is desired and required that each Colony, and every particular Town, present their ablest and most suitable men, to be improved in that service; and the Governor and Council of this Government request that our people in the several plantations thereof will express their wonted cheerfulness and courage in engaging therein. And

for your encouragement thereunto, you may please take notice that our Governor is designed to have the conduct of
all the United Forces, of whose particular favor and kindness
you may be well assured; and also that special and effectual
care is and shall be taken, that those that go forth shall in
all respects be comfortably provided for, according to the
season and service, and that the lands and other profits of
the war that have been obtained, or by the blessing of God
shall be gained, shall be kept as security for the soldiers' pay
that have been and shall be improved, and shall not be sold
or disposed but to answer that end. The worshipful Captain
Bradford and Captain John Gorham are your particular commanders. Such as cheerfully tender themselves to the expedition, or to press, shall be looked upon with singular respect.

Governor Josiah Winslow had succeeded Myles Standish
as commander of the Colony's militia. As general of a mixed
force from three colonies, he proved a valiant leader.

On 18 December the three contingents made rendezvous
at a place then called Pettyquamscott (now Wickford, Rhode
Island) on the west side of Narragansett Bay. The one house
at Pettyquamscott, a garrison, had been destroyed by the
Indians shortly before, and all the men, women, and children
within it had been killed. Winter struck early that year, and
Winslow's army had to spend the night outdoors in the snow.
The Governor had accurate intelligence from an Indian deserter that the Narragansetts had fortified themselves on an
island in a "hideous swamp" eighteen miles inland, and that
no fewer than 3,500 of them—counting the women and children—were inside the fort.

Winslow knew that time was of the essence of victory;
resolutely he decided to attack at once. Breaking camp before dawn 19 December, the English marched inland through

deep snow, in a long column—the Indian guide and Mosely's company in the van, the Bay troops next, then Governor Winslow on horseback with the Plymouth companies, and the Connecticut forces under Major Treat in the rear. Not even halting to eat, they arrived before the fort in the early afternoon.

The Narragansetts' wigwams were protected by several rows of palisades about fifteen feet thick, and the Indians were well supplied with firearms, powder, and lead. A reconnaissance showed that one entrance only was possible—a gap in the palisade bridged by a big tree trunk. It was covered by a blockhouse, but a breach had to be made there, or nowhere. Drums beat and trumpets blew the signal to charge, and picked troops rushed the bridge. Six officers were killed outright in this rash but necessary assault; four others, including Captain Gorham of Barnstable, were fatally wounded. Captain Bradford was badly wounded but recovered. But the survivors succeeded in getting over the big tree, other troops rushed in, and there ensued a fierce melee of hand-to-hand fighting with clubbed muskets, cutlasses, and pistols. The Indians were driven out, then rallied and returned. But after three hours' bitter fighting they were completely beaten and the survivors fled. The Great Swamp Fight was over.[2]

Winslow now ordered the wigwams to be burned so that the Indian fugitives could not return. As the flames rose above the bare treetops, snow began to fall. At about four

---

[2] The site of this battle, now marked by a stone monument, is in the town of South Kingston, R. I. It may be seen from the New Haven Railroad on the right, going toward New York, shortly after passing Kingston station.

[OPPOSITE] *Great Swamp Fight.*

o'clock, when it was growing dark, the weary army, carrying the wounded on stretchers, started back to Narragansett Bay. All the wounded but twenty, who died en route, reached the house of Richard Smith at Wickford at two in the morning. They had marched at least thirty-six miles in the snow and fought a decisive battle, all within the space of twenty-two hours.

Losses were severe—seventy killed, including half the company commanders, and one hundred and fifty wounded; but those of the Narragansetts were far heavier. No exact count or reliable estimate of them was ever made, and Canonchet escaped. But it is certain that the military power of the tribe was more than half destroyed, together with their winter food supply.

For about six weeks, though short of provisions and devoid of shelter, Governor Winslow's army remained at Wickford lest the Narragansetts return. Conditions were not unlike those at Valley Forge a century later. Although there was a respite in the fighting, Philip and Monoco and their men, and the Narragansett survivors were still at large. On 28 January 1676 Winslow and his army started plodding northward through the snow, in hope of surprising the rest of the Narragansetts in central Massachusetts. They had so little food that this expedition was known as the "hungry march." It was completely fruitless. After marching about seventy miles, Winslow dismissed the Connecticut troops and led the others to Boston, where they disbanded on 5 February. The Narragansett campaign, after one hard blow, had petered out; but it was none the less true that the Great Swamp Fight was one of our most decisive battles. The New Englanders had acted promptly and fought superbly. They would have been stupid and cowardly indeed if they had lost the war after that.

KING PHILIP'S WAR

(2)

❦❦❦❦❦❦❦❦❦❦❦❦❦❦❦❦❦❦❦❦❦❦❦❦❦❦❦❦❦❦❦❦❦

REPEATED RAIDS AND LOSSES

But the war was then far from being won. Philip, returning from his fruitless mission to the Mohawks, Canonchet with the rest of the Narragansetts, and the Nipmuks, were getting ready for a fresh series of assaults. As the Boston poet Benjamin Tompson wrote:

Some breathing time we had, and short, God knows,
But now alarums from recruited foes

Bounce at our ears; the mounting clouds of smoke
From martyred towns the Heavens for aid invoke.

February, March, and April were the toughest season of
the war for New England. On February 10, a large party of
Indians attacked Lancaster for the second time. They were
beaten off by the arrival of Captain Wadsworth's company,
but not before they had burned all the dwelling-houses except five garrisons, and had carried the minister's wife, Mrs.
Rowlandson, into captivity. Some fifty of the townspeople
were killed in that bloody assault, and Lancaster had to be
abandoned. Medfield caught it next, on February 21. The
Indians retired with their plunder, after burning some thirty
houses and leaving an ominous letter of defiance:

> Know ye that the Indians that thou hast provoked to
> wrath and anger, will war these 21 years if you will; we
> come three hundred this time and there are many Indians
> left. Consider, the Indians lose nothing but their lives; you
> must lose all your fair houses and cattle.

Two nights later, buildings were burned at Weymouth on
the seacoast. Boston women were called out to build an
earth barricade across the neck (now Washington Street)
which connected the capital with the mainland. On March
13, Groton was attacked and many houses burned; the garrisons held out and the people retreated to Concord. On
Sunday the 26th, Marlborough was attacked, partly destroyed, and abandoned. A very large force, said to be several hundred strong, attacked and burned Sudbury on 20
April and defeated Captain Wadsworth's company which
came to its rescue, in the Battle of Green Hill. Over thirty of
the troops including their captain were killed.

While these raids were being conducted by the Nipmuks

under Monoco, Muttaump and Sagamore Sam, Philip and Canonchet were moving with their Wampanoags and Narragansetts against their Number 1 enemy, Plymouth. On Sunday 12 March they attacked the Clark garrison house at Eel River in the south part of the township while the men were attending meeting at Plymouth, and killed all the women and children.

PEIRCE'S FIGHT AT PAWTUCKET

◆§ THE Plymouth Council of War, eager to end this menace, sent Captain Michael Peirce with his company of fifty-three Englishmen from Scituate, Duxbury, and the Cape, accompanied by twenty friendly Indians, in pursuit. On 26 March, on the Seekonk plain in Rehoboth, Captain Peirce fell in with a party of Indians led by Canonchet. Feigning a retreat, they lured the English into an ambush on a river bank where they were surrounded by hundreds of warriors.[1] Captain Peirce formed a ring with his little force and fought so bravely that one hundred and forty of the enemy were killed; but he and his little army were wiped out. Only one Englishman and nine friendly Indians survived "Peirce's Fight," the bloodiest battle ever fought on Plymouth soil.

The Indian victors proceeded to burn forty houses in Rehoboth, and thirty or forty more in Providence. The people there could see that Rehoboth was in flames, but, relying on Rhode Island's neutrality, did nothing to help their neighbors or defend themselves. Roger Williams, who parleyed with Conanchet and proposed to make a peace treaty, was told by the Narragansett sachem that he had 1,500 warriors

---

[1] The location of Peirce's Fight is on the Blackstone River about halfway between the centers of Pawtucket and Central Falls, R. I.

under him (doubtless an exaggeration), "that Englishmen were like women"; that he intended to spend the next month burning towns in Plymouth Colony, and that he might then be ready to talk peace.

Philip Walker, the bard of Rehoboth, wrote a long ballad on "Captain Perse and his Coragios Company" which has come down to us. Here are a couple of the stanzas, with Walker's horrible spelling corrected. The first refers to the fact that Peirce pressed incautiously ahead, not waiting to make rendezvous with the famous company under Captain Mosely, the ex-mariner.

> *It fell unlucky that this march was sooner*
> *Than the appointed time to that mariner;*
> *In thy pickeering*[2] *thou lackst those musketeers*
> *And his experience gained 'mongst buccaneers.*

> *Stout hearts stood to't till last, disdained to fly,*
> *Such odds has made the rogues ere since more shy,*
> *Who have no cause to brag of victory;*
> *But give it out they never so were banged—*
> *I hope in time they'll all be shot or hanged!*

Captain Peirce and his men were soon avenged by a Connecticut contingent under Captain George Denison of Stonington, who captured Canonchet in his own country and gave him to the Mohegans and Pequots to be executed.

But the slaughter at Pawtucket had a depressing effect on the morale of Plymouth Colony. The next levy by the General Court was resisted; men would not leave their home towns, for fear of an Indian attack in their absence. All that could be done was to appoint a war council in each village

---

[2] An old word for reconnoitering.

to see that a twenty-four-hour watch was kept, that garrison houses were properly armed and supplied, and that the people were ordered into them whenever Indians were reported near. One can well imagine how people hated to abandon their homes to be burned and their stock to be killed, and crowd into one small house. But that was the only way to save their lives when the Indians were striking here, there, and everywhere.

THE TIDE TURNS

◆§ THE MOST effective fighting in the spring of 1676 was done by Massachusetts Bay and Connecticut. They sent out small, mobile mounted forces to rush to the rescue of threatened towns and keep the Indians on the move. As the enemy had no means of carrying a quantity of provisions, he was on the verge of starvation by July. Mrs. Rowlandson, captured in the raid on Lancaster, and whom Philip kept by him in hope of getting a rich ransom (which eventually he did), tells in the narrative of her captivity that the Indians were eating the guts and feet of dead horses, as well as frogs, turtles, skunks, and rattlesnakes; "Yea, the very bark of trees." When they raided a settlement they had a feast, but a few days later they were hungry again.

Several hundred Indians camped at the rapids (now Turner's Falls) of the Connecticut River, above Deerfield, to appease their hunger with fresh shad and salmon. Captain William Turner, commanding the garrisons in the river towns, led 180 men to the falls and completely surprised the Indians on 19 May. Several hundred were killed at this Falls Fight, at the cost of only one Englishman, and never again did the Indians win a battle.

On the 24th, Captain Thomas Brattle and a troop of horse pulled a similar surprise on three or four hundred Nipmuks who were fishing at the Pawtucket Falls on Blackstone River, and killed a considerable number, with a loss of only one man killed.

Plymouth Colony now began to pluck up her courage. Governor Winslow reported on 23 May 1676 that all the towns except Scituate—which had been attacked in April, and many of whose fighting men had been wiped out in Peirce's Fight—were eager to march against the enemy. The General Court decided to make more use of friendly Indians, and to order one hundred and fifty white men and fifty Indians to be raised in June for a mobile force; any Englishman who declined to serve to be compelled to run the gantlet or stand a fine of five pounds.

During the hot summer this strategy of attrition began to bear fruit. Indians when attacked now put up a poor fight and many surrendered. A party of two hundred became so desperate for want of food that they "came and submitted themselves to mercy in Plymouth Colony." The Nipmuk sachem Monoco (One-eyed John) surrendered, with one hundred and eighty followers, plus the much-wanted Matoonas as his prisoner. Matoonas, regarded by both sides as a No. 1 war criminal, was promptly executed on Boston Common by Monoco. Sagamore Sam surrendered. Pomham, the one Narragansett sagamore at large, was captured with fifty followers. And Captain Benjamin Church shortly got on the trail of Philip, who, like a modern generalissimo, had not shown himself at the front. He had not been seen, or at least not recognized, by any Englishman since the war began.

CAPTAIN CHURCH'S CAMPAIGN

ᴥ§ CAPTAIN BENJAMIN CHURCH, a native of Duxbury who was living at Little Compton when the war broke, had shown such skill in fighting Indians that Governor Winslow gave him a sort of roving commission, under which he could choose his own officers, recruit his own men, pursue the enemy wherever he might be, and grant quarter to any Indian except certain notorious war criminals. Church was a hero to the Plymouth youth, and the idol of friendly Indians; so he had no trouble in recruiting a mixed force of some one hundred and fifty to two hundred of both races. He and his merry men now combed the swamps and thickets of Plymouth and Bristol Counties in search of human game.

On Sunday, July 30, the captain took time out from campaigning to attend divine worship at Plymouth. Suddenly Governor Winslow at the head of a body of troopers clattered into town, drew up at the meeting-house, and summoned Captain Church to come outside for important news. A main body of the enemy had been sighted near Bridgewater! There wasn't much more preaching that day, for the captain promptly called his men to arms by beat of drum and bustled around collecting provisions. By early afternoon, mounted and waving to the Plymouth girls who were crying "Get Philip! Catch the rogue!" Church's company rode out of town. Next day it was joined by a company of "brisk Bridgewater lads," as Church called them, who en route had captured Unkompoin, Philip's uncle and chief counselor. Unkompoin admitted that the sachem himself was in the neighborhood. Philip was trying to fight his way through to

Pocasset to make a last stand, if need be, at the seat of his ancestors on Mt. Hope.

Church's men now crossed Taunton River and began to beat the woods in search of their wanted prize. They captured his latest wife and his young son, killed a number of Wampanoags, and returned to Plymouth with a pack of prisoners; but no Philip. The Bridgewater boys and Taunton militia continued the mopping up, in the course of which they found the dead body of Weetamoe, the squaw sachem of Pocasset, drowned while trying to cross Taunton River. But still, no Philip.

Dartmouth, where bands of Indians were reported, now needed help. So Church's company got on the march to Buzzards Bay where Lieutenant Jabez Howland—son of *Mayflower* John, and described by Church as "a worthy good Souldier"—captured a sagamore named Sanballet or Sam Barrow. It was he, "as noted a rogue as any among the enemy," who had massacred the women and children at Clark garrison, Eel River. For that he had been given a prominent place on Plymouth's list of war criminals, to whom no quarter was to be given. When informed of this, Sam admitted he deserved to die, but asked the favor of smoking one more pipe of tobacco. When he had taken a few whiffs, he said: "I am ready;" whereupon one of Captain Church's Indians "sunk a hatchet into his brains."

DEATH OF PHILIP

⋙ CAPTAIN CHURCH, "weary and worn" from continuous campaigning, hoped to be excused for the rest of the summer. But Governor Winslow insisted that he go at once in pursuit of Philip. So off he marched with his veterans, red and white,

and reached Mt. Hope without meeting an Indian. Crossing
over to Aquidneck Island with a few of his men, Church
borrowed some horses and rode to Newport to see his wife,
who was staying in the Sanford house. She "fainted with
the surprise"; but before the captain had revived her, even
before his horse was unsaddled, his attention was attracted
by Major Sanford and Captain Golding who dashed up on
horseback. "What would you give to hear some news of
Philip?" cried Golding to Church. "That's what I want!" said
the captain. They then told them that an Indian deserter,
furious with Philip because he had killed his brother, had
come down to Tripp's Ferry (where Mt. Hope Bridge now
crosses) and told them that Philip had reached Mt. Hope.
"Capt. Church thank'd them for their good news, and said,
he hoped by tomorrow morning to have the Rogue's head."

So the captain kissed his wife good-by after a visit that
lasted barely a quarter-hour, mounted, and with his companions "set spurs to their horses and away." Crossing the
ferry to Tripp's house, where Church's company were
resting, they queried the Indian deserter. He confirmed his
story that Philip was camping on a hummock in the "Miery
Swamp" at Mt. Hope, not two miles away. That night Church
silently deployed his men to surround the swamp. Following
his accustomed tactics, his men (in pairs—one Englishman
and one Indian) crept up to the target area "on their bellies,"
crawling from tree to tree, with orders to hold gunfire until
they heard an Indian shout or shoot, when all should open
fire. This was done under cover of night, while the enemy
Indians were sleeping.

It worked perfectly; and we may as well let Captain
Church tell the story.

At break of day, "one of Philip's gang, going forth to ease

himself, when he had done, look'd round him, and Capt. Golding thought the Indian looked right at him, so fired at him; and upon his firing the whole company that were with him fired upon the enemy's shelter before the Indians had time to rise from their sleep. . . . They were soon in the Swamp and Philip the foremost, who, starting at the first gun threw his Petunk [3] and powder horn over his head, catch'd up his gun, and ran as fast as he could scamper, without any more clothes than his small breeches and stockings. They let him come fair within shot; and the Englishman's gun missing fire, he bid the Indian[4] fire away; and he did so to purpose; sent one musket bullet thro' his heart, and another not above two inches from it; he fell upon his face in the mud and water with his gun under him. . . . One of the enemy who seem'd to be a great surly old fellow, halloo'd with a loud voice, and often called out *iootash, iootash* (fight! fight!). . . . It was Annawon, Philip's great captain, calling on his soldiers to stand to it and fight stoutly. . . . When they had drove the Swamp thro' and found the enemy had escaped, or at least the most of them, and the sun now up, and so the dew gone, that they could not so easily track them; the whole Company met together at the place where the enemy's night shelter was; and then Capt. Church gave them the news of Philip's death; upon which the whole Army gave three loud *Huzza's.* Capt. Church ordered his body to be pull'd out of the mire onto the upland; so some of the Captain's Indians . . . drew him through the mud unto the upland, and a doleful, great, naked, dirty beast, he look'd like."

---

[3] The Indian name for a haversack or musette bag.

[4] The former was Caleb Cooke, grandson of Francis, the *Mayflower* passenger; the Indian's name was Alderman, a Pocasset who had been friendly to the English throughout the war.

Philip's body was given the treatment of an English traitor. It was quartered and hung up in the trees; his hands were cut off and sent to Boston, and his head to Plymouth, where it was set up on a pole next Thanksgiving Day.

"For this March," says Captain Church of his company, "they received four shillings and six pence a man, which was all the reward they had, except the honour of killing Philip."

Philip fell on 12 August 1676. Two weeks later Captain Church with two Englishmen and six friendly Indians surprised Annawon, the "great captain," who had escaped to Rehoboth, and he surrendered. The Plymouth General Court condemned Annawon and Philip's brother-in-law Tispaquin to death because they had tortured prisoners. Captain Church pleaded for their lives in vain.

The deaths of Philip and Annawon ended the war in southern New England. Some of his diehard subjects made their way westward through the Iroquois country to the present State of Indiana, where the great French explorer LaSalle found them in 1680.

On Assonet Neck, on the Taunton River opposite Dighton, is a pathetic relic of the once powerful Wampanoags. The Dighton Rock, as it is called, is carved all over with crude outlines of human figures and odd squiggles made by Philip's men and their ancestors.[5] And, a short distance inland, under a pine forest, we can still see the checkerboard

---

[5] Dighton Rock has excited the interest of scholars from the seventeenth century down to the present, and the carvings on it have been at various times ascribed to the Northmen, Phoenicians, Wandering Jews, Chinese, and, of late, Portuguese explorers. But students of Indian culture recognize them as the sort of thing done by Indians of Algonkian stock all over New England. What, if anything, they mean, nobody knows.

outline of an Indian cornfield, untilled since the red men who planted it gathered their last harvest in 1675.

In New Hampshire and Maine, the war dragged on for two years more. The Abnakis had no love for Philip or Canonchet but were so encouraged by the early successes of the Wampanoags and Nipmuks that they decided to have some fun on their own. And before Massachusetts was able to send any substantial help to her Maine district, every little settlement on the coast had either been destroyed or evacuated. New England was too exhausted to push the war against the Abnakis to "unconditional surrender." A negotiated peace, the Treaty of Casco, was made in April 1678. The Indians retained their lands and most of their strength, which they threw against the English in later wars, as allies of the French.

LAST YEARS
OF THE
OLD COLONY

❮❮❮

AFTERMATH OF THE WAR

KING PHILIP'S WAR was a terrible scourge to New England. About twelve settlements were totally destroyed, and forty others damaged. The frontier was flung back almost to the coast; much of the territory lost in Massachusetts and Connecticut was not resettled for forty years. Between five and six hundred men of military age were killed—a loss of eight to ten per cent, far greater than the United States suffered in either World War I or II. Hundreds of families who had lost their homes were living as refugees with families who had been more fortunate; and there was no insurance or government aid to help them rebuild.

No assistance, financial or otherwise, was given by King Charles II, although he managed to send a thousand red-coats to Virginia to put down Bacon's Rebellion. The only succor that came from abroad was a contribution of almost £1,000 for the needy, from the Protestant churches of Dublin in Ireland. Plymouth spent on the war amost £12,000, a sum probably greater in value than the entire personal property of the Colony.[1] No aid came from any other English colony, except a little grain from Bermuda. Ships were sent to Virginia to buy corn, beef, and pork, but Governor Berkeley, who looked on the war as a judgment of God on the New Englanders for disloyalty to Charles I, forbade them to buy provisions in Virginia. No help came even from neighboring New York, where Governor Andros maintained a friendly neutrality.

If Plymouth suffered less than Massachusetts Bay, it was because her Praying Indians remained loyal to their Christian friends, and even helped in the fighting. The Colony showed its gratitude by setting up a system of Indian government in 1682. Every ten adults elected an officer called a tithing-

---

[1] The United Colonies of New England reported to the Crown in 1679 that their total disbursements for the war were: Massachusetts, £46,292; Connecticut, £22,173; Plymouth, £11,743. There is no valuation of the property in New Plymouth at this time, but the burden of the war may be guessed by the taxes. In July 1676, the total tax on the twelve towns of the Colony was £3692 16s. 2d. Scituate had the highest, over £586; Rehoboth came next with £485; while Plymouth and Barnstable tied for third place with £351. In 1677, the first post-war year, the total tax was only £203 15s. 6d., Scituate again leading with £30 10s.; while Rehoboth had fallen down the list to £12, owing to its sufferings in the war.

man, and the tithingmen of each Praying Indian town held court, appointed native constables, and assessed taxes for the native church. "One able discreet man" (the first being John Freeman) was appointed Overseer of the Indians. It was his duty to visit each Indian village at least once a year, assemble the natives, and read the capital and criminal laws of New Plymouth aloud, as they were the only laws that Indians were held to obey. And the Overseer had power to see that justice was done in cases between white men and red. Under this system the number of Praying Indians in the Colony increased fifty per cent in ten years, numbering 1,439 in 1685. By that time they had a dozen preachers of their own race, with names such as Great Tom, Indian Manasseh, Jeremy Robin, Old John, Will Skipeag, and Mr. Sam.

In the course of time, these Praying Indians were absorbed into the white population through intermarriage. Probably there are now more people in the former territory of New Plymouth with Indian blood in their veins than there were when the Pilgrim Fathers landed.

Although the Colony was benevolent to friendly Indians, it treated the prisoners taken in King Philip's War with the utmost severity. They were not considered entitled to civilized usages of war because they had killed women and children and tortured some of their prisoners. Women and children, from whom no danger was feared, were allowed to remain in the Colony, and many were employed as domestic or farm servants. But the General Court ordered that all male captives be sold as slaves outside New England. The free Indian of northern forests made a very poor servant or slave. Nobody wanted him, and one shipload of these poor wretches was hawked about from port to port, with no takers, until purchased by the Moors in Tangier. Proceeds from these sales were looked upon as a proper way to discharge part of the war costs.

Even Indians who took refuge in neutral Rhode Island were sold into servitude. Roger Williams, friend to the natives before the war, took stock in a Providence trading company that sold twenty-seven Indians for less than a pound each to people on Aquidneck and the other islands of Narragansett Bay. But this was on condition that they be set free after a term of years, if they behaved themselves.

THE DOMINION OF NEW ENGLAND

༄ THE GOVERNMENT of New Plymouth went on just as before the war. Josiah Winslow was annually re-elected governor until his untimely death, in December 1680, at the age of fifty-two. "He was a worthy and well-accomplished gentleman," wrote Josiah Cotton, the minister's son; "deservedly beloved by the people, being a true friend to their just liberties; generous, facetious, affable and sincere—qualities incident to the Winslow family."

John Alden, the senior Assistant, who normally would have succeeded Governor Winslow, was now over eighty years old and infirm; Priscilla, still sprightly though a great-grandmother, persuaded him to pass up the honor. So Thomas Hinckley of Barnstable, a comparatively young man of sixty-two, who had been an Assistant for twenty-two years and had fought in the Great Swamp Fight, became Governor of the Colony. His salary was fifty pounds a year. Major William Bradford—a mere stripling of fifty-seven—was now elected to the new office of Deputy Governor, and continued in it until the Colony ended. The same Assistants were elected year after year until they died, when they were suc-

ceeded by such respected leaders as Daniel Smith of Rehoboth, Barnabas Lothrop of Barnstable, and John Thacher of Yarmouth.

The General Court thought that in view of the Colony's
sacrifices, and the fact that it had received no help from England, the King might now be persuaded to grant them a
charter. Governor Winslow wrote to Charles II in 1677, asking for his gracious favor and sending some of Captain
Church's best "souvenirs" of the war—King Philip's wampum
coronet and wampum belt. Unfortunately Winslow's brother-
in-law in England, who was supposed to present the letter
and gifts, kept everything for himself. Charles II of England
never received the regalia of Philip I of Pokanoket.

Early in 1679, the King wrote to the Colony inquiring why
he had not heard from Plymouth since the war. The General Court then drafted a loyal address, to which the King
graciously replied in 1680, confirming Philip's territories to
the Colony and promising a charter "upon due application."
Governor Winslow intended to go to England and see about
it himself; but he sickened and died. James Cudworth was
then appointed the Colony's agent, but he died in England
before he could see the King. And the second substitute, the
Rev. Ichabod Wiswall of Duxbury, crossed the ocean too
late.

There was to be no royal charter for New Plymouth.
Charles II was canceling colonial charters, rather than granting new privileges. One of the last acts of his reign, in 1685,
was to declare the charter of Massachusetts Bay null and
void. Plymouth Colony "solemnly proclaimed" the accession
of James II, hoped for the best, and got the worst.

As James Stuart was intent on suppressing representative
government at home, the English colonies could expect noth-

ing better. In December 1686, Sir Edmund Andros, former Governor of New York, arrived at Boston with a royal commission to govern all New England. This Dominion of New England, as it was called, was to be ruled by Andros with the sole assistance of a council appointed by the King; all elected bodies were abolished. In order to make this Council representative of all parts of New England, the King appointed to it Governor Hinckley, Deputy Governor Bradford, two members of the expiring Court of Assistants, and one other Plymouth man, Nathaniel Clarke. Some of these declined; but Governor Hinckley, thinking he could serve his Colony better by being present rather than absent, attended the several Council meetings, in which he frequently protested against Andros's proceedings. Clarke not only attended but became one of the new government's most pliant tools.

New Plymouth, like her sister colonies, was denied her hard-won liberties while the Dominion lasted. In particular, she lost the right to vote taxes; the Council merely informed each town how much money it must send to Boston annually, and these sums were much higher than the people had been used to paying. In addition, they were told that their land titles were worthless, and they must bring their deeds to Boston and pay to have them confirmed. A particular grievance had to do with the blackfish. Andros, advised by his henchmen that blackfish were whales and that whales were "royal fish," sent sheriffs to seize all the oil that Cape Codders had tried out from stranded blackfish. And a barrel of whale oil was not something that you could easily hide.

For the most part the people of the Colony grumbled but submitted, biding their time. Taunton, however, took part in the resistance to "taxation without representation," which was led by the Rev. John Wise of Ipswich. Taunton town meeting voted that they did not "feel free to raise money on the inhabitants without their own assent in an assembly." Both the town treasurer and town clerk were heavily fined and given jail sentences.

This oppressive government lasted less than three years, because the people of England forced James II to flee to France, and brought in King William III and Queen Mary II as joint sovereigns.

In early April 1689, when the first news of these joyful events reached Boston, the people rose in rebellion, clapped Governor Andros in jail and set up their former elected government. Plymouth promptly followed suit. The Freemen assembled, put the renegade Councilor Clarke in custody, requested Hinckley to resume the governorship (which he did), and summoned a General Court. That body re-elected everyone who had been deposed in 1686, declared a Thanksgiving Day, and proclaimed the new sovereigns. Rhode Island, Connecticut, New York, and New Jersey (which had been added to the Dominion) did the same, thus proving that scrambled eggs can be unscrambled.

For three years more, the Government of Plymouth Colony went on as before Andros. William and Mary were doubtless amused, and perhaps touched, upon receiving an official address from the Colony in which the King is hailed as "another Joshua," and a discreet hope is expressed that the Queen "may prove another Deborah, a nursing mother in our Israel."

In the meantime, the Old Colony had slowly been recovering from Philip's War and even expanding into Philip's old domain, the Pokanoket Peninsula, as well as Weetamoe's Pocasset, and Awashonks's Sakonnet. Upon these lands Bristol, Little Compton, and Freetown were settled after the war. Bristol, which eventually became an important seaport, and Little Compton and Pocasset (renamed Tiverton), were set off to Rhode Island in the following century. Freetown remained in Massachusetts and became the parent town of the city of Fall River.

KING WILLIAM'S WAR

❧ UNDER her restored independent government, New Plymouth took part in the next colonial war, which broke out in 1688. Known in the Colonies as King William's War, it was fought between New England, New York, and the Iroquois on one side, and the French and Abnakis on the other. The Colony raised £750 by taxation in 1689 and levied two hundred men from the militia and fifty Indians, who were placed under the command of Benjamin Church, now promoted major. Church took the Plymouth contingent by sea to Casco Bay in 1689 and marched to the Kennebec, without accomplishing anything.

The following year, Plymouth took part in a very ambitious attempt to capture Quebec. In preparation for it, a new valuation and partial census was made of the Colony, which, according to Mr. Bowen's calculations, indicated that the total white population had risen to 10,105.[2] Some 215 soldiers were drafted for the Canada expedition, together with fifty friendly Indians.

The commander-in-chief of this expedition was Sir William Phips, the self-made knight of Massachusetts Bay. His

---

[2] This increase seems all out of proportion to the other facts known about Plymouth Colony at that time. In my opinion, Mr. Bowen's estimate of the population in 1675—4,884—is too low.

second in command was John Walley of Bristol, an Assistant
of the Old Colony, son of the Rev. Thomas Walley of Barnstable, and forty-six years old. Nobody has ever explained
why Walley was so chosen. Although an active officer of the
militia, he had not even fought in King Philip's War. Benjamin Church apparently was passed over because he preferred to command another raid on the Abnakis in Maine.

The Quebec expedition, two thousand men in thirty-two
ships, sailed from Boston in August 1690. Besides her contingent of fighting men, Plymouth furnished the whaleboats
that were used as landing craft. The fleet made a slow
voyage, arriving off Quebec on October 6. Count Frontenac,
Governor of Canada, had only a thousand troops to defend
his capital, but they put on a very good show; General Walley, after landing the New England troops, made so many
blunders that they were badly beaten by the French and
Indians. Phips then decided to retreat, took the men on
board, and sailed for Boston, losing some of his ships in a
great storm on the passage home. The Canada expedition
was a costly failure.

ANNEXATION TO MASSACHUSETTS

❧ IN THE MEANTIME a struggle was being waged by "pres-
sure groups" at the English court over the fate of New Plymouth. The Colony sent a fulsome address to William and
Mary, and had this one printed so that it could not be lost.
For the last time, New Plymouth begged to be granted a
royal charter. The Rev. Ichabod Wiswall made a second
ocean crossing to try to obtain it; but he had no encouragement in London and proved to be no match for other colonial
lobbyists—the Rev. Increase Mather from Massachusetts

Bay and those from New York. The latter colony had already detached Long Island, Martha's Vineyard, Nantucket, and most of Maine from New England, and wanted to round out its eastern provinces with Cape Cod and the Plymouth Colony.

Wiswall was loath to "trot after the Bay horse," as he put it, but he had no choice. Mather discovered just in time that a new royal commission to Governor Slaughter of New York placed Plymouth under that government; but he had enough influence at court to get Plymouth struck out of the New York document and added to the new charter for Massachusetts Bay. Thus the Bay horse, under its skillful clerical jockey Mather, won the Plymouth prize.

Massachusetts Bay, in the new charter granted by William and Mary in 1691, included all Maine, Nantucket and the Vineyard, and the whole of New Plymouth. As a sop to Plymouth, the Governor, Deputy Governor, and Assistants last elected in the Old Colony, and three or four other leading men, were appointed to the first royal council of the new Province of Massachusetts Bay.

The last General Court of New Plymouth, consisting of Governor Hinckley, Deputy Governor Bradford, six Assistants, and twenty-four deputies of the towns, met on 7 July 1691. It noted that a few towns in Bristol County were not paying their taxes on the excuse that they didn't know whether they belonged to New York or what; and it adjourned after declaring "a day of publique fasting and prayer." For no definite news had yet come from England.

When Sir William Phips, the first royal governor of Massachusetts Bay, arrived with the new charter (May 1692), the Old Colony submitted, glad to be spared from joining New York. The charter was duly proclaimed at Plymouth, and the deputies to the General Court elected that spring took their seats in the new House of Representatives at Boston.

So ended the seventy-two-year history of New Plymouth. The transition was made without trouble or friction, since the laws and institutions of Massachusetts and Plymouth were very similar and the people of both colonies were of the same stock. There is no doubt that annexation was a good thing for the Old Colony; she was now able to take a share in the more abundant life of her wealthier neighbor. Within a few years Plymouth, Duxbury, Barnstable, Falmouth, and Dartmouth had begun to build seagoing vessels and to take a direct part in New England's foreign and West Indies trade. The fisheries at Scituate and on Cape Cod expanded and prospered. Taunton Iron Works established branches elsewhere. Bristol became a lively rival to Newport, R. I. And although many ambitious young men moved to Boston for better opportunities, the Old Colony as a whole marched ahead with the rest of New England.

It is interesting to speculate what might have happened if Plymouth Colony had been granted a royal charter by Charles II. In that event, it would not have been annexed to Massachusetts Bay, because William and Mary respected the charters granted by their predecessors. New Plymouth would have made a fourteenth continental colony in 1775, and a fourteenth State of the Union in 1776. That there was nothing impossible about this may be seen in the United States Census of 1950. The territory of the Old Colony, as now divided between Massachusetts and Rhode Island, had a total population in 1950 of 780,949, which is more than that of New Hampshire, or of Vermont, or of ten other States; more, in fact, than the combined population of Nevada, Delaware, and Wyoming.

Time has a way of changing people's values. Massachusetts Bay has been the main target of dislike or object of admiration among the New England colonies. And it is true that some of the most enduring features of Puritanism, such as the town meeting, the free school, and the college, stem from the Bay rather than from little Plymouth. Yet today, when we look at our past for things to admire, we tend to overlook the proud and arrogant colony of Massachusetts and turn either to her "problem child," Rhode Island, as the seedbed of religious liberty; or to her modest elder sister Plymouth, as a model of successful government under law, and a symbol of faith and pioneer courage. For, after all, the Pilgrims came first; and for years they were alone. Their stout hearts won out, when there was nobody to help them.

There is still a magic in the "Land of the Pilgrims' Pride": the sand dunes of Cape Cod, which to straining eyes on board the *Mayflower* seemed "goodly" after sixty-five days at sea; the pine and oak woods of Plymouth County; the long salt inlets and snug harbors of Buzzards Bay; and Mt. Hope, where the belated challenger to the Pilgrim Colony met his death. In Plymouth Town itself one can still recapture some of the atmosphere of the 1620's, when that little settlement was the only one in North America between Virginia and Canada. Walk, if you will, some day at the close of the year, up to the summit of Burial Hill where the old fort was built. You can look out over the roofs of the modern town to the harbor and the blue bay and the ocean beyond; that "vast and furious ocean" which separated the Pilgrims from the rest of the civilized world. You may rest your eyes on the slender sandpit of Long Point, on the Gurnet, and on the high, wooded promontory of Manomet, looking almost exactly as they did when the Pilgrim Fathers were alive. Then visit the little green park below, which once was Elder Brewster's "meerstead" or garden. There the Pilgrim Spring is still bubbling with pure, sweet water. That spring, it seems, is a symbol of the Pilgrim spirit; it, too, is immortal and will refresh and inspire mankind for hundreds, even thousands of years to come.

Statue of the Pilgrim Maiden

READING
SUGGESTIONS

[◆

WILLIAM BRADFORD's *Of Plymouth Plantation,* the prime source for Plymouth history to 1646, has been frequently printed. The latest edition, with spelling and punctuation modernized so it can easily be read, edited by the author of this book, was published by Alfred A. Knopf, Inc. (New York) in 1952. It may be considered a companion volume to this.

Mourt's Relation, extracts from the Journals of Bradford and Winslow, was printed at London in 1622 and has frequently been reprinted. The best edition, with notes, is that of H. M. Dexter (1865). Another reprint is in Alexander

Young's *Chronicles of the Pilgrim Fathers* (1844). Also in that book are reprinted Edward Winslow's *Good Newes from New England* (1624) and his *Briefe Narration* (1646), important sources and interesting reading.

The official records of the Colony were printed in twelve large volumes, edited by N. B. Shurtleff, in 1855-61. The wills and inventories from which we have quoted are printed in early volumes of *The Mayflower Descendant*, published by the Society of Mayflower Descendants, 9 Walnut Street, Boston (to whom inquiries about ancestors and pedigrees should be addressed).

Of the general histories of the Colony, Roland G. Usher's *The Pilgrims and Their History* (1918) is the best; but there is much good material in John A. Goodwin's *The Pilgrim Republic* (1888 and 1920). Almost every town in the Old Colony has had its history written. Perhaps the two best are W. T. Davis's *Ancient Landmarks of Plymouth* (1883) and Richard LeB. Bowen's *Early Rehoboth* (4 vols., 1945-50).

Frederick Freeman's *History of Cape Cod* (2 vols., 1860-62) is still the standard history of the Cape towns.

David Bushnell's "The Treatment of the Indians in Plymouth Colony," in *The New England Quarterly* XXVI (1953) 193-218 is recommended. Some of the contemporary narratives of King Philip's War are in C. L. Lincoln (ed.) *Narratives of the Indian Wars* (Original Narratives of American History series). But the most readable is Captain Benjamin Church's *Entertaining Passages Relating to Philip's War*, first printed in 1716. The best edition is H. M. Dexter's of 1865. Douglas E. Leach's "the Military System of Plymouth Colony" in *The New England Quarterly* XXIV (1951) 342-64 is an introduction to the history of that war which he is writing. H. L. Peterson's "The Military Equipment of the Plymouth and Bay Colonies" in same, XX (1947) 197-208 is also important.

For additional references see Oscar Handlin and others, *The Harvard Guide to American History* (1954) pp. 266, 270-72.

INDEX

A NOTE ON THE

TYPE

IN WHICH THIS BOOK IS SET

THE TEXT of this book is set in Caledonia, *a Linotype face designed by* W. A. DWIGGINS. *It belongs to the family of printing types called "modern face" by printers—a term used to mark the change in style of type-letters that occurred about 1800. Caledonia borders on the general design of Scotch Modern, but is more freely drawn than that letter.*

The book was composed, printed, and bound by H. WOLFF, *New York. Paper made by* P. H. GLATFELTER Co., *Spring Grove, Pa. Typography by* S. R. JACOBS *and* CHARLES FARRELL.

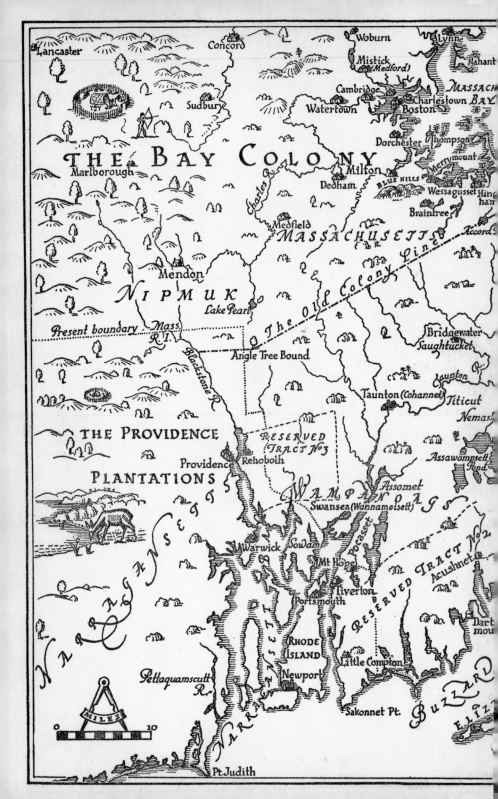